A Feast of Fish

A Feast of Fish

IAN McANDREW

Macdonald Orbis

Acknowledgements

The publishers wish to thank Harrods Ltd, Knightsbridge, London, for the generous loan of some of the tableware used in the photographs.

Photography
Simon de Courcy-Wheeler: pages 17, 18, 19, 20, 61, 62, 63, 64, 117, 118, 119, 120, 189, 190, 191, 192.
Chris Lee: pages 97, 98, 99, 100, 121, 122, 123, 124, 141, 142, 143, 144, 161, 162, 163, 164.

A Macdonald Orbis BOOK
Text © Ian McAndrew 1987
Photographs © Macdonald & Co (Publishers) Ltd 1987

First published in Great Britain in 1987
by Macdonald & Co (Publishers) Ltd

This edition published in Great Britain in 1989
by Macdonald & Co (Publishers) Ltd
London & Sydney

A member of Maxwell Pergamon Publishing Corporation plc

British Library Cataloguing in Publication Data
McAndrew, Ian
  A feast of fish
  1. Cookery (Fish)
  I. Title
  641.6'92   TX747
  ISBN 0-356-12164-X Hardback
  ISBN 0-356-17644-4 Paperback

Editor	Jennifer Jones
Design	Dave Goodman
Photography	Chris Lee
	Simon de Courcy-Wheeler
Stylists	Maggie Heinz
	Andrea Lampton
Illustrations	Lorraine Harrison

Filmset by SX Composing Ltd, Rayleigh, England
Printed and bound in Great Britain by Purnell Book Production Ltd
Member of the BPCC Group

Macdonald & Co (Publishers) Ltd
Greater London House
Hampstead Road
London NW1 7QX

Contents

To Jane, my reason for everything

With special thanks to all of my staff for their help, to all our customers who have had to put up with my experiments, and to Jenny to whom I have given a hard time.

———————————————

indicates that this dish is suitable as a first or fish course; where two serving quantities are given, it is also suitable as a light main course

indicates that this dish is suitable for a light main course, for example lunch or supper

indicates that this dish is suitable as a main course

———————————————

NOTE
Use either metric or imperial measurements, not both

All spoons are level unless otherwise indicated
1 tsp = 5 ml
1 dessertsp = 10 ml
1 tbsp = 15 ml

Foreword

It is a great pleasure to be asked to introduce this book. I have watched with interest the progress of Ian McAndrew and have always wished him well with his task of bringing good food to the people of Canterbury. Despite its proximity to the sea, I feel sure that Ian, like me, has found a lack of enthusiasm for fish from some of the English, which belies the fact that their island is surrounded by prime fishing grounds. They have, for example, assigned that wonderful fish the cod to be buried in batter and thrown into a sea of oil. I hope that many people will begin to learn from the book how to properly cook some *good fresh* fish.

Although fish is a versatile food, it is also delicate and requires careful handling and subtle sauces. How many traditions there are though in the world of fish; for example, I much prefer brill to turbot, crab to lobster. Whatever your own preference, you must insist that your fishmonger serves you only the freshest fish. Ian has created some excellent recipes to deal with all sorts of fish, and you will certainly be on to a winner if your specimen is clear-eyed and shiny.

Much has been written about the 'young English chef', and Ian McAndrew is certainly one of the most talented. A brave man, too, to set up a restaurant in a provincial town at a time when, despite many reports to the contrary, there is often little support for such enterprising young men. I am glad he has been such a success; I have enjoyed his food, and I have enjoyed his book: I now strongly urge you to do the same.

NICO LADENIS

Introduction

Fish: A New Approach

Fish! Most of us like it, but are often not sure what to do with it. 'Although we like fish, we never buy it. I just never know what to do with fish.' is a common cry the world over.

Amazingly, here in the British Isles, where we are surrounded by prime fishing grounds, not only is fish seldom used, but it is often difficult to obtain. Think how many fishmongers you have in your area, and then compare them to the number of butchers.

In this book I will show you some new ideas, as well as some old ones; enough, I hope, to whet your appetite and have you diving into the kitchen! ... but first find a fishmonger, encourage him and, hopefully, one day there may be more and better fish more widely available.

By all means follow the recipes in this book – that, after all, is what it is for – but also improvise. If there is an ingredient in a recipe you cannot get hold of, don't just give up – substitute it. Good food and good cooks are created and creative, not made from books. I hope you will use my book as a guideline, as a source of inspiration – not a bible.

Choosing Your Fish: Freshness and Quality

Choosing your fish is probably the most important and crucial part of your intended dish: without good quality fresh fish, your dish will be ruined before you start.

My first rule is: do not use anything frozen. However, before I go any further, I must admit that this is as much a personal preference as it is for any other reason. Let me clarify my reasoning before the frozen food industry accuses me of overreacting.

Firstly, I have a policy (and always have had) of not using anything frozen, tinned, bottled or preserved in any way unless I have either done it myself or it is absolutely necessary. Secondly, there are a lot of dishes where frozen fish is definitely unsuitable. Mousselines are a prime example of this. The freezing of fish seems to break down the gluten content of the meat and therefore a good binding of egg white and cream cannot be achieved.

Thirdly, have you ever noticed how much ice you get with frozen fish (or glaze as the manufacturers call it!)? Prawns and scallops are both heavily-glazed items; when defrosted, see how much smaller, limp and tired looking they are compared to those lovely, plump, shiny examples of their species sold fresh.

Now I come to the last, most controversial and yet most important reason why fresh fish is preferable to frozen. We all know that the majority of fish caught is frozen at sea when it is at its best. This is, of course, true. However, it is equally true that a lot of fish landed fresh today finds itself unsold in a few days time – then what? In my experience, it finds its way into a freezer and then, of course, it is sold as frozen. How old was it before it was frozen? In fact, it may even have been frozen once already, thawed, then refrozen to extend its shelf life. That glaze on it, is it natural sea slime? Or is it slime from decomposition? I know this is a little hard hitting and certainly the exception rather than the rule, but I make no apologies for it. After all, it is definitely harder to tell how fresh a fish is when it is frozen!

Now that I have, I hope, persuaded you not to buy frozen fish, how can you tell whether the fresh fish you are looking at is really fresh? Well, most of it is commonsense. A fresh fish looks fresh (obvious, isn't it?), bright and shiny; an old fish looks dull and lifeless. The first sign is the skin. It should look shiny, have a slight natural slime, and the scales should look bright and fresh. The eyes should be nicely rounded and once again have a good shine, not sunken and dull. The gills should be a bright red. As the fish ages, the gills go very grey and dirty looking. Another way to test for freshness is to press the fish quite firmly with your forefinger. If it leaves a mark that will not go away, then the fish is old. If it springs back and leaves no mark, you have a good fish. There is, of course, yet another way to test for freshness. I once read in a book on fish how you should bend down so that your nose is about 5 cm/2 inches away from the victim, then inhale deeply. Believe me, if that poor fish is bad you will know about it long before you get that close!

Choosing Shellfish

Choosing fresh shellfish is easy – if it's alive, then it is fresh. However, shellfish can also be bought cooked. Once again, as with frozen fish, I would strongly advise against buying cooked shellfish. I have heard of cases where they have not been completely cooked; not only that, but whoever cooked it probably didn't take as much care over the court bouillon as you would, assuming, of course, that a court bouillon was used at all, which is very doubtful. More than likely, the shellfish were only cooked in plain boiling water and, therefore, their flavour must be affected.

Crabs and lobsters should be alive and feel heavy in relation to their size. A lobster or crab with only one or even no claws is classed as a cripple and is more often than not cheaper. Decide what you want it for and it may be better to use a cripple. Oysters, clams, scallops, and mussels should always be tightly shut or if not snap shut as soon as they are disturbed.

Choosing and recognizing good quality fish is the easy part! The hard part is finding a good supply. Basically, find a good fishmonger, nurture and encourage him, and let him know that you will not accept second best. It may take time, but if he cares about what he sells, then your efforts will pay dividends in the long run.

Preparing Fish

Probably what puts most people off fish is having to prepare it. Yes, it can be a smelly and messy business, but at least in doing it yourself you will know how fresh the fish really is. The alternative is either to buy fish pre-prepared or to ask your fishmonger to prepare it the way you need it for the recipe.

Here I have described the basic methods of preparation. The most important tool in fish preparation is the knife. Without a sharp knife the job becomes a chore. It should have a blade of at least 15 cm/6 inches and be slightly flexible; in other words, a filleting knife. The fish cook's filleting knife is as indispensible as a boning knife is to a butcher. It must, however, be kept sharp at all times, as a blunt knife will not cut but tear and slip, more pressure is then needed in using it, and this can result in more cut fingers than when using a sharp knife.

Scaling

There are three basic preparations for fish: scaling and filleting, then, depending on the recipe, skinning. Scaling should always be your first step; it is an important part and one that people often try to get out of doing, but believe me it must be done – why spoil a beautiful dish just because you cannot be bothered to do the job correctly. If the fish is not first scaled before filleting, then the knife, no matter how sharp it is, will not cut through the scales, which are always very tough. This is not, however, the only reason for scaling; as well as being inedible, scales are also quite loose and some will come off during cooking and removing them from the meat or sauce before serving will consequently be impossible. To scale, hold the fish by the tail using a cloth to keep a grip, then, using the back of a knife, scrape the skin with the knife from tail to head. This is best done over a sink full of water or under running water as the scales do have a tendency to fly off in all sorts of directions. Once scaled, the fish should be rinsed to remove any remaining loose scales.

SCALING FISH
1 *Holding the fish by its tail, scrape away from you with a knife towards the head.*
2 *Place the fish under running water to wash off the scales.*

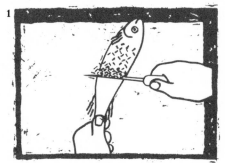

Filleting

Depending on the recipe, the fish may require filleting. Although most fish can be bought ready filleted, it is just as well to know what to do. As fish come in two basic shapes, round and flat, there are also two ways of filleting. Flat fish are probably the easiest fish to cope with as they have a flat bone that is easy to negotiate, and there is also a line, the lateral line, down the fish from head to tail which acts as a cutting guide. This line runs from the centre of the tail up the middle of the fish towards the head; just before the head, it curves off to one side around the pectoral fin and finishes behind the gills. Round fish have a curved rib cage, which makes it more difficult to negotiate, and a line of small bones that have to be freed from the backbone.

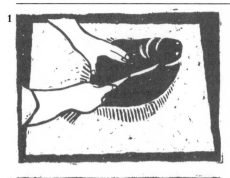

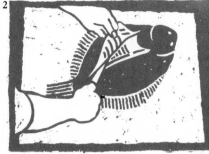

FILLETING FLAT FISH

1 *Lay the fish on the work surface with its head away from you. Make an incision along the dark line through to the bone from head to tail.*
2 *Slide the knife under each fillet, angling it towards the bone as you cut.*
3 *Continue cutting until free.*
4 *Remove the other fillet, turn the fish over and repeat.*

PREPARING FLAT FISH

1 *Using a heavy knife, cut off the head at an angle.*
2 *Trim off the fins and tail with a pair of kitchen scissors.*
3 *With the point of a knife, scrape away the blood clot from just behind the head.*
4 *Pull out any roe. Wash the sole well, especially the cavity, and pat dry.*

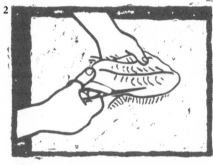

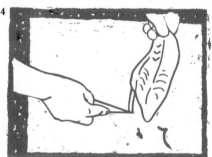

For flat fish, first cut round the side of the head, then down the centre of the fish following the line once it straightens out. Slide the knife under each fillet, angling it towards the bone as you go. For round fish, lay the fish on its side and make a cut just behind the gills at an angle towards the head, then cut along the back just above the dorsal fin from head to tail. Using the

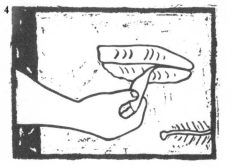

FILLETING COOKED SOLE

1 *Lay the cooked fish on a flat surface and, using a palette knife, scrape away the skirt on both sides.*
2 *With the head of the fish towards you, run the knife down the centre line of the fish. Slide the knife under the fillets and lift off.*
3 *Slip the knife under the bone and carefully lift out the bone.*
4 *Replace the top two fillets on the bottom two.*

point of the knife, carefully cut the fish away from the bone, turn the fish over and repeat on the other side.

Once filleted, always wash the fish and pat dry. There is a line of small bones that runs down the centre of each fillet on a round fish, and these should always be removed before cooking. Depending upon the fish, these bones may only run for about an inch or they may run for two-thirds of the fillet. Bass, mullet, haddock and cod have only a few bones, four or five, whereas salmon and trout have a line of over 20 bones on each fillet. If you do not know where they are – and they are hard to see – run your finger down the length of the fillet from head to tail and they will be easily found. I find it best to remove these with a small pair of pliers.

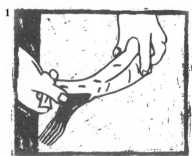

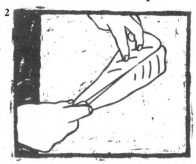

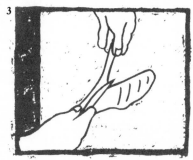

FILLETING MONKFISH
1 *Holding the fish firmly, pull away the skin.*

2 *Put the fish flat on its back and cut the fillet away from the bone.*

3 *Repeat with the second fillet.*

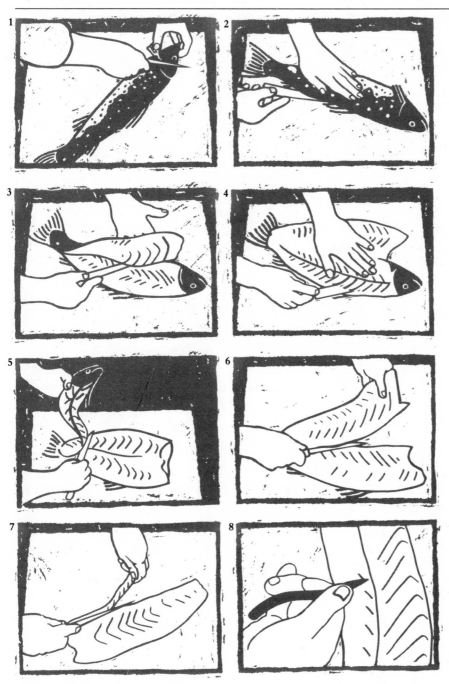

FILLETING ROUND FISH

1 *Lay the fish on its side and make a cut through to the bone at an angle just behind the gills. Turn the fish over and repeat.*
2 *Starting just above the dorsal fin, cut in one movement towards the tail, finishing just above the tail fin. Finish by cutting from the dorsal fin to the cut behind the gills.*
3 *Using the point of a sharp knife, carefully cut along the bone towards the backbone, moving from head to tail, until the top fillet is free but still attached to the bottom fillet.*
4 *Insert the knife under the bone at the tail end and slide it towards the head.*
5 *Free the bottom fillet by gently lifting away the bone.*
6 *Cut the fish down the middle into two fillets.*
7 *Trim the edges of the fillets.*
8 *Using a pair of pliers, remove the line of small bones that runs two-thirds of the length of the fillets. To make the bones easier to find, run your fingers or the back of a knife down the fillet.*

Skinning

Again, depending on the recipe, the fillets may need skinning. Lay each fillet on the board, head end away and skin side down, then make an incision at the tail end through the flesh but not the skin. Work the blade from side to side between the flesh and the skin, pushing with the knife and at the same time pulling the skin with the other hand. Once filleted, the skirt that runs around the edge of all flat fish should be removed.

Once scaled, filleted and skinned, the fish is then ready for cooking. All that needs to be done now is to portion it if it is too large. When cutting a fillet into two or more pieces, I always cut across the fillet holding the knife at a slight angle; this tends to give it a more attractive shape. Sometimes I also cut at an angle diagonally across the fillet; this is normally when the fillet is narrow and a longer strip is required.

SKINNING FILLETS
1 *Lay the fillet skin side down and make an incision through the flesh at the tail end. Grip the skin, tilt the knife away from you and work towards the head.*
2 *Trim off the skirt.*

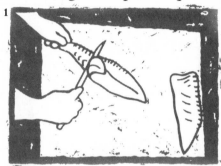
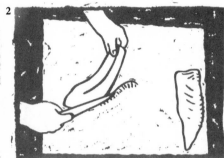

SKINNING DOVER SOLE
1 *Make an incision through the skin on the tail and scrape away enough skin to hold onto.*
2 *Using a cloth, hold the tail firmly in one hand and pull the skin away towards the head.*

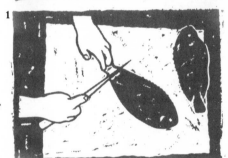

Preparing Shellfish

The preparation of shellfish is a little more varied than that of other fish because there are so many types and so many ways of using them.

Lobsters, when bought alive, must first be killed before using. Depending on the recipe, there are a number of ways of carrying out this task, some of which are definitely not for the squeamish. If cooking the lobster whole, it should first be killed by plunging a trussing needle deep into its head between the eyes; a method that is supposed to be quick and humane, although I am a little dubious as to whether it is or not. It can also be plunged into boiling court bouillon while still alive, and again death is quick. Crabs too are treated in the same way, although if a live crab is plunged straight into a boiling liquid it has a tendency to shed its claws. When roasting or grilling a lobster or removing its meat for a mousseline,

(continued on page 21)

Poached Fillet of Turbot with
Black Chanterelle Sauce
(see page 140)

ABOVE *Parcel of Fresh Salmon with*
Foie Gras
(see page 51)

RIGHT *Lobster and Chicken Sausage*
with Spring Onion Purée
(see page 223)

LEFT *Halibut rolled in Sesame Seeds with Sorrel Butter Sauce* **(see page 108)**

BELOW *Fillet of Sea Bass Baked in Filo Pastry with Fresh Sorrel* **(see page 77)**

Sea Bass Marinated in Fresh Herbs
and Olive Oil
(see page 81)

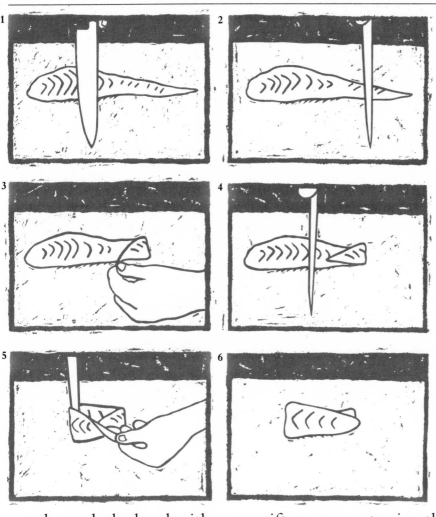

FOLDING FILLETS OF SOLE

1 *Lay the fillet skinned side uppermost and lightly flatten with the side of a heavy knife.*
2 *Using the blade of the knife, tap the fillet across its width about 2.5 cm (1 inch) from the tail end.*
3 *Fold the tail over.*
4 *Tap the fillet again with the blad of the knife but this time across the middle.*
5 *Fold the head over towards the tail.*
6 *The folded fillet is now ready for use.*

cut through the head with one swift movement using the point of a heavy, sharp knife. Whichever way you prepare the lobster, once killed it will not just lie still. Nervous reaction will make the fish jump and move about, sometimes quite considerably, so it is best to be mentally prepared for this happening.

Many people are understandably a little frightened of handling a live lobster or crab, and live crayfish are particularly active. As long as you remember to hold the fish behind the claws, there is no cause for alarm, it will not be able to reach your hand. Both crabs and lobster, if bought really fresh, can normally be kept alive for a couple of days by wrapping them in wet newspaper and keeping them in the refrigerator. Crayfish will also keep several days; put them in a covered container and store in the refrigerator.

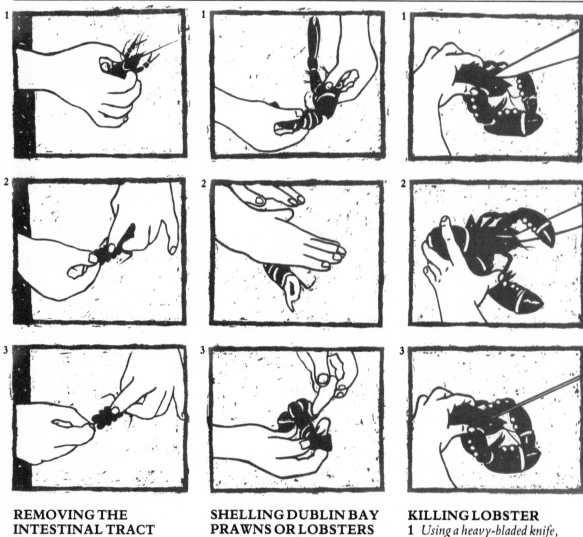

REMOVING THE INTESTINAL TRACT FROM CRAYFISH
1 *Hold the crayfish firmly behind the head and claws.*
2 *Grip the middle of the tail with your thumb and forefinger.*
3 *Twist and pull.*

SHELLING DUBLIN BAY PRAWNS OR LOBSTERS
1 *Pull away the head.*
2 *Crack the shell with the palm of your hand.*
3 *Carefully pull away the shell.*

KILLING LOBSTER
1 *Using a heavy-bladed knife, place the point just behind the head.*
2 *With one swift movement, push the knife through the head.*
3 *Alternatively, plunge a trussing needle between the eyes.*

When preparing mussels, scallops and clams, it is as well to remember that they are always full of sand and therefore cannot be washed too often. With both mussels and clams, allow them to sit in clean water for about 15 minutes, having first checked that they are alive, then change the water, allow them to sit for another 15 minutes, and repeat the process one more

PREPARING CRAB

1 *Turn the crab onto its back and break off the claws.*

2 *Pull off all the legs.*

3 *With the crab still on its back and with the eyes away from you, push the body up and away with your thumbs to separate it from the carapace.*

4 *The gills, or dead man's fingers, can now be pulled away from the body and discarded.*

5 *The only inedible part of the crab is its stomach. To remove this, press down on the mouth part of the crab until it cracks off. It can now be pulled out and discarded. All the remaining meat can be removed and eaten.*

6 *Any brown meat in the centre of the body can be eaten.*

7 *Using a thin-bladed knife or oyster knife, pick the white meat out of the body where the legs have been pulled away.*

8 *Using the back of a heavy-bladed knife or mallet, carefully crack the claws and legs to remove the meat.*

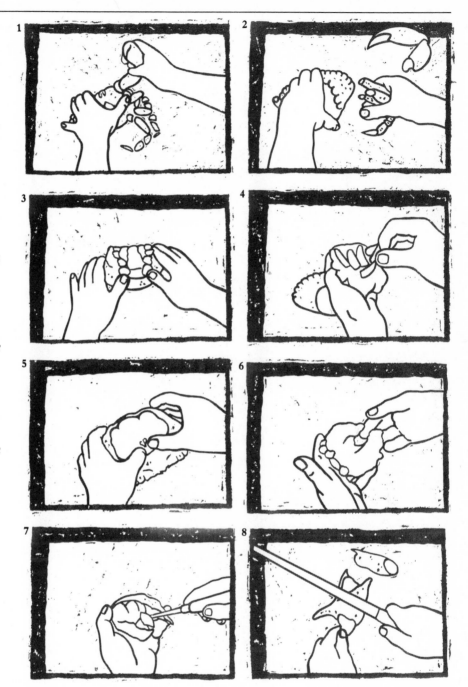

time. Mussels should be scraped to remove any barnacles and the beards pulled away. If a mussel feels too heavy for its size, then it is probably full of mud and should be discarded. Mussels and clams can also be kept for a couple of days before cleaning and cooking; simply cover them with wet newspaper, place a heavy weight on top, and store them in the refrigerator.

A few will die, but the majority will be alive and perfectly good.

Scallops are quite difficult to clean, so it is probably best to buy them ready cleaned, although even then they will still need a good wash. It is important to remember that although all fish, especially shellfish, must be washed, they should not be left standing in water for too long as this will impair their flavour.

Oysters, although molluscs, do not need the same careful cleaning as, for example, mussels. The shells should be scrubbed, especially if they are to be eaten raw straight from the shell, but soaking is not necessary. When using them for cooking, always save their juice; strain it through muslin and add it to the sauce. Like mussels, oysters can be stored for a few days in exactly the same way, but always check that they are still alive before using.

OPENING OYSTERS

1 Hold the oyster in a cloth so that the flat side is uppermost. Using an oyster knife, push into the hinge and twist.
2 Slightly prise the shells apart down the inside of the flat shell. Pull off the shell.
3 Remove the oyster from the concave shell by freeing it with the knife.
4 The oyster is now ready for use. If liked, keep the shells for decoration.

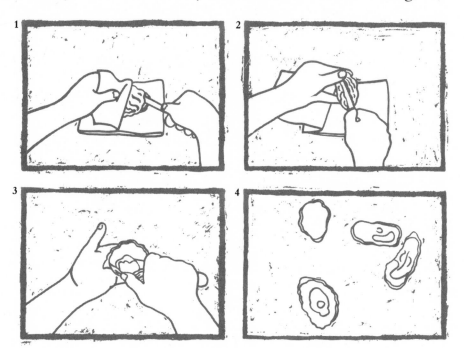

Cooking Fish

The actual cooking of the fish is probably the most difficult and crucial part of any of these recipes. Fish is so easy to overcook and so difficult to get just right – it is almost done, just needs a few seconds more and it will be ready, when the telephone rings or the door bell goes, you answer it and, too late, you are having dry, tasteless fish again!

Fish is cooked at a much lower internal temperature than other meats and therefore it cooks quicker – when it reaches about 63°C/145°F, it is ready;

once over that temperature, the water in the structure of the fish runs out, the meat becomes dry very quickly and, as the flavour is contained in the water, tasteless.

There are many ways in which fish can be cooked, but one way that should be avoided is boiling unless you are cooking shellfish or making a soup, and even then they should only simmer. You will see by the recipes that my preferred ways of cooking are poaching and steaming, although I also use grilling, baking and frying. The cooking times mentioned in the recipes work for me, although there are a few variables that must be taken into consideration. The efficiency of your oven or grill will be a major factor in determining the cooking time; if the thermostat in your oven is not working properly, then the cooking time may vary slightly. The thickness of a fish will also play its part in upsetting your timing. Where I have called for a 150 g/5 oz fillet of turbot, for example, it could be 1 cm/½ inch thick and 12.5 cm/5 inches long or, if the fish it came from is larger, it may be 2 cm/¾ inch thick by 10 cm/4 inches, and this extra depth will mean that it must be cooked a little longer. Use the cooking times supplied as a guide, but do not take them as being absolutely correct in every case. They do, however, emphasize how little time fish needs to cook, and even if the fish is not cooked after the specified time, it will probably only take a matter of seconds more, rather than minutes, to finish the process. Once the fish has been cooked, it must be served as soon as possible. Remember that while it is being kept warm, the fish will continue to cook and that if it is kept too warm for too long, it will overcook and become dry and flavourless. At all times be aware, do not overcook!

Finally, you can tell whether fish is cooked or not in a number of ways: its colour will change and become opaque and even; it should just give to the touch; or, if on the bone, the meat should just pull away, not fall off easily.

Poaching
To poach means to cover or partially cover the fish in liquid, such as stock or court bouillon, which is then gently heated until the liquid just starts to tremble. The liquid should then be held at this point until the fish is cooked. I find it best to transfer the pan to the oven to complete the cooking process; this will prevent the liquid from boiling, which must be prevented if the fish is to poach correctly and retain its flavour and moisture. If the poaching stock is allowed to boil, the fish will toughen and shrink considerably. It is

important when poaching that the pan or tray used is large enough to take the fish without touching or overlapping with each other. If you do not have a pan large enough, use two pans rather than using the same one twice. If the fish is to be served cold once poached, it is best to allow the fish to cool in its stock until ready for serving; this will greatly improve its flavour and is particularly good for shellfish. When cooking shellfish, they should always be plunged into boiling liquid and then the heat turned down and the liquid allowed to just simmer, not boil.

Steaming

Fish is steamed by placing it in a tightly fitting perforated container over a pan containing boiling water or stock so that the steam produced by the boiling liquid envelopes the food. It is a quick and clean method of cooking that was, until quite recently, much maligned in the West as being fit only for invalids, but it is a method that is extensively used by the Chinese. Its main advantage over other methods is that it retains more of the natural flavour, moisture and nutrients of the food, needs nothing adding to enable it to be cooked, and is, therefore, better suited to those on calorie-conscious diets. Another advantage is that more than one food can be cooked in the container at the same time without any loss of individual flavour. It is important when steaming not to allow the boiling liquid to touch either the fish or the steaming basket, and to keep the liquid boiling continuously and not allow the pan to boil dry.

Grilling

Grilling is suitable both for small, whole fish, such as mullet, or for fillets of fish, and even for some shellfish such as prawns or lobsters. It also takes two forms: over heat on a charcoal grill or barbecue; or under a grill giving top heat only. If the fish is thin or only a fillet, the flesh or cut side should be done first to seal in its juices; alternatively, a tray can be used instead of a rack, in which case the fish will not need turning. Always preheat the grill on its highest setting so that the fish seals quickly, trapping its juices; if it is a large piece, then turn the heat down a little so that the fish cooks gently and without burning. When grilling whole fish, it is best to score the flesh a few times so that the heat can penetrate more effectively, and remember that it will need basting occasionally. If it is not scored, the outside of the fish will dry and burn before the inside is cooked.

Shallow-frying or sautéeing

This method is often called pan-frying and differs from deep-frying in that only a small amount of fat is needed; in fact, since the arrival of the non-stick frying pan, food can be sautéed dry, which is a lot more acceptable to the health conscious. When using fat to fry in, a combination of oil and butter is best; butter for the flavour it gives, and oil to prevent the butter from burning. If you wish to use only butter, then it must be clarified first; clarified butter will not burn, whereas unclarified will. The food should always be started in a very hot pan to seal in its juices, then the heat reduced to allow it to finish cooking gently. It is a very quick way of cooking and is more suited to thinner cuts than to whole fish.

Baking

Baking is cooking in an oven with butter or oil and with a little liquid, although the addition of fat or liquid is not strictly necessary. It is normally reserved for whole fish or the thicker cuts of fish, and also includes cooking fish in pastry or foil, such as *en papillote*.

Braising

As with baking, braising is also a method of cooking in an oven; the fish is normally braised on a bed of vegetables with the addition of stock and wine. Braising is a slower method of cooking, and it is always carried out in a covered pan in a moderate oven (160-180°C/325-350°F/Gas Mark 3-4). The fish must be basted occasionally with the cooking liquor and it is normally served in its own liquor or with a sauce made from it. Again, like baking, this method is more suited to whole fish or cuts of firm fish such as turbot and brill.

Roasting

This is probably a method that not many people would associate with the cooking of fish. It is, however, very good for cooking whole fish and cuts of firm fish. It is also an excellent way of cooking lobster, and a few recipes for roasting lobster are included in this book. Roast lobster has a far different flavour to that of poached one that, to my mind, is superior. To roast, a fairly hot to hot oven is needed (200-230°C/400-450°F/Gas Mark 6-8). If the oven is not hot enough and the roasting pan not heated up first, the juices from the fish will escape and it will boil rather than roast.

Stocks, Sauces and Basic Recipes

The sauce chef is generally regarded as the most important member of any kitchen brigade. He is the person who can make or break a good meal more than anyone else. To make a good sauce takes practice and, moreover, patience. A really first-class sauce takes time and, most importantly, it also requires perfect ingredients and excellent base stocks.

Concentrate on making a good stock, in this case fish stock. All it needs is 20 minutes cooking time, but careful preparation of the bones and the vegetables, and nursing while it cooks will result in a finished product to be proud of.

Never discard a bone or a shell if it can be used to make a stock or sauce, store these in the refrigerator for use another day. Keep things like fish stock and veal stock in small containers in the freezer so that all you need to take out is the amount that you will need for that particular recipe. It is interesting to note that a friend of mine freezes her fish stock in the ice cube tray and then stores the cubes in a bag. In this way she can be more precise about the amount to take out. It's not too good in a gin and tonic mind you!

The way I cook means that most of my sauces are made as required from the ingredients for that particular dish, but I have tried to include a few general sauces that will accompany any plainly grilled, poached or steamed fish, whether hot or cold. Why not try inventing a few new dishes yourself using a base sauce with ingredients of your fancy? It is a very rare for me to season a sauce; if the base stock is good and the fish has been seasoned, then, unless you prefer highly-seasoned food, this is normally sufficient.

Once made, the finished sauce should be served as soon as possible. If, however, you find that you must make a particular sauce a little time in advance, then keep it away from direct heat. Store it in a water bath or bain-marie over a very low heat and drop a few small pieces of butter on top to help prevent a skin from forming. If you do not have a proper bain marie, put a few sheets of newspaper in the bottom of a saucepan with a few inches of water and sit the pan with the sauce in on top of this over a very low heat.

Above all else take time – a sauce to be proud of can never be hurried.

Fish Stock

MAKES ABOUT
1 litre/1¾ pints

450 g/1 lb fish bones and trimmings
900 g/2 lb white vegetables (white of leek, celery, onions, fennel)
25 g/1 oz butter
150 ml/¼ pint white wine
Juice of 1 lemon
About 1.2 litres/2 pints water
Bouquet garni (parsley or parsley stalks, thyme, bay leaves)

Next to your fish, fish stock is undoubtedly the most important item you will need. Without it, a sauce will not be a sauce only something to wet the meat. A good stock takes little time to prepare or cook, yet it is surprising how few people bother to make it.

The best bones to use are those from turbot, brill, Dover sole, whiting and most white flesh fish. However, I do not normally use the bones of cod or haddock as I find they leave the stock with a dirty appearance. The stock will keep very well in a refrigerator for up to 7 days or can be frozen down into usable amounts.

Method

Remove any blood from the bones and, if using the heads, then remove the gills. Soak the bones in cold water for a short time. Peel and wash the vegetables and roughly chop them. Heat the butter in a heavy-based pan, add the vegetables and sweat for a few minutes. Add the white wine, reduce slightly, and then add the lemon juice and sufficient water to just cover the bones. Bring to boil and skim frequently. When no more scum comes to the surface, after about 4-5 minutes, add the bouquet garni and simmer for 20-25 minutes. When ready, strain the stock through muslin or fine cloth.

Veal Stock

MAKES 1.2 litres/2 pints

1.5 kg/3-3½ lb veal bones, coarsely chopped
25 g/1 oz tomato purée
3 litres/6 pints water
2 medium carrots, chopped
1 small onion, chopped
1 small leek, chopped
2 sticks celery, chopped
50 g/2 oz mushrooms, chopped
2 medium tomatoes, chopped
1 sprig fresh thyme
1 sprig fresh rosemary
½ bay leaf
225 ml/8 fl oz dry white wine

Without a good base stock, a finished sauce can never be a good one, and the one thing that a good stock needs is time. Many people only simmer their veal stock for a couple of hours; I much prefer to cook it for at least 6 hours. It is not until after 6 hours that the bones will have given up all their flavour.

Method

Preheat the oven to 230°C/450°F/Gas Mark 8.

Brown the bones in a roasting tray in the oven, turning from time to time. When lightly browned, dot the tomato purée over them and continue browning for a further 10 minutes. Drain the bones of any fat and transfer them to a large saucepan, then add the water and bring to the boil. Once the stock comes to the boil, lower the heat and skim – a lot of fat and scum will have risen to the surface. Allow to simmer for 5 minutes, skimming as necessary. Add the vegetables and the herbs, pour in the white wine and continue to simmer gently for 6 hours.

After 6 hours, strain the stock through muslin or a fine strainer. If there is more than 1.2 litres/2 pints of stock, reduce it over a high heat until only this amount remains. If you do not do this, the finished stock will not have sufficient strength.
NOTE Once cold, the stock should keep in the refrigerator for up to 2 weeks or, alternatively, you can freeze it for longer.

Court Bouillon

MAKES 1.5 litres/2½ pints

Court bouillon is used to cook all kinds of fish and shellfish, both for eating hot or cold. If the fish is to be eaten cold or is to be used at a later date, it is best to leave it in the court bouillon – this will prevent the fish from drying out and will also improve its flavour. If the fish is to be served in the court bouillon, then the vegetables can be cut into attractive shapes; otherwise, the vegetables need only be roughly cut. The court bouillon can be kept for 2 or 3 days in the refrigerator.

2 medium onions
2 medium carrots
I leek
2 sticks celery
¼ bulb fennel
25 g/ I oz butter
50 ml/2 fl oz white wine vinegar
300 ml/ ½ pint dry white wine
1.2 litres/2 pints water
2 stalks parsley
2 bay leaves
I clove garlic
10 g/ ¼ oz black peppercorns
25 g/ I oz salt

Method
Peel and wash all the vegetables and roughly cut them up into small pieces. Melt the butter in a saucepan, add the vegetables, cover with a lid and sweat for 8-10 minutes. Pour in the vinegar, wine and water and bring to the boil. When boiling, add the herbs, garlic, peppercorns and salt and simmer for 15 minutes.

Avocado Sauce

MAKES 600 ml/1 pint

This sauce is delicious with any terrine or cold fish mousse and is also good with any poached or steamed fish or shellfish that is served cold. It can also be used as a dip for prawns.

2 ripe avocados
300 ml/ ½ pint double cream
300 ml/ ½ pint natural yoghurt
Juice of I lemon
Salt, freshly ground white pepper and sugar

Method
Peel and stone the avocados. Cut them up quite small and place in a food processor or blender. Scrape all the flesh from the skins and add this to the machine. Blend the mixture to a smooth paste, then remove from the machine and rub through a fine sieve. Add both the cream and the yoghurt to the avocado purée together with the lemon juice. Mix in well and season to taste with salt, pepper and a little sugar.

Watercress Yoghurt Sauce

MAKES ABOUT
600 ml/1 pint

115 g/4 oz watercress

25 g/1 oz cooked spinach

300 ml/½ pint live natural yoghurt

300 ml/½ pint double cream

Juice of ½ lemon

Dash of Worcestershire sauce

Salt and freshly ground white pepper

This is a perfect accompaniment for any cold fish, such as poached salmon, and is also good for cold mousses and terrines. I do tend to use a lot of yoghurt-based sauces for cold food, simply because yoghurt gives the sauce a light, fresh, clean taste. This sauce does not keep very well, as the lemon juice and the yoghurt turn the watercress grey. It is best made no more than half an hour before required and kept at room temperature – if it is kept in the refrigerator, it will become too cold and impair the flavour.

Method

Pick through the watercress to remove any leaves that are yellowing and wash well. Blanch the watercress in boiling salted water for a few seconds, then refresh in iced water and drain.

Place the watercress in a blender or food processor with the cooked spinach and blend until it is really smooth. Rub the purée through a sieve. Add the yoghurt, cream and lemon juice, mix together well and season to taste with the Worcestershire sauce, salt and pepper.

Tomato Sauce

MAKES ABOUT
450 ml/¾ pint

5 medium tomatoes

85 g/3 oz cold butter

50 g/2 oz shallots, roughly chopped

25 g/1 oz tomato purée

1 small clove garlic, crushed

120 ml/4 fl oz fish stock

120 ml/4 fl oz dry white wine

15 g/½ oz fresh tarragon

Sea salt and freshly ground white pepper

This sauce is good with any kind of fish or shellfish, and can be served either hot or cold. It is also excellent with chicken or veal; just substitute the fish stock for chicken stock.

Method

Blanch and skin the tomatoes and roughly cut them up. Melt 25 g/1 oz of the butter in a saucepan and gently soften the shallots for a minute without colouring. Add the tomatoes and soften for a further minute, again without colouring, then stir in the tomato purée. Now add the garlic, fish stock and white wine, bring to the boil briefly and then simmer over a very low heat for 20 minutes. After 10 minutes, add the tarragon. Season to taste with sea salt and freshly ground pepper.

When cooked, allow to cool, then rub the sauce through a sieve. To use, simply reheat, then whisk in the remaining butter in knobs and continue whisking until all the butter has melted.
NOTE The sauce will keep perfectly well for up to 4 days if stored in the refrigerator.

Lobster Sauce

675 g/ 1 ½ lb lobster shells
25 ml/ 1 fl oz oil
225 g/8 oz mirepoix (leek, celery, carrot, onion)
½ clove garlic, crushed
85 ml/3 fl oz brandy or Armagnac
1 ½ tbsp tomato purée
1.7 litres/3 pints fish stock
1 bay leaf
1 sprig fresh rosemary
10 g/ ¼ oz fresh tarragon
Pinch of saffron

Method

Preheat the oven to 180°C/350°F/Gas Mark 4.

Chop up the shells so that they are quite small. Heat the oil in an ovenproof pan, add the mirepoix of vegetables and the garlic, cover with a lid and sweat over a medium heat, stirring occasionally, until the vegetables start to soften. Add the lobster shells and continue to sweat for a further 10 minutes, then add the brandy and allow it to reduce by about half. Stir in the tomato purée, fish stock and herbs and bring to the boil. Continue cooking in the oven for 1½ to 2 hours (the liquid should be just simmering). When the sauce is cooked, strain through muslin or a fine sieve.

NOTE This recipe should yield at least 1.2 litres/2 pints of finished sauce which can be used for many things. It can be served as a sauce in its own right (it is delicious with chicken) or reduced with cream to make a richer sauce. It can also be used as a base for consommé.

To make a soup, add 1½ tablespoons of flour before putting in the brandy. Place in a hot oven (230°C/450°F/Gas Mark 8) for 10 minutes to singe the flour, then remove, add the brandy and continue with the recipe. Finish by stirring in double cream to taste.

The finished sauce can also be kept in the freezer for several months.

Crayfish Sauce

MAKES ABOUT
900 ml/1½ pints

450 g/1 lb live crayfish
900 ml/1½ pints fish stock
1 bay leaf
300 ml/½ pint dry white wine
115 g/4 oz mirepoix (celery, onion, carrot, leek)
1 tbsp oil
25 g/1 oz shallots, chopped
1 tomato, roughly chopped
2 cloves garlic, crushed
120 ml/4 fl oz brandy
25 g/1 oz tomato purée
About 450 ml/¾ pint double cream

Crayfish sauce, or sauce Nantua as it is sometimes known, is traditionally made with a creamy béchamel sauce to which crayfish butter has been added (see opposite). As I use very little flour in the kitchen, my variation is slightly different. It is a sauce that will complement all types of fish and it is also very good with veal, chicken and lamb. To finish the sauce, an equal amount of cream is added and then the sauce is boiled until it thickens.

Method

Make a court bouillon from the fish stock, bay leaf, white wine and mirepoix: place together in a saucepan, bring to the boil and simmer for 5 minutes. Remove the intestinal tract from the crayfish by pinching the middle section of the tail between your thumb and forefinger, then twist and pull. Plunge the crayfish into the court bouillon and cook for 4 minutes. Remove and allow to cool, then strain, reserving the liquid.

Shell the crayfish tails and save all the shells and heads; crush the heads. Put the shelled meat in a little of the cooking liquor; either use the meat for garnishing the dish for which you are making the sauce or, if it is only the sauce you want, use the meat for another dish. Heat the oil in a heavy-based saucepan, add the shallot and sweat for about a minute, stirring to prevent browning. Add the crayfish heads and shells, tomato and garlic, and continue to sweat for a further minute. Pour in the brandy, ignite and allow to burn out, then stir in the tomato purée and pour in the court bouillon. Bring to the boil and simmer for 20 minutes.

After 20 minutes, place the sauce in a food processor or blender and blend for a few seconds. Strain the sauce through a sieve into a saucepan. Return the sauce to the boil and reduce until it thickens and only about 450 ml/¾ pint remains.

To finish the sauce, add an equal quantity of double cream, return to the boil and continue boiling until it thickens. Strain through a sieve before serving.

Crayfish Butter

MAKES ABOUT
675 g/1½ lb

24-28 (450 g/1 lb) live crayfish
350 g/12 oz butter
115 g/4 oz mirepoix (onions, leek, celery, carrot)
1 small clove garlic, roughly chopped
50 ml/2 fl oz brandy
175 ml/6 fl oz dry white wine
120 ml/4 fl oz fish stock
1 bay leaf
1 sprig fresh thyme

As an alternative to crayfish sauce, try making crayfish butter, which is mainly used to enrichen sauces. By incorporating it in a cream sauce, it will improve both the flavour and depth of the sauce – lobster butter is also made in the same way. Only the shells are needed and it can be made from shells left over from another recipe. If using fresh crayfish, save the tail meat either as an accompaniment to the dish incorporating the butter, or possibly use it in a salad. The keeping quality of the butter is very good – 1-2 weeks in the refrigerator, or even longer in the freezer. Make a roll of it using greaseproof paper and cut off as much as you need while still frozen – it will keep for many weeks. I find it is better to chop up the shells a little before putting them in the blender, as the machine will accept them better this way.

Method

Melt about 25 g/1 oz of the butter in a saucepan, add the mirepoix of vegetables and the garlic and sweat over a medium heat without colouring until the vegetables start to soften. Meanwhile, remove the intestinal tract from the crayfish by pinching the middle section of the tail between the thumb and forefinger, then twist and pull. When the vegetables are soft, add the crayfish and continue to sweat over a high heat for about 3 minutes. Pour in the brandy and ignite, allow the flame to burn out and add the white wine and fish stock together with the herbs. Simmer for 5 minutes, then remove the crayfish and allow to cool. Reduce the stock by about half, remove from the heat and allow to go cold.

Extract the meat from the crayfish tails and use in another recipe. Roughly chop up the shells. Put the shells and vegetables in their cooking liquid in a blender or processor with the remaining butter and blend until a smooth paste. When ready, rub this through a sieve. Store the finished butter in either the refrigerator or the freezer.

Green Sauce

MAKES ABOUT
450 ml/ ¾ pint

50 g/2 oz potatoes
120 ml/4 fl oz fish stock or water
175 g/6 oz spinach
50 g/2 oz fresh dill
50 g/2 oz fresh parsley
50 g/2 oz fresh tarragon
Salt and freshly ground white pepper
1 egg yolk
2 tsp Dijon mustard
175 ml/6 fl oz salad oil
85 ml/3 fl oz single cream

This sauce makes a good accompaniment for any cold fish or shellfish, and it is also very good for serving with terrines. If the pronounced flavour of a particular herb, such as tarragon, is required, then increase the amount of tarragon and reduce the other herbs accordingly. Once made, the sauce should keep perfectly well in the refrigerator for a couple of days.

Method

Wash and peel the potatoes, then cut them up into small pieces. Cook them in the fish stock until soft. When cooked, allow them to cool in the stock. Pick the spinach of its stalks, and wash well. Pick all of the herbs of their stalks and add to the spinach. Cook the herbs and spinach in boiling salted water until just soft, then refresh in iced water and drain.

Once cold, place all the cooked ingredients, including the potatoes, and a little salt and freshly ground pepper in a food processor or blender and process until smooth. Add the egg yolk and the mustard, and, with the machine on, slowly add the oil as if making mayonnaise.

Remove the sauce from the machine, stir in the cream, pass through a fine strainer or muslin, then check the seasoning. If the sauce is a little too thick, it can easily be thinned down by whisking in a little water or fish stock.

Sauce Hollandaise

MAKES ABOUT
300 ml/ ½ pint

175 g/6 oz unsalted butter
50 ml/2 fl oz white wine vinegar
Pinch of crushed peppercorns
1 small shallot, finely chopped
2 egg yolks
2 tbsp water
Juice of ½ lemon
Pinch of cayenne pepper
Salt

Method

Clarify the butter by placing it in a double saucepan over simmering water until it has melted and cleared. Remove the scum from the top and carefully pour off the pure fat, leaving behind the thin milky liquid which can be discarded. Keep warm.

Put the vinegar, crushed peppercorns and shallot in a saucepan and bring to the boil. Continue boiling until reduced to a quarter of its original volume. Allow this to cool, then place it in a round-bottomed bowl over a saucepan of very hot but not quite boiling water. Add the egg yolks and water and whisk together until the mixture becomes as thick and smooth as double cream. Then very slowly add the warm butter, whisking continuously. The butter must be added slowly as it will separate if added too fast or not whisked in properly. If the mixture becomes too thick, add a few drops of warm water to thin it slightly.

When all the butter is incorporated, season with the lemon juice, cayenne pepper and salt. Pass the sauce through muslin or a fine sieve to remove both the peppercorns and the shallot. The sauce can be kept warm in a double saucepan over a low heat.

Sauce Maltaise

Make up the basic sauce hollandaise as above and add the juice and zest of 2 blood oranges which have been reduced by two-thirds and mixed with a few drops of Orange Curaçao liqueur. Ordinary oranges can be substituted for the blood oranges if they are not available.

Sauce Hollandaise with Mustard

SERVES 4

An excellent accompaniment to any grilled or sautéed fish. The cream lightens the sauce, but it can be made without it.

175 g/6 oz unsalted butter
50 ml/2 fl oz white wine vinegar
Pinch of crushed white peppercorns
1 small shallot, finely chopped
2 egg yolks
2 tbsp water
Juice of ½ lemon
Pinch of cayenne pepper
Salt
2 tbsp whole grain mustard
50 ml/2 fl oz double cream, whipped (optional)

Method

Clarify the butter by placing it in a double saucepan over simmering water until the butter has melted and cleared. Remove the scum from the top and carefully pour off the pure fat; discard the thin milky liquid left behind. Keep the fat warm.

Combine the vinegar, peppercorns and shallots in a saucepan and bring to the boil. Reduce the liquid to a quarter of its original volume and then allow to cool. Take a round-bottomed bowl and set it over a saucepan of very hot but not quite boiling water. In this, whisk together the vinegar mixture and the egg yolks with the 2 tablespoons of water. Continue whisking until the mixture becomes as thick and smooth as double cream. When it has reached this stage, very slowly add the warm butter, whisking continuously. The butter must be added slowly; if it is added too fast or not whisked in properly, it will separate. If the mixture becomes too thick, add a few drops of warm water to thin it slightly. When all the butter is incorporated, season with the lemon juice, a pinch of cayenne and a little salt. Pass the sauce through muslin to remove both the peppercorns and the shallots. Then whisk in the grain mustard and fold in the whipped cream.

Once made the sauce cannot be kept warm and must be used straightaway.

115 g/4 oz watercress

25 g/1 oz cooked spinach

300 ml/½ pint fish stock

85 ml/3 fl oz dry white wine

300 ml/½ pint double cream

Juice of ½ lemon

Salt and freshly ground white pepper

Hot Watercress Sauce

Watercress sauce will complement almost any type of fish whether poached, grilled or steamed. It is also good with a fish mousse.

Method

Pick through the watercress to remove any yellowing leaves and wash well. Blend the cooked spinach and the watercress together in a food processor or blender for at least 5 minutes until really fine. If you find that the watercress is a little too dry to go round the machine, add about 25 ml/1 fl oz of the fish stock just to dampen it. If you add too much, however, it will go round but not purée.

Bring the fish stock to the boil along with the white wine and reduce over a high heat until only a quarter of the liquid remains. Add the cream and return to the boil. Just as the sauce starts to thicken, stir in the watercress and spinach purée. Allow the sauce to simmer for a minute, then season with the lemon juice, salt and pepper to taste. Pass the sauce through muslin or a fine strainer, and serve immediately.

3 egg yolks

1 tbsp Dijon mustard

1 tsp salt

450 ml/¾ pint vegetable oil

150 ml/¼ pint olive oil

½ tbsp white wine vinegar

Juice of ½ lemon

Freshly ground white pepper

Mayonnaise

This is the base for numerous different sauces as well as being good in its own right. It is not necessary to refrigerate mayonnaise; it will keep perfectly well in a cool place for many days.

Method

Mix together the egg yolks, mustard and salt. Gradually add the oils in a steady flow, whisking continuously until they are all incorporated, then whisk in the vinegar and the lemon juice and season to taste with freshly ground pepper. If the mayonnaise is a little too thick, beat in a tablespoon of hot water.

Yoghurt Vinaigrette

This is a lighter-tasting, fresher alternative to an ordinary vinaigrette. It is nice to substitute half of the olive oil for walnut oil, depending on what type of salad you are using it for.

Method

Mix all the ingredients together except the water and add this only if the vinaigrette is a little too thick. Season to taste with a little freshly ground pepper and salt if needed.

3 tbsp natural yoghurt
I tbsp sherry vinegar
2 tbsp olive oil
I tsp Dijon mustard
Pinch of sugar
About I tbsp water
Salt and white pepper

Yoghurt Dressing for Salads

This easy to make, light, fresh-tasting dressing will liven up those green salads. For added interest, add 15 g/½ oz finely chopped fresh chives or mixed herbs to the finished dressing.

Method

Mix together the yoghurt and the cream, and add the lemon juice to taste. Season with a pinch of sugar and freshly ground pepper.
NOTE This dressing will not keep very long as the yoghurt will act on the cream and turn it all to yoghurt.

65 ml/2½ fl oz natural live yoghurt
65 ml/2½ fl oz double cream
Juice of ½ lemon
Pinch of caster sugar
Freshly ground white pepper

Tomato Vinaigrette

Method

Blanch and skin the tomatoes and roughly cut them up. Heat the olive oil in a saucepan, add the shallots and gently soften for a minute without colouring. Add the tomatoes and stir in the tomato purée, followed by the garlic and the sherry vinegar. Bring to the boil and then simmer over a very low heat for 10 minutes. Season to taste.

When cooked, allow the vinaigrette to cool and then pass it through a sieve. Do not force it through; all you want is the resulting liquid.
NOTE The vinaigrette will keep perfectly well for up to 4 days if stored in a refrigerator, but allow it to come to room temperature before using; if it is too cold, it will lose some flavour.

5 medium tomatoes
120 ml/4 fl oz olive oil
50 g/2 oz shallots, roughly chopped
25 g/I oz tomato purée
I small clove garlic, crushed
50 ml/2 fl oz sherry vinegar
Salt and freshly ground white pepper

MAKES 450 ml/¾ pint

50 g/2 oz white bread, crusts removed

About 175 ml/6 fl oz crab or lobster soup (see page 33, 154)

1 egg yolk

Pinch of Saffron

2 cloves of garlic, crushed

½ pint (300 ml) salad oil or olive oil

Salt and freshlyt ground white pepper

Rouille

This is the perfect and traditional accompaniment to fish soups – they really are not the same without it.

Method

Cut the bread into small pieces and soak in the soup until soft. Place the egg yolk, soaked bread, saffron and garlic in a blender and process until smooth, then gradually add the oil as if you were making mayonnaise. Season to taste with salt and pepper. If you think it is a little too thick, then add a little more fish soup. This is best made a few hours before required.

To Serve

Serve the rouille separately in a sauceboat. Float pieces of thinly sliced, toasted French bread in the soup and dollop the rouille on top of the bread.

MAKES 300 ml/ ½ pint

225 g/8 oz sugar

300 ml/ ½ pint water

Sugar Syrup

Method

Bring the sugar and the water to the boil in a saucepan. When it comes to the boil, skim off any scum that comes to the surface (this is the impurities in the sugar coming out). If you use sugar cubes instead of granulated, there should be less scum as it is normally purer. Boil for a couple of minutes until syrupy, then allow to go cold. The syrup will keep for weeks in a cool place.

Basic Fish Mousse

MAKES 6 *quennelles or*
6 × 85 *ml/3 fl oz moulds
for a first course*

275 g/10 oz trimmed fish (with bone and skin removed)

1 tsp salt

1 egg white

150 ml/1/4 pint double cream

25 ml/1 fl oz dry sherry

Pinch of grated nutmeg

Salt and finely ground white pepper

A mousse can be made either from raw fish and then cooked or from cooked fish, and can be served either hot or cold. There are also many ways of making a mousse. The former, which appears most frequently in the book, is used for making quenelles, for cooking in a mould, as the basis for a fish terrine, and for filling or spreading on to other fish.

It is not easy to make a perfect mousse every time without practice, but it is not as difficult as many people seem to think as long as certain rules and procedures are followed every time. All the ingredients must be chilled beforehand and should not be allowed to warm up too much during preparation. Always use fresh fish for a mousse, never frozen – although frozen fish will do, it is much more difficult to achieve a good result. Finally, always test the mousse when you have finished preparing it and before cooking. To do this, do not use all of the cream called for in the recipe, but hold a little back, about a third. To test, drop a teaspoon of the mousse mixture into simmering water until it is cooked. If the texture is rubbery or too firm, then add more cream and test again until the desired consistency is reached. A mousse should be so light that it almost floats away, but not so light that it falls apart.

The best fish to use for a mousse are any of the firm white fish such as turbot, brill, monkfish, and Dover sole. Salmon also makes a very good mousse, as does pike. In the shellfish line, scallops and lobster make excellent mousses.

Method

First, make sure that all the ingredients are well chilled. Place the trimmed fish in a liquidizer or food processor and blend until it is a fine, smooth paste. Add the salt, beat in well and then add the egg white and beat again until the mixture stiffens. Gradually stir in two-thirds of the cream slowly by hand. Add the sherry and season with the nutmeg and salt and pepper.

NOTE If while making the mousse you think it has become a little warm, then place it in the refrigerator until it is cold again. To ensure that it stays cold, add the last half of the cream over a bowl of iced water.

Shortcrust Pastry

MAKES ABOUT
350 g/12 oz

225 g/8 oz plain flour
1 tsp salt
150 g/5 oz butter
1 egg
25-50 ml/1-2 fl oz cold milk

This light, crumbly pastry is mainly used for flans and tartlets and will keep in the refrigerator for 4 or 5 days. If required, water can be substituted for the milk. The amount of water or milk needed will depend upon the flour used; the better the flour the more liquid.

Method

Sieve together the flour and the salt, then rub the butter and the flour together with your fingertips. Add the egg and the milk and mix together. When they are mixed in, knead the pastry into a smooth dough, but do not overwork; the finished dough should be quite firm.

Wrap in greaseproof paper or in a polythene bag and store in the refrigerator. Allow to rest for at least an hour before using. NOTE Small scallop-shaped pastry shells make an impressive garnish suitable for a number of fish dishes. To make 4 pastry shells, you will need 4 scallop shells and about 150-175 g/5-6 oz shortcrust pastry, rolled out to a thickness of 3 mm/⅛ inch. Grease the scallop shells, cut the pastry into 4 pieces and, using the point of a sharp knife, trim the pastry to fit the shell. Each pastry shell should be about 6.5-7.5 cm/2½-3 inches in length, starting from the bottom of the shell. Place on baking tray, brush with egg wash, and bake in a hot oven (230°C/450°F/Gas Mark 8) for 5-6 minutes or until golden brown.

Puff Pastry

MAKES ABOUT
1.25 kg/2 lb 12 oz

450 g/1 lb plain flour
2 tsp salt
225 ml/8 fl oz cold water
450 g/1 lb cold unsalted butter

Method

Sieve the flour and form into a mound on the work surface. Make a well in the centre. Dissolve the salt in the water and pour into the well. Gradually mix together the flour and water using your fingers. When the ingredients are thoroughly mixed, work the dough with the palms of your hands until completely smooth. Wrap the dough in a cloth or greaseproof paper and leave to rest in the refrigerator for at least 2 hours.

Dust the work surface with a little flour and roll out the dough to form four flaps of about 10 cm/4 inches wide, each at right angles to one another, and leaving a thick piece of dough in the middle. Knead the butter to form one supple slab; it must still be cold as well as supple. Place this in the centre of the dough. Fold over each of the flour flaps to completely enclose the butter. Return to the refrigerator, covered, for a further 30 minutes.

Again, lightly flour the work surface and gently roll the dough into a rectangle about 60 cm/24 inches long and 40 cm/16 inches wide. Keep the surface of the table dusted with flour while rolling and always roll the pastry away from yourself. Mark the rectangle into three sections. First fold one end section over the middle section and then fold the final section over the other. This is called a 'turn'. Now turn the dough through 90 degrees and roll it out again into a rectangle as before, flouring the work surface as you go. Once again, mark out three equal sections and fold over as before. The pastry has now had two 'turns'. Cover the pastry and leave to rest and firm up again in the refrigerator for at least 30 minutes.

Give the pastry another two 'turns' exactly as the first two, cover and return to the refrigerator for another 30 minutes. Give the pastry two final 'turns' so that it has now had six 'turns' in total. After resting again for 30 minutes, the pastry will be ready for use. It will last for about 4 days in the refrigerator or, if you wish, freeze it and then you can keep it for a few weeks.

Filo Pastry

Method

Sieve the flour, cornflour and salt together, make a well and add the oil and about half the water. Mix into the flour and continue adding more water until the dough is smooth and does not stick to the hands. The dough should then be covered with a damp cloth and left to rest in the refrigerator for a minimum of 2 hours. (The paste will not be elastic enough if left for a shorter period.) I prefer to leave the paste for a longer period, and find 24 hours about right. It will keep for up to 2 days in the refrigerator, as long as it is covered with a damp cloth.

To use, roll out the pastry as far as you can, using plenty of flour on the work surface at all times. When you have rolled it out as thin as possible, place the sheet over the backs of your hands and pull gently downwards, stretching all the time, until you can virtually see through it.

Once rolled out, the pastry should be used straightaway.

NOTE You can buy ready-made filo pastry from Greek and Turkish delicatessens.

MAKES ABOUT
175 g/6 oz

85 g/3 oz strong plain flour
25 g/1 oz cornflour
Pinch of salt
1 dessertsp oil
50 ml/2 fl oz cold water

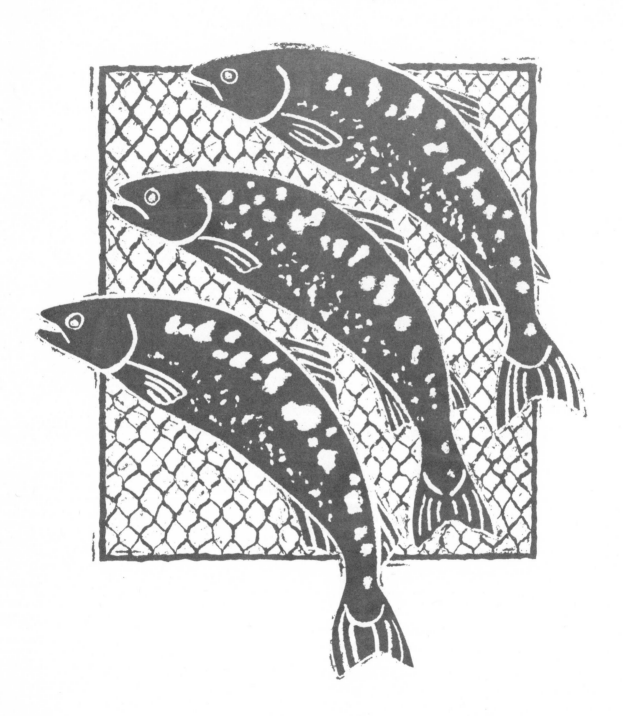

Freshwater Fish

Unfortunately, I have not included in this section as many types of fish as I would have liked because of limited availability. The range of freshwater fish does not match that of seawater fish although salmon, salmon trout and trout are always in good supply. However, pike, carp, tench and perch seem to be fished only for sport these days, so, unless you are a keen coarse fisherman, you will find they are difficult to obtain with any certainty.

Carp, although often found in large ornamental ponds, is also a fish of the rivers. It is a bottom feeder and, therefore, the flesh tends to be slightly muddy in taste; nevertheless, it has a fine flavour and a firm-textured flesh. Perch is a member of the bass family and it is well worth the effort of either catching or tracking down one for sale. It can be found across Europe and America and it is a shame it is not easier to purchase. Most recipes for river trout would also be suitable for perch. The tench has a very delicate flavour and is probably best just shallow-fried in a little butter and lemon juice. Now, the pike is a different fish again; it is delicate of flavour, and quite difficult and time-consuming to prepare because of its seemingly thousands of peculiar-shaped bones. I do, however, believe it is well worth every second it takes to prepare, especially in a mousse.

Pike
(FRENCH: *brochet* GERMAN: *hecht*)

There are very few freshwater fish that I use – not because I dislike them, but more because I cannot get them. The pike is one that I really do like, although it is difficult to fillet.

Hated by anglers yet providing great sport, pike, the shark of fresh water, used to be eaten a lot many years ago, but now it is hardly ever used. Its delicate, soft flesh is best poached or used in a mousseline to produce what the French are famous for, Quennelles de Brochet.

Terrine of Pike with Herbs and Wrapped in Salmon

SERVES 18-20

1 × 1.75 kg/4 lb pike
1 × 675 g/1½ lb fillet of salmon
1 tsp salt
1 egg white
450 ml/¾ pint double cream
120 ml/4 fl oz dry sherry
2 egg yolks
6 spinach leaves
50 g/2 oz mixed fresh herbs (tarragon, dill, chervil, chives, basil, parsley), finely chopped
15 g/½ oz butter
Freshly ground white pepper

Picture: page 64

A very delicate terrine – layers of white and green fish mousse with a centre of pike and salmon rolled in spinach – which makes an excellent first course. Once cooked, it will keep perfectly well in the refrigerator for up to 7 days. It is best served with a green sauce (see page 36) sprinkled with a few fresh herbs.

Method

Scale, fillet, skin and wash the pike. Cut a strip of meat from the thick part of each fillet about 2 cm/¾ inch wide and set to one side. Remove any dark meat from the skin side of the fish and discard. Cut the rest of the fish into small pieces, place in a blender or food processor along with the salt and egg white and blend for a few minutes until you have a smooth paste, then rub the mixture through a sieve into a bowl set on crushed ice. Gradually add two-thirds of the cream, mixing in well, then add the sherry and egg yolks and season to taste. Test the mousse (see page 41); if it is too firm, add a little more cream and test again. Leave in the refrigerator until needed.

Pick over and wash the spinach leaves. Blanch in boiling water for a few seconds, then refresh in iced water and drain.

Butter a 28 cm/11 inch terrine mould. Cut the salmon into long thin slices and line the terrine with these. Make sure there are no holes or gaps and allow an overhang of at least 6.5 cm/2½ inches all the way round. After lining the terrine, there should be enough salmon left over to wrap round the two strips of pike that have been set aside. The strips of pike should be laid on top of each other, so you will need to cut the remaining salmon into long enough slices to go round. Lay the slices of salmon out flat and slightly overlapping with each other, place the pike on top and roll. Then lay out the leaves of spinach in the same way as the salmon and roll up the salmon and pike in these.

To make the green mousse, mix the herbs with a quarter of the fish mousse. Use half of this mixture to spread an even layer at the bottom of the terrine. On top of this, spread half of the white mousse evenly, but leave a groove down the centre for the salmon and pike roll. Lay in the roll and gently press into place. Top this with the remaining white mousse and smooth out until even. Finally, top with the last of the green mousse. Fold over the overhanging salmon to completely cover. If there are some gaps fill with any scraps that you have left.

Cover the terrine with buttered foil and top with its lid. Cook in a bain-marie in a moderate oven (180°C/350°F/Gas Mark 4) for 45-50 minutes. After 30 minutes, remove the lid but not the foil. To test whether it is cooked, insert a long trussing needle into the centre. if the needle meets no resistance when entering and comes out slightly warm in the middle, then the dish is ready. Allow to cool. A terrine is best eaten 24 hours after being made.

Poached Fillet of Pike with Butter Sauce

SERVES 4

Method

Preheat the oven to 180°C/350°F/Gas Mark 4.

Butter a pan large enough to take the fillets without overlapping and sprinkle the shallots over the base. Cover with buttered paper or foil and poach in the oven for about 5-6 minutes. When cooked, remove the fish, cover and keep warm.

Set the liquor over a high heat and reduce until it is syrupy, then add the cream and bring back to the boil. When boiling, remove the pan from the heat and gradually whisk in the butter, and continue whisking until it has all melted.

To Serve

Arrange the pike on to serving dishes and coat with the sauce. Sprinkle with the sprigs of fresh parsley.

4 × 150-175 g/5-6 oz fillets of pike (a 1.5-2 kg/3-4 lb pike should be large enough)

25 g/1 oz shallots, finely chopped

225 ml/8 fl oz fish stock

175 ml/6 fl oz dry white wine

50 ml/2 fl oz double cream

175 g/6 oz cold unsalted butter

Garnish

Sprigs of parsley

Salmon
(FRENCH: *saumon* GERMAN: *lachs*)

One of the finest, most beautiful, well-known and popular fish in existence, the salmon is a king among fish.

It is a migratory fish, born in a river, living in the sea and returning to the river of its birth to spawn. It is thought that once the salmon returns to fresh water it stops feeding and does not start again until it returns to the sea. Accepting this fact is difficult, because it is caught using a rod and line by those dedicated fishermen, so it must take the bait.

The salmon is suffering badly because of over-fishing. Thankfully, however, it is now farmed quite extensively and this is helping to alleviate the problem. Nevertheless, the threat of the poacher is a great problem and one that appears to be getting worse, simply because the salmon is greatly prized and commands a high price. Man is not the only predator of the salmon, however – its flesh is also highly prized by some fish and birds. On many an occasion I have witnessed a salmon floundering in a shallow part of a river close to a weir being attacked by hungry sea gulls, who peck large holes in the sides of the salmon and then leave it to die.

A great drawback with salmon is that, if it is overcooked, it will be very dry; it should always be cooked so that the centre is still slightly pink. So when dealing with such a magnificent fish, take care!

Personally, I prefer a fish weighing about 2.25 kg/5 lb and am not overkeen on the larger ones. A 2.25 kg/5 lb fish will give 8-10 good-sized portions.

Salmon with Salmon Mousse, Crayfish and Tangy Sauce

SERVES 4

Method

Preheat the oven to 230°C/450°F/Gas Mark 8.

Bring the court bouillon to the boil. Remove the intestinal tract from the crayfish by pinching the middle section of the tail between your thumb and forefinger, then twist and pull. Plunge the crayfish into the bouillon and cook for 3 minutes, then remove and allow to cool. Save four of the crayfish for garnish and shell the rest (save the shells and heads to make crayfish sauce or butter). Butter 4 × 85 ml/3 fl oz moulds. Blanch the spinach leaves, refresh in iced water, drain and dry in a cloth. Use these to line the moulds, leaving enough over the edges to cover. Cut each crayfish tail into four or five pieces and mix into the salmon mousse. Fill the moulds with the mousse and fold over the spinach leaves to cover completely. Seal each mould with buttered foil, place in a bain-marie and poach for 8-10 minutes in the oven. Remove and keep warm. Turn down the oven to 190°C/375°F/Gas Mark 5.

Remove the zest from both limes, segment one and set aside for garnish. Squeeze the juice from the second lime and combine with the fish stock. Put the salmon in a buttered, ovenproof pan, add the fish stock, and cover with buttered paper or foil. Heat the liquid over a high heat until it just starts to tremble, then transfer the pan to the oven and poach for about 4 minutes. When cooked, remove the salmon, cover and keep warm.

To make the sauce, reduce the stock by at least two-thirds. Then pour in the cream, bring back to the boil and add the lime zest. Turn the heat down to very low and gradually add the butter using a small whisk and whisking until it has all melted. On no account allow the sauce to boil again once you have started to add the butter or it will separate.

To Serve

Gently reheat the salmon and remaining crayfish in the oven for a minute, then arrange on the plates. Pour the sauce over the fish, and place the mousse alongside. Garnish each plate with a crayfish and the lime segments and finish with a sprig of dill.

---

4 × 115 g/4 oz fillets of salmon

28 live freshwater crayfish

1.2 litres/2 pints court bouillon (see page 31)

8 large spinach leaves

½ recipe for salmon mousse (see page 54)

2 limes

300 ml/½ pint fish stock

50 ml/2 fl oz double cream

115 g/4 oz cold unsalted butter, cut into 1 cm/½ in cubes

Garnish

4 sprigs fresh dill

SERVES 4

4 × 150 g/5 oz fillets of salmon

4 baby beetroots (with their tops), weighing about 25 g/1 oz each

50 ml/2 fl oz vinegar

50 g/2 oz beetroot

A little butter

300 ml/½ pint fish stock

120 ml/4 fl oz dry white wine

300 ml/½ pint double cream

Garnish

Flat parsley leaves

Poached Salmon with Beetroot

An unusual combination? I think so too, but it does work, honestly!

Method

Preheat the oven to 180°C/350°F/Gas Mark 4.

Scrub the baby beetroots clean and cut their tops back to about 2.5 cm/1 inch long. Place them in a pan, add the vinegar and cover with cold water. Bring to the boil and simmer until cooked – this will take about 15 minutes. When cooked, remove from the heat and allow to go cold in the juice. Peel and cut the other beetroot into fine strips, about 2.5 cm × 3 mm/1 × ⅛ inch, and place these in cold water until needed. (This is to remove some of the colour, without this soaking the sauce may well be a little too dark.) When the baby beetroots are cold, peel them carefully – try to retain their original shape and leave their tops on and intact.

Butter an ovenproof pan and put in the salmon. Add the fish stock and the white wine and cover with buttered paper or foil. Heat the liquid over a high heat until it starts to tremble, then transfer the pan to the oven and poach gently for about 5-6 minutes. When cooked, remove the fish from the stock, cover and keep warm. Set the stock over a high heat and reduce until syrupy. Add the cream and reduce until it starts to thicken.

To Serve

Gently reheat the baby beetroots in a little of their cooking liquor. As the sauce starts to thicken, add the strips of beetroot and continue to boil until the beetroot is cooked but still retains a slight crispness – this should take no more than 2 or 3 minutes. As the beetroot cooks, the sauce will slowly change colour from white to a bright pink.

Place the fish back in the oven for a couple of minutes to warm through. Strain the beetroot from the sauce and make a little pile of it in the centre of each plate. Pour the sauce around and place the fish half on and half off the beetroot. Drain the baby beetroots from their liquor and place alongside each piece of salmon. Scatter a few leaves of flat parsley over the plate to finish it off.

Colourful, isn't it?

Steamed Fillet of Salmon with Elder Flowers

SERVES 4

Method

Preheat the oven to 230°C/450°F/Gas Mark 8.

Take four squares of foil large enough to make a bag to hold the individual pieces of salmon, and butter one half of each square. Arrange the flowers on the buttered pieces of foil, place each piece of salmon on top and season. Sprinkle the onion over the fish and then top each with a sprig of parsley. Fold the foil over to enclose the fish and seal tightly on three sides. Pour in the fish stock and white wine and then seal completely.

Place the four bags on a baking sheet and cook in the oven for about 6 or 7 minutes.

To Serve

Leave the fish in the bags – your guests should be allowed to have the experience of breaking them open and savouring the heavenly aroma. All you need to do is sit back and bask in their envious praise!

4 × 175 g/6 oz fillets of salmon
25 g/1 oz butter
4 sprigs elder flowers
Salt and freshly ground white pepper
4 small carrots, finely sliced
8 button onions or spring onions, finely sliced
4 sprigs parsley
225 ml/8 fl oz fish stock
120 ml/4 fl oz dry white wine

Parcel of Fresh Salmon with Foie Gras

SERVES 4

Method

Place a slice of foie gras, about 5 cm/2 inches square × 4 cm/1½ inches thick, in the middle of each slice of salmon. Season well and wrap the salmon around the foie gras to make four parcels. Heat the oil and half the butter in a pan and sauté the parcels gently for about 4 minutes, turning only once (the fish should only be slightly coloured). Remove the salmon from the pan and keep warm. Tip off the fat, add the remaining butter and stir-fry the julienne of vegetables until cooked, but still crisp.

Put the fish stock and dry sherry in another pan and reduce by about two-thirds, then add the cream and reduce again until thickened. Add the chives and season to taste.

To Serve

Pour the sauce on to the plates, add the vegetables and arrange the salmon parcels on top.

4 slices of salmon (5 mm/¼ inch thick and 10 cm/4 inches square)
4 slices fresh foie gras
Salt and freshly ground white pepper
1 tbsp oil
25 g/1 oz unsalted butter
300-450 ml/½-¾ pint fish stock
50 ml/2 fl oz dry sherry
300 ml/½ pint double cream
115 g/4 oz julienne of vegetables (carrot, leek, celeriac, turnip)
25 g/1 oz fresh chives, chopped

Picture: page 18

SERVES 4

1 × 350 g/12 oz fillet of salmon
115 g/4 oz cucumber
2 limes
4 dessertsp natural yoghurt
1 dessertsp chopped fresh dill
Salt and freshly ground white pepper
4 lettuce leaves

Garnish

4 sprigs fresh dill

Tartare of Salmon with Cucumber and Dill Dressing

Method

Skin the salmon, remove the line of small bones that run down the middle of the fillet using a pair of pliers, and cut into 3 mm/⅛ inch dice, discarding any grey meat (it doesn't taste very good and it also looks unappetizing).

Peel the cucumber, discard the centre core of seeds, and dice finely. Ideally, this should be cut into smaller dice than the salmon. Peel one lime and cut the zest into short, fine strips and blanch in boiling water for about 3 seconds – this will greatly enhance its colour. Set to one side. Now squeeze the juice from both the limes. To make the dressing, add one third of the juice to the cucumber, season, and mix in the yoghurt and the dill.

Add the remaining juice to the salmon, season to taste, and mix in well.

To Serve

Place a dessertspoon of the cucumber and yoghurt dressing on each of the plates just off centre. Divide the salmon mixture into four equal parts, shape each portion into a thick circle and place on top of the lettuce leaf at the side and slightly on top of the cucumber.

To garnish, sprinkle each plate with the lime zest and top with a sprig of dill.

Fillet of Scottish Salmon on a Bed of Spring Vegetables

SERVES 4

Method

Prepare the vegetables as attractively as possible: turn the courgettes into small barrels, pick the calabrese and cauliflower into small florets, choose small carrots and turnips and peel to preserve their original shapes. Trim the spring onions, leaving 1 cm/½ inch of green stalk. Blanch the vegetables separately and lightly. Refresh in iced water, then drain.

Season the salmon fillets, heat the oil in a pan with half of the butter and gently cook the fish 3–4 minutes each side; be careful not to overbrown. Remove the salmon from the pan and keep warm. Tip off the excess fat from the pan and add the remaining butter. Toss the vegetables in this and then season. Add the Noilly Prat, fish stock and lemon juice, bring to the boil and reduce the liquor slightly.

4 × 175 g/6 oz fillets of salmon
85 g/3 oz each mangetout, carrots, turnips, courgettes, calabrese, French beans, cauliflower
20 spring onions
I tbsp oil
50 g/2 oz butter
Salt and freshly ground white pepper
50 ml/2 fl oz Noilly Prat
300-450 ml/½-¾ pint fish stock
Juice of I lemon

Picture: page 190

To Serve

Strain the vegetables from the liquor and arrange attractively on the plates. Place the salmon in the middle and pour a little of the liquor over the vegetables and fish.

Fresh Salmon Marinated in Pink Grapefruit with Avocado

SERVES 4

Method

Slice the salmon as thinly as possible and remove and discard any dark meat from the slices. Remove the zest from the grapefruit and squeeze out the juice. Mix these with the cayenne pepper, then place the slices of salmon in this marinade so that they are completely covered. The salmon can be left for anything from 1 hour to 24 hours – personally, I think it is at its best after only 1 hour.

450 g/ I lb fresh boneless salmon
I large pink grapefruit
Pinch of cayenne pepper
½ frizzy lettuce
I ripe avocado

Garnish

Sprigs of fresh dill

To Serve

Wash the lettuce and arrange on the plates. Peel and slice the avocado thinly and lay the slices of salmon and avocado on top of the lettuce. Pour over some of the marinade and, to complete the picture, garnish with sprigs of dill.

SERVES 6

Mousse

275 g/10 oz fillet of salmon

½ tsp salt

I egg white

About 150 ml/¼ pint double cream

50 ml/2 fl oz vermouth

Freshly ground white pepper and a little grated nutmeg

Filling

225 g/8 oz fresh girolles

50 ml/2 fl oz Madeira

25 ml/1 fl oz veal stock (optional)

120 ml/4 fl oz double cream

Sauce

50 ml/2 fl oz Madeira

300 ml/½ pint fish stock

120 ml/4 fl oz double cream

175 g/6 oz cold butter

Garnish

6 sprigs fresh dill

Picture: page 63

Salmon Mousse with Girolles in Creamy Madeira Sauce

Although this is quite a long and complicated dish to prepare, the reward of seeing the faces of your guests when they cut into the mousse and out flows the creamy girolle filling must be worth it.

Method

Preheat the oven to 230°C/450°F/Gas Mark 8.

To make the mousse, skin and bone the salmon, cut it into small pieces and then blend in a food processor or blender with the salt until smooth. Add the egg white and blend for a few seconds more until it is well mixed in. Remove from the blender and rub the mixture through a sieve to get rid of any sinews – only by doing this can you be sure of a really fine texture. Set the bowl of salmon on crushed ice, gradually add two-thirds of the cream, then stir in the vermouth and season with salt and pepper and a little nutmeg. Test the mousse (see page 41) – it should be soft and not rubbery and should hold together. If the consistency is not quite right, add a little more cream and test again.

For the filling, prepare the girolles by scraping away any dirt or soil, but do not wash. Put 12 nice, small girolles to one side and cut the rest into 1 cm /½ inch pieces. Bring the Madeira and veal stock to the boil (the veal stock will improve the flavour of the sauce, but if none is available, use extra cream instead). When it has reduced slightly, add the cream and return to the boil. Reduce the sauce until it becomes very thick – as soon as it starts to thicken, it will reduce and thicken very quickly. Remove from the heat and add the diced girolles, stirring in well, and leave the sauce to go cold.

Butter six 175 ml/6 fl oz moulds. Line both the base and the sides of each mould with a layer of the salmon mousse about 5 mm/¼ inch thick. Make sure there are no holes and that the inside surface is smooth, then spoon the filling into the mould to fill each two-thirds full – the filling must be cold before it goes in. Place a spoonful of the salmon mousse on top and gently smooth this over to form a seal; do not allow any of the filling to seep out. Cook the moulds in a bain-marie in the oven for 12 minutes.

Meanwhile, make the sauce. Bring the Madeira and fish stock to the boil and reduce until only a quarter of the liquid remains. Add the cream and the whole girolles, return to the boil, then turn the heat down to low and gradually whisk in the butter until it has all melted.

To Serve

When the mousses are cooked, remove them from their moulds and place one on each plate. Spoon the sauce over the mousse, arranging two of the girolles at the side of each plate, and finish with a sprig of fresh dill.

Salmon en Papillote with Thyme and Vegetables

SERVES 4

This is an extremely simple dish, but so full of flavour as the fish is cooked sealed in its own natural juices.

4 × 176 g/6 oz fillets of salmon
50 g/2 oz butter
Salt and freshly ground white pepper
115 g/4 oz julienne of vegetables (carrot, leek, celery)
4 sprigs fresh thyme
225 ml/8 fl oz fish stock
85 ml/3 fl oz vermouth

Garnish

Sprigs of parsley

Method

Preheat the oven to 230°C/450°F/Gas Mark 8.

Take four squares of foil large enough to make a bag to hold the individual pieces of salmon and butter each square using all the butter. Place each piece of salmon on one of the buttered halves, season, and divide the vegetables out equally over the portions of salmon. Place a sprig of thyme on each. Fold the other half of the foil over and tightly seal by folding over the edges two-thirds of the way round. Pour in the fish stock and the vermouth and then seal completely.

Place the four bags on a baking sheet and cook in the oven for 8 minutes.

To Serve

Either serve the bags as they are, unopened, and let your guests experience breaking their own bag open. In this case, the parsley should be added with the vegetables before cooking. Otherwise, open the bags in the kitchen, arrange on the plates, pour the liquor over and garnish with the sprigs of parsley.

SERVES 4

1 × 675 g/1 ½ lb fillet of salmon

115 g/4 oz fresh sorrel leaves

450 ml/¾ pint fish stock

120 ml/4 fl oz dry white wine

450 ml/¾ pint double cream

1 tbsp oil

85 g/3 oz unsalted butter

Salt and freshly ground white pepper

Juice of ½ lemon

Pan-fried Salmon with Sorrel Sauce

This classic dish is so simple to make. Fresh sorrel is a must – although it is not widely used, it is very easy to grow and it is best picked when it is needed, as it does not keep well once picked.

Method

Remove the line of small bones that runs down the middle of the fillet using a pair of pliers. Skin the fillet and cut it into four long, thin slices, weighing about 175 g/6 oz each.

Remove the stalks and central vein from the sorrel and wash well. Tear the leaves into fairly small pieces – it is important to tear the leaves and not cut them, as cutting causes an almost total loss of flavour.

Put the fish stock and white wine together in a saucepan and reduce until the liquid is syrupy. Add the double cream and reduce further until it just starts to thicken.

Heat the oil in a large frying pan, adding 25 g/1 oz of the butter once it is hot. Season the fillets of salmon and gently fry in the fat, top side down first, for about 45 seconds, then turn and cook for a further minute. Do not allow the fat to become too hot as the salmon should only be slightly browned. The flesh should also remain slightly pink to retain its moisture and to stop it from becoming tough. When the fish is cooked, remove from the pan and keep warm.

Add the sorrel to the sauce and return to the boil. Remove from the heat and, with a swirling motion of the pan or stirring with a wooden spatula, add the remaining butter in small pieces. Season the sauce with the lemon juice and a little freshly ground pepper and salt.

To Serve

Divide the sauce out between the plates, drain the fillets of salmon to remove any excess fat and place the fish in the middle of each plate. Serve immediately.

Gravlax with Mustard and Dill Dressing

1 × 1.75 kg/4 lb salmon
25 g/1 oz white peppercorns, coarsely crushed
115 g/4 oz coarse sea salt
8 juniper berries
115 g/4 oz sugar
175 g/6 oz fresh dill
Juice of 1 lemon

Sauce

15 g/½ oz fresh dill
1 egg yolk
2 dessertsp Dijon mustard
Good pinch of sugar
150 ml/¼ pint salad oil
Juice of ½ lemon

Picture: page 164

Although this recipe is for a lot of portions, it will keep in a refrigerator for up to a week as long as it is kept covered. If you want to keep this dish for any length of time, then baste the salmon with its juices once a day to keep it moist.

Method

Fillet the salmon, removing the line of small bones that runs half the length of each fillet using a pair of pliers, rinse and dry each fillet. Mix the peppercorns with the sea salt, juniper berries and sugar. Roughly chop 115 g/4 oz of the dill stalks, reserving the rest for later.

Take a sheet of foil large enough to wrap the salmon in and lay the fillets side by side on the foil. Evenly spread each fillet with the salt and sugar mixture, using it all up, and cover with an even layer of chopped dill, then squeeze the lemon juice over the fillets. Place one fillet on top of the other, fold over the foil and seal it tightly all the way round. Leave to stand in a refrigerator for 36 hours, turning the parcel over every 6-8 hours. After 36 hours, open the parcel, separate the fillets and scrape them clean, but save the juice and use to baste the fillets. Finely chop the reserved dill, spread an even layer over each fillet and baste again with the juice. Lay one fillet on top of the other, reseal the foil bag and leave to stand for further 12 hours, turning again after 6 hours.

To make the sauce, finely chop the leaves of the dill. Mix the egg yolk with the mustard and sugar in a bowl and then gradually whisk in the oil as if making mayonnaise. If the mixture becomes too thick, then thin it down with a little warm water. Add the chopped dill, season to taste with a little salt, the lemon juice and a little more sugar if necessary. If the sauce is still too thick, a little warm water can be added until it is of a good consistency.

To Serve

Carve thin slices of the salmon as you would smoked salmon. Arrange the slices attractively on the plates and accompany with the mustard dressing and possibly some green salad.

SERVES 6

900 g/2 lb white asparagus (see below)

4 leaves gelatine

I tbsp dry sherry

150 ml/ ¼ pint double cream

I egg white

Pinch of sugar

¼ head frizzy lettuce

50 g/2 oz salmon caviar

Sauce

175 ml/6 fl oz natural yoghurt

175 ml// fl oz double cream

Juice of ½ lemon

Pinch of sugar

Garnish

Sprigs of fresh chervil or dill

Picture: page 163

Mousse of White Asparagus with Pearls of Salmon Caviar

This mousse will keep perfectly well in a refrigerator for up to 2 days.

Method

Peel and trim the asparagus and poach in salted water until cooked, then refresh in iced water and drain. Save the tips of 15 stalks, cutting them to about 4 cm/1½ inches long. Chop up the rest of the asparagus and purée in a blender or food processor until smooth. Rub this mixture through a sieve into a bowl. Soak the leaves of gelatine in cold water to cover until soft and then melt them in the sherry over a low heat. While the gelatine is still warm, mix it into the asparagus, making sure that it is well incorporated. Place the bowl of mixture in a bowl of iced water, stirring occasionally until it starts to set. Half whip the cream and whisk the egg white with a pinch of sugar until stiff. Gently fold the cream followed by the egg white into the asparagus purée, then leave to set in the refrigerator for at least an hour.

To make the sauce, mix together the yoghurt and the cream, add the lemon juice and season to taste with a little sugar.

To Serve

Break up the frizzy lettuce, wash well and dry on a cloth. Make a nest of it in the centre of each plate. Form the mousse into equal-sized egg shapes using two tablespoons and place one in the middle of each nest. Pour a thread of sauce around each one, cut the reserved asparagus tips in half lengthwise and arrange five pieces around each mousse. Place a little of the caviar on top of the tips, then finish off with a little on top of each mousse. Finish the arrangement with sprigs of fresh chervil or dill.

NOTE For 900 g/2 lb of asparagus you will need about 18-20 stalks; green asparagus can also be used with an equally good result.

Tartlet of Salmon with Cucumber

SERVES 4

Method

Skin the fillet of salmon and remove the line of small bones that runs down the middle of the fillet using a pair of pliers. Cut off the dark meat on the skin side and discard. Cut the flesh into 5 mm/¼ inch cubes.

Cut the cucumber across its width into three equal pieces. Either cut these, having removed the seeds, into batons about 3 mm/⅛ inch wide, or turn them into barrel shapes, allowing five or six pieces to each portion.

Pick the dill of its stalks, saving four good sprigs to use as garnish. Break the rest up to make them a little finer. Wash the frizzy endive well and break up the leaves into large pieces.

Combine together the vinegar, oil and mustard to make a vinaigrette and season.

Butter a small saucepan, place in the cubes of salmon along with the vermouth and fish stock, and season. Cover with a tightly fitting lid and heat until the liquid begins to tremble, then reduce the heat and allow to cook for about 15 seconds. Drain the salmon from the stock, cover and keep warm. Reduce the stock over a high heat until it is syrupy. Add the cream and cucumber, bring back to the boil and reduce slightly until thickened.

To Serve

Place the pastry cases in a hot oven (200°C/400°F/Gas Mark 6) for a minute to reheat. Return the salmon to the sauce and allow to soak for 30 seconds. Place a pastry case in the middle of each plate, toss the frizzy endive in the vinaigrette and arrange around the cases. At the last minute, add the dill to the sauce and salmon and fill each case with the mixture, making sure not to overfill the cases or to allow the sauce to run out. Top each filled case with a sprig of the reserved dill. Serve before the pastry has a chance to go soft.

Ingredients
1 × 225 g/8 oz fillet of salmon
7.5 cm/3 inch piece of cucumber
15 g/½ oz fresh dill
¼ head frizzy endive
1 tbsp white wine vinegar
3 tbsp olive oil
½ tsp Dijon mustard
Salt and freshly ground white pepper
A little butter
50 ml/2 fl oz vermouth
200 ml/7 fl oz fish stock
120 ml/4 fl oz double cream
4 × 10 cm/4 inch shortcrust pastry tartlet cases (see page 42)

Salmon Trout and Rainbow Trout
(FRENCH: *truite saumonée, truite*
GERMAN: *meerforel, forel*)

These are two completely different fish: the salmon trout, like the salmon, spends its adult life in the sea; the rainbow trout is confined to fresh water. However, their flesh is of a similar texture and any recipe for one will suit the other.

To look at, the difference between a salmon trout and a salmon is minimal and therefore it can be difficult to tell them apart, but their flesh is very different. The tail fin of the salmon also has a slight fork, whereas the salmon trout's is straighter, and whereas the spots of the salmon tend to be confined to the area above the lateral line, the trout's are not.

For salmon trout I prefer fish of about 1-1.25 kg/2-2½ lb in weight, this will give four good portions. With rainbow trout 400 g/14 oz fish are probably the best and will give one portion.

Paupiette of Rainbow Trout with Leeks on Caviar Sauce

SERVES 4-8

3 × 450 g/1 lb rainbow trout
½ tsp salt
1 egg white
120 ml/4 fl oz dry white wine
400 ml/14 fl oz double cream
350 g/12 oz young leeks
Salt and freshly ground white pepper
300 ml/½ pint fish stock
25 g/1 oz caviar
25 g/1 oz cold butter

Picture: page 62

This recipe is for a first course, but it is also good as a light meal for four people. I know that caviar is expensive, but it really does go rather well with the trout; if you cannot stretch to caviar, then try adding leaves of fresh thyme instead. They are obviously not quite the same, but are definitely a lot cheaper and almost as good. Use the youngest, thinnest leeks possible (pencil thickness if possible) as they have a far superior flavour and are that much more tender.

Method

Preheat the oven to 200°C/400°F/Gas Mark 6.

Scale and fillet the trout, trim the edges and remove their skins. Remove the line of small bones that runs down the middle of each fillet using a pair of pliers.

Put four of the fillets aside in the refrigerator until needed. Cut the remaining two fillets into small pieces and blend in a food processor or blender along with the salt until smooth. Add the egg white and blend again to beat in well. Rub the mousse through a sieve into a bowl set on crushed ice. Stir in 25 ml/1 fl oz of the wine. Gradually add 120 ml/4 fl oz of the cream, mixing in

(continued on page 65)

Terrine of Crab Wrapped in Smoked Salmon
(see page 155)

LEFT *Paupiette of Rainbow Trout with Leeks on Caviar Sauce*
(see page 60)

BELOW *Mousseline of Scallops with Ginger*
(see page 200)

RIGHT *Salmon Mousse with Girolles in Creamy Madeira Sauce*
(see page 54)

BELOW RIGHT *Crab Mousse with Asparagus and Chervil Butter Sauce*
(see page 156)

*Terrine of Pike with Herbs and
Wrapped in Salmon (shown left)*
(see page 46)

*Three-fish Layered Terrine with
Avocado Sauce (shown right)*
(see page 208)

well, then test the consistency of the mousse (see page 41). If it is a little too firm, add a bit more cream and test again. Leave in the refrigerator until needed.

Trim the leeks and cut them into small pieces about 5 mm/¼ inch square, and wash them really well. Blanch in boiling, salted water for about 15 seconds, then refresh in iced water. Drain and dry thoroughly on a cloth, and season with a little salt and pepper.

Place the remaining four fillets of trout between two sheets of polythene or cling film and carefully flatten using a cutlet bat or the side of a heavy knife until they are about 3 mm/⅛ inch thick. Lightly season the skin side of each fillet, then spread a thin layer of mousse over the skin side of each fillet to cover completely. Sprinkle each fillet with an even layer of the leeks. Starting at the tail end, roll each fillet over as if rolling a Swiss roll, then roll each fillet in a sheet of greaseproof paper long enough to wrap round the fillet twice.

Lay the paupiettes in an ovenproof pan, pour in the fish stock and the remaining white wine, and cover with buttered paper or foil. Heat the liquid until it just starts to tremble, then transfer the pan to the oven for 10 minutes. After 5 minutes, turn the paupiettes over to allow them to cook evenly. When cooked, remove the paupiettes from the pan and keep them covered, still in their greaseproof paper, in a warm place.

Return the stock to a high heat and reduce rapidly until it is thick and syrupy.

To Serve

When the stock has reduced sufficiently, add the remaining cream, return to the boil and reduce until the sauce just starts to thicken. Meanwhile, return the paupiettes to the oven for a further minute to reheat. When hot, carefully remove their paper sleeves and slice each one into six equal pieces. At the last minute, add the caviar to the sauce and remove from the heat. Gradually add the butter in pieces, shaking the pan until all the butter has melted. Arrange the slices of trout in a semi-circle in the middle of the plates and pour the sauce around. Serve at once.

SERVES 4

2 × 450 g / 1 lb salmon trout

115 g / 4 oz hop shoots

1 tbsp oil

25 g / 1 oz butter

300 ml / ½ pint sauce Maltaise (see page 37)

Garnish

1 orange, segmented

Salmon Trout with Hop Shoots

Between the end of April and the beginning of May salmon trout start to appear. Similar to look at as the salmon but with the flesh of a trout, this delicate fish can be used in the same ways as the salmon. Hop shoots – a little known delicacy – also appear at the end of April. These are the trimmings of the hop fields. Each plant throws out a large number of shoots, but only a few are required by the farmer; the rest are picked out and discarded. Long ago the shoots were considered a delicacy, but over the years they seem to have been forgotten. Picked and cooked like asparagus, they make a good vegetable or first course. Here I have combined the shoots with the trout to provide a perfect combination.

Method

Scale the fish and fillet them. Remove the line of small bones that runs down the middle of each fillet. Skin each fillet – this is not strictly necessary but I prefer to remove the skin. Wash the hop shoots well and tie into bundles of about 20 shoots each. Trim to equal length, about 10 cm/4 inches long. Segment the orange and place to one side; this is to be used as garnish.

Have ready a pan of boiling salted water. Heat the oil in a frying pan, then add the butter. Season each fillet and gently fry in the oil and butter, skin side up, for about 1 minute. Carefully turn the fillets over and cook for a further minute. Do not allow the fat to become too hot as the salmon should come out only slightly browned. The flesh should be slightly undercooked and still be a little pink in the centre so that it remains tender and is not dry. While the salmon trout are cooking, add the bundle of hops to the boiling water for 30 seconds, then remove from the water and drain. When the fish is cooked, drain off any excess oil.

To Serve

Place a fillet in the centre of each plate, cut the strings from the shoots and place a bundle across each fillet. Spoon some of the warm sauce Maltaise over the fish and the shoots and the rest around the fillets. Garnish with the orange segments. (If you find the sauce is a little too thick, thin it down with a little warmed orange juice until it pours easily.)

Pan-fried Fillet of Salmon Trout with Grapes and Walnuts

SERVES 4

1 × 1.25-1.5 kg/2½-3 lb salmon trout
150 g/5 oz green grapes
50 g/2 oz walnut halves
1 tbsp oil
150 g/5 oz butter
Salt and freshly ground white pepper
1 tbsp walnut oil
Juice of ½ lemon

One of the best ways to eat salmon trout is pan-fried – in this case topped off with walnuts and green grapes – with a little salad. This recipe is equally suitable for river trout or salmon.

Method

Scale and fillet the salmon trout. Remove the line of small bones that runs down the middle of each fillet. Skin each fillet and cut across into two equal-sized portions.

Peel the grapes, cut them in half and remove the pips. Rub the walnuts in a dry cloth to remove any loose skin.

Heat the oil in a frying pan, then add 25 g/1 oz of the butter and heat until it starts to sizzle. Season the fillets on the skin side. Gently lay the fillets in the pan, skin side up, and fry gently until they are lightly browned, then turn them over and continue cooking over a gentle heat until lightly browned on the other side. Remove the fish from the pan, drain on kitchen paper and keep warm. Tip out the fat from the pan, wipe the pan and return to the heat. Add the walnut oil and, when this is hot, add the grapes and walnuts. Toss them in the oil and then add the rest of the butter and shake the pan until it has all melted. Finally, pour in the lemon juice.

To Serve

Lay a fillet of salmon trout on each plate, spoon the walnuts and grapes over each fillet and pour the butter over the top. Serve immediately.

SERVES 4

1 × 900 g/2 lb salmon trout

10 cm/4 inch piece of cucumber

24 small girolles

150 ml/¼ pint dry vermouth

300 ml/½ pint fish stock

85 ml/3 fl oz double cream

225 g/8 oz cold unsalted butter

Garnish

Sprigs of fresh fennel or dill

Poached Salmon Trout with Girolles and Cucumber

If fresh girolles are not available, then use dried ones – which are not, of course, quite as good. It really is a very pretty dish if you take time and care over the final presentation.

Method

Preheat the oven to 190°C/375°F/Gas Mark 5.

Scale and fillet the salmon trout. Remove the skin and any bones from both fillets and cut across each fillet into two equal portions.

Cut the cucumber across into four 2.5 cm/1 inch lengths, then cut each piece into six and 'turn' each section into small barrel shapes, leaving the skin on. Alternatively, cut each piece into six thick batons. Scrape the girolles clean of any dirt or grit, but do not wash. To prepare dried girolles, soak in cold water for about 20 minutes before using.

Butter an ovenproof pan large enough to take the fillets without overlapping and put in the fillets. Add the vermouth and fish stock and cover with buttered paper or foil. Set the pan over a high heat until the liquid just starts to tremble, then transfer the pan to the oven and cook for 4–5 minutes. When cooked, remove the fillets from the pan, cover and keep warm.

To make the sauce, return the stock to a high heat and reduce until syrupy. Add the girolles and the cucumber along with the cream. Bring back to the boil, then remove from the heat and gradually add the butter, shaking the pan with a swirling motion until it has all melted. Do not allow the sauce to boil once the butter has been added. If you need to keep it warm for a few minutes, then stand it in a saucepan of warm water over a low heat.

To Serve

Return the fillets of fish to the oven for about a minute to reheat. Cover the plates with sauce, alternating the girolles and cucumber around the plates, and place the fillets in the centre. To complete the picture, garnish with sprigs of fennel or dill.

Salmon Trout in a Buttery Court Bouillon

SERVES 4

Either fillet the fish or cook it whole. Salmon trout, river trout or even salmon can be used – that's how versatile fish can be.

1 × 1.25-1.5 kg/2½-3 lb salmon trout
6 button onions or large spring onions
4 small carrots
1 stick celery
About 450 ml/¾ pint fish stock
About 50 ml/2 fl oz white wine vinegar
2 bay leaves
About 10 g/¼ oz whole black peppercorns
About ½ tsp coarse sea salt
2 stalks parsley
225 g/8 oz unsalted butter

Picture: page 162

Method

Peel and thinly slice the onions into rounds. Peel the carrots and cannelize, then also thinly slice into rounds. Peel the celery and cut across into crescents.

Scale the salmon trout. If cooking and serving whole, remove the insides and wash well. If cooking as portions, fillet and skin both fillets. Remove the small bones that run down the middle of each fillet using a pair of pliers. Cut each fillet across into two equal portions.

Combine the fish stock, vinegar, bay leaves, peppercorns, salt and parsley in a large deep tin (it must be big enough to take all the fillets without overlapping) and bring to the boil. If the pan is on the small side, it is probably best to cook only two fillets at a time – don't try and cram them all in at once. If cooking whole, use a salmon kettle instead and increase the amount of stock so you have enough to cover the fish. When the stock is boiling, reduce the heat until it is barely simmering and gently put in the fish. Cook the fillets for 5 minutes; a whole fish will need about 20 minutes. When cooked, remove the fish, cover and keep warm.

Strain 450 ml/¾ pint of the stock into a saucepan, set over a high heat and reduce until only a quarter of its original volume remains. Add the vegetables, return to the boil, then reduce the heat to low and gradually add the butter, shaking the pan as you do until all the butter has melted. Stir in the parsley and test the vegetables; they should still be slightly crunchy. If they are a little too hard, allow the sauce to sit over a very low heat for a further minute or so.

To Serve

Place the fillets on the plates and pour over the sauce. Arrange the vegetables attractively on the plates and serve.

NOTE If serving the fish whole, serve the sauce separately in a sauce boat.

SERVES 4

1 × 800 g / 1 ¾ lb salmon trout
2 small carrots
4 large spring onions
1 small courgette
8 asparagus tips
16 mangetout
1 red pepper, weighing about 150 g / 5 oz
175 ml / 6 fl oz fish stock
1 tsp sea salt
50 ml / 2 fl oz olive oil
25 ml / 1 fl oz white wine vinegar

Garnish

Leaves of red lettuce (optional)

Steamed Salmon Trout with Sea Salt and Slivers of Vegetables

This is a quick and simple dish, especially if your fishmonger fillets the salmon trout for you. It can be prepared well in advance and cooked when needed. The actual cooking only takes a matter of minutes so it is ideal for a dinner party. For the calorie-conscious, leave the oil out of the sauce and add a little more fish stock instead.

Method

Scale and fillet the salmon trout and remove the line of small bones that runs down the middle of each fillet using a pair of pliers. Skin the fillets, then cut across into two equal portions.

Peel the carrots and cut diagonally into thin slices about 5 cm/2 inches long. Peel the spring onions and cut each one into four or five slices. Cut the courgette in the same way as the carrot, peel the asparagus and once again cut into slices diagonally. Top and tail the mangetout.

Quarter the red pepper and remove its seeds, cut it up quite small and put in a pan with the fish stock. Bring to the boil and simmer for about 15 minutes or until very soft. Purée in a blender or food processor until smooth, then pass through a fine sieve or muslin.

Place the fillets of trout into a steaming pan, sprinkle with the sea salt and strew the vegetables over the top. Place over boiling water and steam for 3 minutes. After 3 minutes, the fish should still be slightly pink in the centre and the vegetables should retain a little crunch. While the fish is cooking, bring the pepper purée to the boil along with the olive oil and the white wine vinegar. Season with a little sea salt and boil rapidly for about a minute until the oil and the pepper purée emulsify.

To Serve

When the trout is cooked, pour the sauce in a circle around the plates, place a fillet of the fish in the centre of each and evenly distribute the vegetables over and around the fish. If you wish, scatter a few small leaves of red lettuce around the sauce.

Steamed Salmon Trout with Basil and Tomato Vinaigrette

SERVES 6

1 × 675 g/1 ½ lb salmon trout
18 asparagus tips
Salt and freshly ground white pepper
3 tomatoes
3 tbsp walnut oil
3 tbsp sherry vinegar
18-20 fresh basil leaves
⅓ head oak leaf lettuce

Picture: page 98

Have everything ready in advance for this warm first course, leaving only the cooking of the fish and the final touches until the last minute.

Method

Scale, fillet and skin the salmon trout. Remove the line of small bones that runs down the middle of each fillet using a pair of pliers. Cut each fillet slightly on an angle into six pieces.

Peel the asparagus and tie in bundles of six. Cook in boiling salted water so that they are cooked but still retain a little bite. Refresh in iced water and drain.

Blanch and skin the tomatoes, then deseed and cut the flesh into small dice. Mix together the oil and the sherry vinegar and add the tomato. Tear the basil leaves into small pieces and add to the vinaigrette. Season to taste.

To Serve

Lay the pieces of salmon in a steaming pan, season and steam over boiling water for 2 minutes. Alternatively, lay the fillets in a buttered pan or tray, add about 85 ml/3 fl oz of fish stock, cover and poach for 2 minutes. While the salmon is cooking, gently warm the vinaigrette through – it should not be hot, but just take off the chill. Remove the fish from the heat and drop the asparagus tips into boiling water for about 30 seconds to reheat.

Cut each asparagus tip in half. Lay three leaves of lettuce on each plate, and place two slices of the fish in the centre. Scatter the asparagus around the fish and spoon the warm dressing over and around the fillets.

SERVES 8

3 × 450 g/1 lb rainbow trout
½ tsp salt
1 egg white
25 ml/1 fl oz dry white wine
About 85 ml/3 fl oz double cream
Freshly ground white pepper
175 g/6 oz fine French beans
1 dessertsp sherry vinegar
1 tbsp walnut oil
50 g/2 oz shallots, finely chopped
85 ml/3 fl oz yoghurt vinaigrette (see page 39)

Galantine of Rainbow Trout with French Bean Salad

Although this is not one of the easiest starters to make, it is certainly very effective. It can be made the day before, but its flavour and texture will be so much better if it is stored in a cool, dry place instead of the refrigerator. Serve with a small salad of lettuce hearts tossed in the dressing. This would also be an ideal dish for a buffet, in which case brush each slice with a little fish aspic (see page 213).

Method

Scale and fillet the trout, then trim the edges and remove the skin. Remove the line of small bones that runs down the middle of each fillet. Put four of the fillets in the refrigerator until needed.

To make the mousse, cut the remaining two fillets into small pieces and process them in a food processor or blender with the salt until smooth. Add the egg white and process again until it is well mixed in, then remove and rub through a sieve into a bowl set on crushed ice. Stir in the wine and gradually add two-thirds of the cream, mixing it well. Test the mousse (see page 41). If it is too firm, add a bit more cream and test again. Leave in the refrigerator until needed.

Have ready a pan of boiling water, making sure it is large enough to take the finished roll and that there is sufficient water to allow the roll to float. If you do not have a large enough pan, make the galantine in two pieces.

To make the galantine, flatten out the four fillets of trout with a cutlet bat or the side of a heavy knife until they are about 3 mm/ ⅛ inch thick. Trim the edges so that the fillets are square in shape and save the trimmings. Lay out the fillets, skin side up and side by side, on a sheet of cling film at least 45 cm/18 inches wide. Fill any gaps with the trimmings. Lightly season the fish and then carefully and lightly spread the mousse over the fillets to form a layer the same thickness as the fish. Gently roll the fish over as if rolling a Swiss roll. Roll in cling film and tie off the ends tightly. Place the galantine into the boiling water, reduce the heat so the water is barely simmering and cook for 12 minutes, then remove from the pan and place the galantine in iced water until it is cold.

Top and tail the French beans and cook in boiling salted water – they should still retain a slight crunch. Refresh in iced water and drain. Mix together the vinegar and walnut oil. Add the beans to the shallots and lightly season, then thoroughly toss in the oil and vinegar dressing so that everything is nicely coated.

To Serve

Divide the beans out between the plates, forming a small pile in the centre of each plate. Slice the galantine into 24 slices about 5 mm/¼ inch thick. Lay three slices in a semi-circle around the bean salad, and pour a little yoghurt sauce around the slices of galantine.

Rainbow Trout Marinated with Ginger and Lime

SERVES 4

1 × 450 g/1 lb rainbow trout
2 limes
50 ml/2 fl oz sugar syrup (see page 40)
25 g/1 oz fresh ginger
120 ml/4 fl oz walnut oil
1 dessertsp sherry vinegar
Salt and freshly ground white pepper
¼ head frizzy lettuce

This easy-to-prepare recipe is also suitable for salmon and salmon trout, but it is important to use only the freshest of fish. If you don't have any limes, use lemons instead.

Method

Scale and fillet the trout. Remove the line of small bones that runs down the middle of each fillet. Skin each fillet, then cut slightly at an angle across the fillets to give 20 slices altogether.

Peel the limes and cut the zest into fine strips. Place the zest into the syrup, bring to the boil and simmer until almost all of the syrup has gone, then allow to go cold. Peel and finely grate the ginger, and juice the limes. Mix together the ginger, lime juice, walnut oil and sherry vinegar, and add a good pinch of salt and a few turns of the pepper mill. Lay the trout in a shallow tray, lightly season and pour the dressing over. Allow to sit in the refrigerator for about 6 hours.

To Serve

Break up the frizzy lettuce and wash well, shake dry and scatter the leaves on the plates. Divide the trout out across the plates, strain the dressing and spoon it over the trout and frizzy lettuce. Scatter the strips of lime zest over the top.

Seawater Fish

There are so many hundreds of different types of fish in the sea, and most of them are edible. Catch or buy one and someone somewhere will have a recipe for it. It would take a much bigger book than this to include even one recipe from every single fish, so I have not tried. What I have done, however, is to include recipes for the fish I use most frequently and the fish that are readily available to most people. If I have been unable to get a particular fish (which has often been the case), then there is no recipe for it. Having said that, however, all fish are so versatile, especially those from the sea, that a recipe that suits one fish will definitely suit at least two other types of fish – so experiment! Where a recipe calls for Dover sole, try using witch or lemon sole instead. Is sea bass not available, or even too expensive? Well, try using haddock. The sea holds a wealth of food still not appreciated as much perhaps as it ought.

Bass, salmon bass, sea bass
(FRENCH: *bar, loup de mer*
GERMAN: *seebarsch*)

Much prized by sea anglers, it is not until more recent years that bass has found favour with gourmets. For me, it is certainly one of my favourites, and is probably best eaten plainly grilled or baked. Bass has always been a great favourite of the Chinese. Owing to its present, rightly-deserved popularity, it has become a very expensive fish and also a difficult fish to find, except during the summer months when it is at its best.

Sea bass, or salmon bass as it is also known (only because of its silvery colour), is armed with very sharp fins and great care is needed in its preparation if you are not to cause yourself an injury. Its scales are large and thick and must be removed before preparing and cooking.

The bass found in America, although not exactly the same as those found in European waters, are equally good and can be used in the same ways.

SERVES 4

1 × 450 g/1 lb sea bass
48 small girolles, or 24 large ones cut in half
A little butter
85 ml/3 fl oz vermouth
350 ml/12 fl oz fish stock
50 ml/2 fl oz Madeira
450 ml/15 fl oz double cream

Garnish

Sprigs of fresh dill or fennel

Sea Bass with Girolles

Use dried girolles if fresh ones are not available; dried are not as good, but they will do just as well. Be careful when handling the sea bass as their fins can cause nasty injuries.

Method

Preheat the oven to 190°C/375°F/Gas Mark 5.

Carefully scale the sea bass – avoid handling the fins and the area around the gills. Fillet the fish but do not skin. Remove the few small bones at the head end of each fillet using a pair of pliers.

Scrape the girolles clean of any dirt or grit but do not wash. If they are large, as they often are, then cut each one in half lengthwise. To prepare dried girolles, soak in cold water for about 20 minutes before using.

Butter an ovenproof pan large enough to comfortably take the fillets (use two pans if necessary). Lay the fillets in, add the vermouth and the fish stock, and cover with a lid or buttered paper or foil. Set the pan over a high heat until the liquid starts to tremble, then transfer to the oven. Cook for about 3-4 minutes – once the surface colour of the fish has changed, it is cooked. Remove the fillets, cover and keep warm.

Add the Madeira to the stock, then return the stock to a high heat and reduce by two-thirds. Add the girolles and the cream, bring back to the boil and reduce until thickened.

To Serve

Return the fillets of bass to the oven for a minute to reheat. Divide out the girolles between the plates and arrange them in an oval around the edge of the plates. Pour over the sauce and place a fillet in the middle of each. To finish, scatter the sprigs of dill or fennel over the girolles.

Fillet of Sea Bass Baked in Filo Pastry with Fresh Sorrel

SERVES 4-8

4 × 150 g/5 oz fillets of sea bass
175 g/6 oz filo pastry
125 g/4½ oz sorrel leaves,
Salt and freshly ground white pepper
Juice of ½ lemon
25 g/1 oz butter
300 ml/½ pint fish stock
25 ml/1 fl oz white wine
450 ml/¾ pint double cream

Picture: page 19

Method

Preheat the oven to 240°C/475°F/Gas Mark 9.

Make the filo pastry (see page 43) at least 24 hours in advance, and allow to rest in the refrigerator until required.

Sweat 115 g/4 oz of the sorrel, lightly seasoned, in the lemon juice and 10 g/¼ oz of the butter for about 2 minutes, then allow to cool. Scale, bone and skin the sea bass, then season and spread the cooked sorrel down one side of each fillet. Divide the pastry into four equal amounts and roll out, stretching each piece as thin as possible, as described in the recipe on page 43. Cover each fillet separately with the pastry, making sure there are no holes. Melt the remaining butter and brush the parcels liberally with it. Bake them on a baking tray in the oven for 10-12 minutes. Baste the pastry with the butter once again after about 4 minutes.

For the sauce, reduce the fish stock and the white wine until thick and syrupy, then pour in the cream and reduce again until it starts to thicken. At the last minute, add the remaining sorrel to the sauce and season.

To Serve

Pour the sauce on to each plate and place a parcel on top. Only when the pastry case is opened is the full impact of the dish felt.

SERVES 4

2 × 550 g/1 ¼ lb sea bass
2 large round lettuces
20 oysters
Salt and freshly ground white pepper
25 g/1 oz shallots, finely chopped
300 ml/½ pint fish stock
175 ml/6 fl oz dry white wine
85 ml/3 fl oz double cream
175 g/6 oz unsalted butter

Sea Bass Wrapped in Lettuce with Oysters

With or without oysters this makes a wonderful dish – the lettuce helping to retain the moisture of the bass. As only the larger outer leaves of the lettuce are used, try poaching the hearts cut in half alongside the bass and serve as a garnish. Alternatively, use them to make a little lettuce salad to accompany the meal.

Method

Preheat the oven to 200°C/400°F/Gas Mark 6.

Scale and fillet the bass. Remove the few small bones that run from the head to halfway down the length of each fillet using a pair of pliers. Skin each fillet.

Discard the very outer leaves of the lettuces and remove the larger leaves so that only the hearts are left. Wash the leaves well, then plunge them into boiling water for a minute to blanch. Refresh in iced water and drain.

Open all of the oysters over a bowl to catch the juices and remove them from their shells; be sure to reserve any juice there may be. Reserve 8 whole oysters and cut the rest into 5 mm/¼ inch dice.

Remove the central rib from each lettuce leaf, season the fillets and wrap them in the lettuce; it will take three or four leaves to wrap each fillet. Lightly butter a shallow ovenproof pan or tray and sprinkle with the shallots. Lay the fillets of fish in the pan, add the fish stock and the white wine and cover with buttered paper or foil. Set the tray over a high heat until the liquid just starts to tremble, then transfer to the oven and cook for 10 minutes. When cooked, drain the fish from the stock, cover and keep warm.

Return the stock to a high heat. Strain any juice from the oysters through muslin into the stock and return to the boil. Add the whole oysters and simmer for 30 seconds, then remove the oysters and keep warm with the fish. Reduce the stock until syrupy, then add the cream and bring back to the boil.

To Serve

Just before serving, remove the sauce from the heat and add the butter in small pieces, whisking continuously until it has all melted. Add the diced oyster and allow to soak for about 30 seconds. Pour the sauce on to the plates, lay a fillet of bass on top, and top each fillet with 2 oysters.

Steamed Sea Bass on a Bed of Watercress and Chive Sauce

SERVES 4

This summery dish is delicious and easy to prepare. The soft texture of the sea bass and the slight crunch of the watercress complement each other really well. Calorie conscious? Then leave out the cream, double the quantity of fish stock and do not reduce it down quite so far.

2 × 450 g/1 lb sea bass
115 g/4 oz watercress
Salt and freshly ground white pepper
300 ml/½ pint fish stock
150 ml/¼ pint dry white wine
25 g/1 oz fresh chives, finely chopped
225 ml/8 fl oz double cream

Method

Scale and fillet the sea bass. Remove the few small bones at the head end of each fillet with a pair of pliers. Wash the watercress well and remove any yellowing leaves and roots. Season each fillet with salt and freshly ground white pepper. Bring the fish stock and the white wine to the boil over a high heat, place the fish in a steaming basket over this and steam. When the fish is cooked – it should take 3-4 minutes – remove it from over the stock and keep warm.

Reduce the fish stock until only about 4 tablespoons remain. Add the chives and the cream and bring back to the boil.

To Serve

Arrange the watercress in a circle in the middle of each plate. Place a fillet of the bass in the middle of each ring and pour the sauce around.

NOTE This should be served immediately, as the longer it stands, the more chance there is of the watercress losing its bite.

SERVES 2-4

2 × 350-400 g / 12-14 oz sea bass
¼ green pepper
¼ red pepper
¼ yellow pepper
15 g / ½ oz fresh fennel or dill
Salt and freshly ground white pepper
A little butter
120 ml / 4 fl oz fish stock
Juice of ½ lemon

Sea Bass en Papillote with Fennel and Peppers

If you cannot get hold of fresh leaf fennel, then dill is an ideal substitute. However, whichever herb you use, it must be fresh; dried will not do.

Method

Preheat the oven to 230°C/450°F/Gas Mark 8.

Scale and fillet the sea bass. Remove the few small bones that run from the head halfway down the length of the fillets with a pair of pliers. Match up the pairs of fillets and spread the fennel evenly across all of the fillets, and season. Skin, deseed and cut the peppers into 5 mm/¼ inch dice. Mix together the different peppers and cover one of each pair of fillets with this mixture, then lay the other fillet on top to re-form the shape of the fish. Take two squares of foil large enough to make two individual bags to hold the fish. Butter an area just large enough for the bass to lie on. Place the prepared fish on this. Fold the foil over and tightly seal the edges three-quarters of the way round. Pour in the fish stock and lemon juice, which should be equally divided between the two bags, and then finish off sealing the bag.

Put the bags on a baking sheet and place in the oven for 10 minutes.

To Serve

When the bags come out of the oven, they should be puffed up like pillows. Cut them open and, using a fish slice, carefully transfer the fish to the plates. Separate the fillets and lay them next to each other, meat and pepper side up. Pour the juices from the bag over the fish and serve immediately.

Sea Bass Marinated in Fresh Herbs and Olive Oil

SERVES 4

Sea bass is probably my favourite fish of all. Use only the freshest of fish for this recipe, but once in the marinade it will keep for a couple of days. This really must be one of the easiest starters of all time.

1 × 675 g / 1 ½ lb sea bass
10 g / ¼ oz fresh mixed herbs (dill, fennel, chives, tarragon, marjoram, parsley, olive oil)
2 tsp sea salt
Freshly ground black pepper
120 ml / 4 fl oz olive oil

Picture: page 20

Method

Scale and fillet the sea bass. Remove the few small bones that run from the head halfway down the length of each fillet with a pair of pliers. Using a thin-bladed, sharp knife, carve thin slices from each fillet as if carving smoked salmon. Each fillet should give at least 12 slices.

Remove the stalks from the herbs and mix the leaves together. Lay the slices of fish in a shallow container so they do not overlap. Sprinkle with half the sea salt and generously grind some fresh black pepper over the slices. Strew the herbs over the top, then pour on the oil. Press it all down to make sure that the oil covers everything. Leave to stand in the refrigerator for between 18 and 24 hours. (If you do not have a container large enough to take all of the fish in one layer, do not worry. Lay in one layer, cover with herbs, salt and pepper, then make another layer on top, repeating the process.)

To Serve

Simply transfer the fish to the plates, leaving the herbs in place on top of the fish. Pour the oil over and sprinkle with the remaining sea salt.

SERVES 2

2 × 350-400 g / 12-14 oz sea bass

40 fresh mint leaves

20 g / ¾ oz unsalted butter

Salt and freshly ground black pepper

150 ml / ¼ pint fish stock

Grilled Sea Bass with Mint

This dish is simplicity itself. It takes only a few minutes to prepare (especially if you get your fishmonger to fillet the bass for you) and a matter of minutes to cook. It is great for a hot summer's day with a crisp green salad and a few boiled Jersey potatoes.

Method

Scale and fillet the sea bass and remove the small bones from each fillet – found just behind the head – with a pair of pliers. With the point of a small knife, make 10 small incisions in the flesh of each fillet at regular intervals, cutting right through to the skin at about a 45 degree angle. Place 1 leaf of mint into each incision. Melt the butter and use a little to butter a grilling tray. Place the fillets on this, season, and brush with melted butter. Place the fish under a hot grill. As it cooks, baste with the butter and the juices as they run off. The fillets will only take 4 or 5 minutes to cook. When cooked, remove them on to serving dishes and keep warm.

To Serve

Bring the fish stock to the boil and swill out the grill tray with it, strain, reduce slightly over a high heat and pour over the fish. NOTE If fresh mint is not available, then try using fresh sage leaves.

Baked Sea Bass with Fennel

2 × 350 g / 12 oz sea bass
115 g / 4 oz fennel
25 g / 1 oz fresh fennel leaves
Salt and freshly ground white pepper
225 ml / 8 fl oz fish stock
½ tbsp Pernod
85 g / 3 oz butter

Whenever I make this dish, I always use very small bulbs of fennel complete with tops and allow one per person, cutting the bulb into four slices and stripping the leaves from the top. These are, of course, difficult to get if you do not grow your own or know a market gardener, as I do, who will let me pick them the size I like. Do try, though, to get them as small as possible, their flavour is not only that much better but they are also more tender. This dish works just as well with a larger sea bass of course; it is just that I prefer everything in individual portions.

Method

Preheat the oven to 200°C/400°F/Gas Mark 6.

Scale the bass, and carefully remove the fillets. Remove the few small bones that run from the head halfway down the length of the fillets with a pair of pliers. If using baby fennels, then leave them whole and blanch for about a minute in boiling salted water. If not, then cut them into quarters or smaller, and blanch. Refresh in iced water, then drain. Pick the leaves from their stalks, and reserve two nice sprigs for garnish.

Cut four slits across the skin side of each fillet, and slide a slice of the fennel into each slit. Lightly season the inside of each fillet and cover the fillets with the fennel leaves. Put the fillets back together to re-form each fish; the scored side should be on top.

Grease a shallow ovenproof tray. Place the fish on this and add the fish stock and the Pernod. Melt about 25 g / 1 oz of the butter and brush over the fish. Cover with buttered paper or foil, and cook in the oven for 15 minutes. Baste the fish once every 5 minutes with a little of the cooking liquor.

When cooked, leave the fish in the pan and tip off the liquid into a saucepan – you need 175-225 ml/6-8 fl oz, so if you have too much reduce it a little. Bring the liquid to the boil, remove from the heat and gradually whisk in the remaining butter until it has all melted.

To Serve

Place the fish on to the plates and pour the sauce around. Place a sprig of the reserved fennel over the top.

NOTE If using baby fennel and it comes with its root on, do not discard this. Instead, peel and coarsely grate it and add it to the leaves in the centre of the fish before cooking.

SERVES 4

2 × 450-550 g/ 1 - 1 ¼ lb sea bass
225 g/8 oz carrots
50 g/2 oz parsley
1 tbsp oil
50 g/2 oz unsalted butter
Salt and freshly ground white pepper
300 ml/ ½ pint fish stock
Juice of ½ lemon

Garnish

A few flat parsley leaves

Fillet of Sea Bass Sautéed with Carrots and Parsley

This is a good dish for those who are having to count the calories. It is also quick and simple to both prepare and finish.

Method

Scale and fillet the sea bass. Remove the small bones from each fillet – found just behind the head – with a pair of pliers. Make three or four cuts diagonally in the skin – this should prevent the fillets from curling when cooking. Peel the carrots and cut into even thin strips about 5 cm/2 inches long by 3 mm/⅛ inch wide. Wash and pick over the parsley and chop coarsely.

Heat the oil in a frying pan, then add half of the butter. Season the fillets of bass and gently sauté them, skin side up, in the oil and butter for about 1 minute until slightly brown. Carefully turn over the fillets and continue cooking for a further minute. Remove them from the pan and keep warm. Tip away the fat, reheat the pan and add the remaining butter. When hot, add the strips of carrot and quickly fry, turning frequently, for about 30 seconds, then add half of the chopped parsley and mix in well.

To Serve

Remove the carrots and arrange in the centre of the plates to form a nest. Add the fish stock and the lemon juice to the hot pan, bring to the boil and reduce slightly. Reheat the fillets of sea bass in a hot oven (200°C/400°F/Gas Mark 6) for about a minute. Place a fillet in the middle of each nest of carrot. At the last minute add the remaining parsley to the sauce and pour the sauce over and around each fillet. Top with leaves of fresh parsley.

Brill
(FRENCH: *barbue* GERMAN: *glattbutt*)

One of the lesser-known of the flat fish, brill resembles turbot in a lot of ways. It is slightly different in shape, being more oval – its body is almost twice as long as it is wide. The main difference between the two fish is that the brill has a covering of very fine scales, whereas the turbot has none. In addition, whereas the turbot has 'stones' embedded in its dark skin, the brill is completely smooth. Like the turbot, the brill is not found in American waters, but it is still finding its way into restaurants and fish markets over there, presumably because so many Americans now come to Europe and try brill and then go back to the States and look for it.

The brill never grows to the same size as a turbot; it is never much bigger than 3 kg/7 lb and the normal sizes found are smaller, up to 2.25 kg/5 lb. Although it has a very good flavour and texture, it is still regarded as inferior to the turbot, which is, of course, normally reflected in the price.

Brill can be used in any turbot, sole, or halibut recipe as well as in the recipes contained here. If you get a small one, try poaching it whole in a court bouillon.

SERVES 6

6 × 150-175 g/5-6 oz fillets of brill

225 g/8 oz shallots, finely sliced

Salt and freshly ground white pepper

175 ml/6 fl oz red wine

600 ml/1 pint fish stock

175 g/6 oz cold butter, cut into 2.5 cm/1 inch cubes

Garnish

Sprigs of fresh chervil (optional)

Fillet of Brill Poached in Red Wine with Shallots

This is a very attractive and colourful dish. The fish and the shallots take on the red of the wine, so they are left with a deep purple hue which contrasts well with the delicate green of the chervil.

Method

Preheat the oven to 160°C/325°F/Gas Mark 3.

Butter an ovenproof pan large enough to take the fillets without overlapping. Cover the base of the pan with the shallots, place the fillets of brill on top, and season. Add the red wine and fish stock, cover with buttered paper or foil and bring to just below boiling point. Transfer to the warm oven (the oven should not be so hot that it makes the liquid boil) and cook for about 4-6 minutes. When cooked, remove the fish and shallots from the stock, cover and keep warm.

Put the stock in a saucepan and reduce by about half, then gradually add the cubes of butter, beating with a small whisk until all the butter has melted. Do not allow the sauce to boil again once the butter has been added.

To Serve

Divide the shallots between the plates, place the fillets on top and pour the sauce around. Garnish with sprigs of chervil, if liked. NOTE One 2 kg/4 lb brill will yield six 150 g/5 oz portions (each large fillet will yield two portions and a small fillet one portion). If brill is not available, turbot will do equally well and John Dory is also very good. A 2 kg/4 lb turbot will yield the same as the brill, but if using John Dory, allow one 450-500 g/16-18 oz fish for two portions.

Poached Fillet of Brill in a Rich Red Wine Sauce

SERVES 6

This has always been a very popular dish with all our customers. The richness of the sauce harmonizes with the brill to give a powerfully-flavoured dish and the turned vegetables offer a wonderful splash of colour as well as providing a contrast in textures. For the sauce, use only a good quality Burgundy; the better the wine, the better the sauce. Turbot or monkfish can be used instead of brill for this dish.

1 × 2.25 kg/5 lb brill
2 medium carrots
2 medium courgettes
2 small turnips
115 g/4 oz calabrese
85 g/3 oz fine French beans
100 g/3½ oz butter
Salt and freshly ground white pepper
600 ml/1 pint red Burgundy
300 ml/½ pint fish stock
350 ml/12 fl oz veal stock

Garnish

Sprigs of fresh chervil

Method

Preheat the oven to 200°C/400°F/Gas Mark 6.

Fillet and skin the brill. Cut the large fillets in half and leave the small fillets whole to give six portions.

'Turn' the vegetables into small barrel shapes about 2.5 cm/1 inch long or, alternatively, cut them into batons 2.5 cm × 5 mm/1 × ¼ inch. Break the calabrese into small florets. Top and tail the beans and break into 2.5 cm/1 inch lengths. Blanch the vegetables in boiling salted water for a few seconds, then refresh in iced water. Drain.

Butter an ovenproof pan large enough to take all of the fillets without overlapping. Lay the fish in and season with a little salt and freshly ground white pepper. Pour over the wine and cover the pan with buttered paper or foil. Set over a high heat and as soon as the liquid starts to tremble transfer to the oven and cook for about 6 minutes. When cooked, remove the fish from the wine, cover and keep warm. Set the wine over a high heat, add the fish stock and bring to the boil and reduce until only 200 ml/7 fl oz remains. Add the veal stock, bring back to the boil and reduce until it starts to thicken.

To Serve

Return the fish to the oven for about 30 seconds to reheat. Gradually whisk 85 g/3 oz butter into the sauce and continue whisking until it has all melted. Strain the sauce through muslin or a very fine sieve. Melt the remaining butter in a pan and roll the vegetables in this until they are hot; lightly season.

Place a fillet on to each plate, pour the sauce over and around. Spoon the vegetables on top, arranging them neatly on the fish. Place a nice sprig of fresh chervil on the vegetables.

1 × 350 g/ 12 oz fillet of brill
350 g/12 oz young leeks
120 ml/4 fl oz fish stock
50 ml/2 fl oz dry white wine
175 ml/6 fl oz double cream
15 g/½ oz butter
Salt and freshly ground white pepper
4 × 10 cm/4 inch shortcrust tartlet cases (see page 42)

Picture: page 141

Tartlet of Brill with Baby Leeks

Turbot or John Dory would be good substitutes for this easy-to-make first course. I much prefer to use really young, pencil-sized leeks, but they are hard to get hold of unless you grow your own.

Method

Preheat the oven to 200°C/400°F/Gas Mark 6.

Cut the leeks into 1 cm/½ inch dice if they are large or just cut them across at an angle if they are small. Wash and dry well.

Skin the fillet of brill and cut 12 slices across the fillet at a slight angle. Lay these in a buttered shallow tray or ovenproof pan, add the fish stock and the white wine and cover with buttered paper or foil. Heat the liquid until it just starts to tremble, then reduce the heat so that the liquid is not moving and allow the fish to poach for about 30 seconds. Remove the fish from the pan and keep warm.

Return the liquid to a high heat and reduce until it has almost gone. Add the cream, return to the boil, then add 225 g/8 oz of the leeks and allow the liquid to boil until it starts to thicken.

To Serve

Heat the butter in a small saucepan until it starts to sizzle, then add the remaining leeks and season lightly. Cover the pan with a lid and gently sweat until cooked – this should take no more than 2 minutes. Spoon the leeks from the sauce into the tartlet cases, place three slices of brill on top and place in the oven to reheat for about 1 minute. While these are reheating, return the sauce to the boil and reduce until it becomes really thick. Place a tartlet on each plate just off centre, spoon enough sauce over them to coat the fish but not so much that it runs on to the plate, and spoon a pile of leeks on the opposite side of the plates.

Fillet of Brill with Two Sauces

The richness of the red wine sauce and the delicate sabayon make a wonderful combination. This is probably best served with a light red Burgundy rather than the traditional white wine served with fish.

Method

Preheat the oven to 190°C/375°F/Gas Mark 5.

Skin and trim the fillets of brill. Butter an ovenproof pan, lay in the fillets and add the fish stock. Bring the liquid to trembling point, cover with a lid, transfer to the oven and gently poach for 4–5 minutes until cooked. When cooked, remove the fillets from the stock, cover and keep warm. Divide the stock out between two pans, add the red wine to one and the dry sherry to the other. Set both pans over a high heat and reduce the one containing the red wine by three-quarters and the one containing the sherry by two-thirds. When the sherry sauce has reduced, remove it from the heat and allow to go cold. When the red wine sauce has reduced, add the veal stock and reduce over a high heat until it thickens.

To make the sabayon sauce, break the egg yolks into a round-based bowl and add the reduced sherry stock. Whisk the egg yolks with the sherry stock over a pan of hot, not boiling, water until they thicken. Meanwhile, pass the red wine sauce through a fine strainer, then gradually whisk in the butter until melted.

To Serve

Place the fillets of fish in the oven for a few minutes to reheat. Place a fillet of fish in the centre of each plate, pour the wine sauce around, spoon the sabayon over the fillets and top each one with a sprig of fresh chervil.

4 × 175 g/6 oz fillets of brill
350 ml/12 fl oz fish stock
175 ml/6 fl oz red wine
120 ml/4 fl oz dry sherry
350 ml/12 fl oz veal stock (see page 30)
3 egg yolks
25 g/1 oz unsalted butter

Garnish
Sprigs of fresh chervil

SERVES 4

4 × 175 g / 6 oz fillets of brill
2 medium carrots
2 small turnips
2 medium courgettes
15 g / ½ oz truffle peelings
300 ml / ½ pint fish stock
25 ml / 1 fl oz Madeira
120 ml / 4 fl oz veal stock (see page 30)
50 g / 2 oz unsalted butter
Salt and freshly ground white pepper

Picture: page 99

Poached Fillet of Brill with Truffle Sauce

This is a dish that should be reserved for that special occasion; the truffle, whether fresh or canned, is always very expensive. There is no substitute for it, but I have included this dish because it is an all-time favourite of mine and never fails to impress. Turbot can be used instead of brill, but as brill is normally the cheaper fish of the two at least it helps to keep the cost down, albeit only slightly. I have also used truffle peelings here as they are only a quarter of the price of whole truffles.

Method

Preheat the oven to 190°C/375°F/Gas Mark 5.

Turn the vegetables into small barrel shapes about 2.5 cm/1 inch long by about 1 cm/½ inch wide. Blanch the carrots and turnips together in boiling salted water for 1 minute, and the courgettes separately for 30 seconds. Refresh in iced water and drain. Finely chop the truffle peelings, making sure to save the juice that they come packed in, and return them to their juice. Skin and trim off any dark meat from the fillets of brill. Butter an ovenproof pan, put in the fish, add the fish stock and cover with buttered paper or foil. Bring the liquid up until it is almost boiling, then transfer to the oven and poach for 4-5 minutes. When cooked, remove the fish from its stock, cover and keep warm.

Reduce the stock over a high heat by about two-thirds, then add the Madeira, the veal stock and the truffles with their juice, and reduce until thickened.

To Serve

Reheat the fish in the oven for about 1 minute. Melt 15 g/½ oz of the butter in a saucepan over a very low heat and toss the vegetables in this to reheat. Season as necessary. Bring the sauce to the boil, remove from the heat and whisk in the remaining butter a little at a time until it is all melted. Pour the sauce onto the serving dishes, place the fillets of brill on top and arrange the vegetables attractively around.

NOTE The colours in this dish are so vibrant – the stark white of the fish against the dark-brown background speckled with black, all topped off with the brightly coloured vegetables – that it is a feast for the eyes as well as the palate.

Fillet of Brill with Banana and a Delicate Curry Sauce

SERVES 4

4 × 150 g/5 oz fillets of brill
1 banana
1 tbsp oil
25 g/1 oz butter

Sauce

1 tbsp oil
50 g/2 oz mirepoix (carrot, onion, celery, leek, cut roughly into smallish dice)
1 small clove garlic, crushed
1 tomato, finely diced
15 g/½ oz desiccated coconut
½ banana, finely diced
15 g/½ oz mango, finely diced
25 g/1 oz tomato purée
1 dessertsp curry powder
600 ml/1 pint fish stock

This is a delightful combination for a little-used fish. This recipe can also be used to the same effect with turbot or John Dory. The sauce really should be delicate, so even if you do like your curries hot, I would advise against having it too hot as the flavour of the fish will soon be lost.

Method

Preheat the oven to 180°C/350°F/Gas Mark 4.

To make the sauce, heat the oil in an ovenproof pan, add the mirepoix of vegetables and the garlic, cover with a lid and sweat until the vegetables start to soften. Add the tomato and the coconut, sweat for a further minute, then add the banana and the mango and continue cooking for a further minute. Stir in the tomato purée and the curry powder. Pour in the fish stock, bring to the boil and place in the oven for 1 hour. The sauce should barely simmer and not be boiling. After 1 hour, remove from the oven, allow to cool and then place in a blender or food processor and blend until smooth. Pass the sauce through a sieve.

Skin and trim the fillets. Cut the banana into 12 long, thin slices and set to one side.

To Serve

Gently reheat the sauce. If it is a little too thick, thin it down with a little fish stock. Heat the oil in a frying pan, then add the butter which should sizzle and not burn. Season the fillets and gently fry for 2–3 minutes each side, allowing to colour only slightly and just turning once. When cooked, place the fillets on a piece of kitchen towel to remove any excess oil.

Arrange the fillets on the plates. Pour the sauce around the fillets and place three slices of banana in a fan at the point of each fillet. Serve with a little rice pilaf.

Dover Sole, tongue, slip
(FRENCH: *sole* GERMAN: *zunge*)

The Dover sole has always been considered by far the best of the flat fish, its flesh being firm, white and delicate of flavour. The cooking is often overcomplicated, especially in more classical dishes. Here I have suggested quite a few ways to use this fish, but what could be better than serving it grilled with a wedge of lemon.

After standing for a day or two, the flesh of the sole improves due to some chemical change in its makeup. Skinning a Dover sole must be the easiest thing yet, as the skin will just pull away from the meat. This cannot be said of all the soles – lemon sole will not do this, but nevertheless it is a fine substitute for the real thing.

Dover sole are graded into sizes, 175-225 g/6-8 oz, 225-300 g/ 8-10 oz, 300-350 g/10-12 oz and so on. Normally a fish weighing 350-400 g/12-14 oz will give one good-sized portion, and once filleted, the sole, as with all flat fish, gives four fillets.

There is an American sole, but it is not of the same family, although it can be used in the same way.

SERVES 4

3 × 450 g/1 lb Dover sole
115 g/4 oz fresh mousserons
50 g/2 oz cold unsalted butter
15 g/½ oz shallots, finely chopped
300 ml/½ pint fish stock
120 ml/4 fl oz dry sherry
225 ml/8 fl oz double cream

Fillets of Dover Sole with Mousserons

This is my favourite of all the wild mushrooms, and served with Dover sole in a little cream sauce you have a dish that is stunning in its simplicity.

Method

Preheat the oven to 190°C/375°F/Gas Mark 5.

Remove and discard the stalks of the mousserons and wipe off any pieces of grass or dirt but do not wash them.

Skin and fillet the Dover sole. Trim the edges and slightly flatten each fillet using the side of a heavy-bladed knife or a cutlet bat – this will prevent the fillets from curling as they cook. Fold each fillet in half; if they prove to be a little too long, then fold the tail over about 2.5 cm/1 inch and then fold in half. Lightly butter an ovenproof pan, scatter the chopped shallot over the bottom and lay the fillets in, keeping them separate. Add the fish stock and the sherry, cover with buttered greaseproof paper and set the pan over a high heat until the liquid begins to tremble. Transfer to the oven and cook for about 4-5 minutes. When cooked, remove the fillets from the stock, drain, cover and keep warm.

Place the stock over a high heat and reduce by three-quarters, then add the cream and reduce slightly until it starts to thicken.

To Serve

When ready to serve, put the fillets of sole into the oven for about a minute to reheat. Add the mousserons to the sauce and bring back to the boil. Remove the pan from the heat and gradually add the remaining butter to the sauce, shaking the pan until it has all melted. Arrange the sole on the plates and pour over the sauce.

Fillets of Dover Sole Véronique

SERVES 4

4 × 350-400 g/12-14 oz Dover sole
48 white grapes
600 ml/1 pint fish stock
175 ml/6 fl oz dry white wine
Salt and freshly ground white pepper
225 g/8 oz unsalted butter

Picture: page 122

This dish is a corner-stone of classical cookery. It is a very simple dish to produce, finished with a wonderful glaze. Although the classical recipe is for Dover sole, lemon sole can also be used. It does not have such a fine flavour or texture as the Dover sole, but it is still good.

Method

Preheat the oven to 190°C/375°F/Gas Mark 5.

Peel the grapes and remove their pips – if the grapes will not peel simply by pulling their skins off, then it may be necessary to blanch them in boiling water for a couple of seconds first. Allow them to cool and store them in the refrigerator. Skin and fillet the sole. With the side of a heavy knife or a meat bat, slightly flatten each fillet and fold in half lengthwise. Place the folded fillets into a lightly buttered ovenproof dish. Pour over half of the fish stock and all of the white wine, season, cover with buttered paper or foil and poach in the oven for about 3-4 minutes. When the fish is cooked, remove the fillets, cover and keep warm.

Add the remaining fish stock to the cooking liquor, bring to the boil and reduce until it is syrupy. When the stock has reduced sufficiently, turn the heat down to low and gradually whisk in the butter until it has all melted.

To Serve

Arrange the fillets on the plates or serving dish, pour over the sauce and place under a very hot grill to glaze – if the grill is really hot, this will only take a few seconds. When browned, arrange a pile of chilled grapes with each portion and serve immediately.

SERVES 4

4 × 225-275 g/8-10 Dover sole
350 ml/12 fl oz fish stock
175 ml/6 fl oz dry sherry
115 g/4 oz fresh white breadcrumbs
225 g/8 oz unsalted butter
5 tsp fresh thyme leaves
Salt and freshly ground white pepper
50 ml/2 fl oz double cream

Whole Poached Dover Sole with Thyme Butter Sauce

This is a very simple dish to prepare and cook and yet it is so effective and tasty. If you cannot get hold of fresh thyme, try chopped chives instead, or even shredded mint leaves. Go on, experiment!

Method

Preheat the oven to 190°C/375°F/Gas Mark 5.

Skin the sole, remove the heads and blood clots behind the heads and rinse well. Trim off the fins and the ends of the tails with a pair of scissors. Butter an ovenproof pan or dish large enough to take the fish without overlapping, put in the fish and add the fish stock and 150 ml/¼ pint of the sherry. Cover with buttered paper or foil and poach in the oven until cooked – about 6–8 minutes. When cooked, remove the fish from the stock and keep warm. Put the liquor into a saucepan and reduce until syrupy.

Meanwhile, moisten the breadcrumbs in the remaining sherry, then melt 50 g/2 oz of the butter and mix into the crumbs. Add 2 teaspoons of thyme and season. Lay the fish on a flat surface and cover each sole with a generous layer of the crumb mixture. Place the fish under a hot grill and brown evenly. Remove from the grill, cover and keep warm.

When the liquor is syrupy, pour in the cream and bring back to the boil. Reduce the heat to low and gradually add the remaining butter in small pieces, beating with a small whisk until it has all melted (once you have added the butter do not let it come back to the boil).

To Serve

At the last minute add the rest of the thyme to the sauce and check the seasoning. Pour the sauce onto the plates, place the fish on top and serve immediately.

Poached Fillets of Dover Sole with Lobster and Lobster Sauce

SERVES 4

3 × 450 g / 1 lb Dover sole
1 × 350-400 g / 12-14 oz live lobster
900 ml / 1 ½ pints court bouillon (see page 31)
A little butter
150 ml / ¼ pint fish stock
50 ml / 2 fl oz dry sherry
225 ml / 8 fl oz lobster sauce (see page 33)
225 ml / 8 fl oz double cream
Salt and freshly ground white pepper

Garnish

15 g / ½ oz truffle (optional)
A few flat parsley leaves

Method

Preheat the oven to 190°C/375°F/Gas Mark 5.

Bring the court bouillon to the boil, plunge in the lobster and cook for 10 minutes. Allow it to go cold in the bouillon, but do not refrigerate. When cold, shell the lobster and keep the shells for another recipe. Slice the tail meat into 5 mm/¼ inch slices, and cut each piece of claw meat in two lengthwise.

Skin, fillet and trim the sole. Flatten the fillets slightly with the back of a knife or cutlet bat to prevent them curling while poaching. Fold the fillets in half; if they prove to be a little too long, then fold the tail over about 2.5 cm/1 inch and then fold in half. Butter an ovenproof pan, lay the fillets in, add the fish stock and the sherry, and cover with buttered paper or foil. Heat the liquid over a high heat until it just starts to tremble, then transfer the pan to the oven and poach for 3-4 minutes. When cooked, remove the fillets from the liquor and cover and keep warm. Pour a few spoonfuls of the liquor over the lobster meat to keep it moist.

Reduce the remaining liquor by at least three-quarters and then add the lobster sauce and reduce again by half. Pour in the cream and reduce further until the sauce just coats the back of a spoon.

To Serve

Reheat the sole and the lobster in the oven for 30 seconds and then drain well as they retain a lot of moisture. Place a fillet on each plate, pour the sauce over the fish and on to the plate, and arrange the lobster on top of the sauce. Garnish with the truffle and flat parsley leaves.

SERVES 4

4 × 450 g / 1 lb Dover sole

2 medium tomatoes

50 g / 2 oz unsalted butter

300 ml / ½ pint fish stock

120 ml / 4 fl oz dry sherry

300 ml / ½ pint double cream

15 g / ½ oz fresh chives, finely chopped

Salt and freshly ground white pepper

Garnish

Fresh chives (optional)

Fillets of Dover Sole with Tomato and Chive Cream Sauce

There really is no better fish than Dover sole treated as simply as possible. It is such a delicate fish with a unique texture – why spoil it?

Method

Preheat the oven to 180°C/350°F/Gas Mark 4.

Blanch the tomatoes, skin and deseed. Cut the flesh into strips about 5 mm/¼ inch wide and set aside. Skin and fillet the sole. Lightly butter an ovenproof pan large enough to take the fillets without overlapping. Slightly flatten each fillet with the side of a heavy knife or cutlet bat (this will prevent the fillets from curling as they cook), then fold each fillet in two lengthwise. Lay them in the pan and add the fish stock and dry sherry. Cover with buttered paper or foil and poach in the oven for about 3-4 minutes. Remove the fillets, cover and keep in a warm place.

For the sauce, place the liquor over a high heat and reduce until syrupy. Add the cream and continue boiling for 1-2 minutes until slightly thickened, and then add the chives.

To Serve

Return the fillets of sole to the hot oven for about 30 seconds to reheat. Add the tomato strips to the sauce at the last minute, correct the seasoning with a touch of freshly ground pepper and, if needed (which is doubtful), a little salt. Place the fillets on the serving dishes and pour the sauce over them. If liked, garnish the dish with a few strands of chives.

Lettuce and Oyster Soup
(see page 188)

ABOVE *Steamed Salmon Trout with Basil and Tomato Vinaigrette*
(see page 71)

ABOVE RIGHT *Roast Quail with a Salad of Quail's Eggs and Crayfish*
(see page 225)

FAR RIGHT *Poached Fillet of Brill with Truffle Sauce*
(see page 90)

RIGHT *Salad of John Dory with Blackcurrant Vinaigrette*
(see page 115)

*Sautéed Fillet of Lamb with Scallops and
Scallop Mousse*
(see page 226)

Whole Poached Dover Sole with Oyster Ragoût

SERVES 4

Method

Preheat the oven to 200°C/400°F/Gas Mark 6.

Skin the Dover sole, trim off the fins and the ends of the tails with a pair of scissors, and remove the heads and blood clot from behind the heads, then rinse. Remove any roe and discard. Shell the oysters over a bowl to catch the juices and reserve. Cut the oysters into 5 mm/¼ inch dice. Leave in the refrigerator until needed.

Butter an ovenproof pan or dish large enough to take the sole without overlapping. Lay the sole in the pan and season with salt and freshly ground white pepper. Add the fish stock and the white wine – if there is a little too much stock, reserve it and add after the fish are cooked and the stock is reducing. Cover the fish with buttered paper or foil. Heat the liquid over a moderate heat until it starts to tremble, remove from the heat and transfer to the oven for about 8-10 minutes until cooked. When cooked, remove the fish from the stock to a shallow dish, cover and keep warm.

Pour the stock into a saucepan and set over a high heat to reduce by three quarters.

While the stock is reducing, trim and fillet the fish, and then replace the fillets to re-form the shape of the fish.

When the stock has reduced far enough, add the cream. Continue to boil until the sauce starts to thicken.

To Serve

When ready to serve, reheat the fish in the oven for about 1 minute. Strain the oyster juices through muslin into the sauce, then add the oysters. Remove the pan from the heat and gradually add the remaining butter in small amounts, shaking the pan or stirring with a wooden spoon until it has all melted – be careful not to crush the pieces of oyster. Check the seasoning – it should not need any more salt because of the addition of the oyster juices. Place the fish on each plate and pour over the sauce, making sure you divide the oysters out equally. Garnish each with a sprig of dill.

4 × 225-275 g/8-10 oz Dover sole
20 oysters
25 g/1 oz shallots, finely chopped
50 g/2 oz cold unsalted butter
Salt and freshly ground white pepper
450 ml/¾ pint fish stock
150 ml/¼ pint dry white wine
300 ml/½ pint double cream

Garnish

Sprigs of fresh dill

SERVES 4

3 × 400 g/ 14 oz Dover sole (this allows 3 fillets per portion)
A little butter
85 ml/3 fl oz fish stock
85 ml/3 fl oz dry white wine

Sauce

65 g/2½ oz butter
85 g/3 oz shallots, roughly chopped
½ clove garlic, crushed
450 g/ 1 lb tomatoes, roughly chopped
1 tbsp tomato purée
85 ml/3 fl oz dry white wine
120 ml/4 fl oz fish stock
10 g/ ¼ oz fresh tarragon

Garnish

1 medium tomato
32 fresh tarragon leaves

Poached Fillets of Dover Sole with Tomato and Tarragon

A beautifully simple dish that is ideal as a light main course – marvellous for a warm summer's evening with a bowl of salad and a chilled bottle of wine. The tomato sauce can be done the day before, leaving only the cooking of the sole and the finishing off of the sauce to the last minute.

Method

For the sauce, heat 15 g/½ oz butter, add the shallots and garlic and gently sauté without browning. Add the tomatoes, tomato purée, white wine, fish stock and tarragon and cook over a low heat for about 20 minutes. Rub the sauce through a sieve.

Blanch the tomato for garnish and skin it, remove the seeds and cut the flesh into small dice. The seeds and skin can be added to the sauce while it is cooking.

Fillet and trim the sole. Slightly flatten each fillet with the side of a heavy knife or with a meat bat – this will prevent the fillets from curling while cooking. Butter a large, shallow pan and lay the fillets in flat. Add the fish stock and white wine, cover with buttered paper or foil and poach for about 10 minutes. When the fish is cooked, remove it from its liquor and keep warm. Reduce the stock until syrupy, then add the tomato sauce.

To Serve

Bring the sauce up to the boil, then turn the heat down to low and gradually whisk in the remaining butter until it has all melted. Pour the sauce onto the plates, lay 3 fillets on top and sprinkle with the tarragon leaves and diced tomato.

Whole Poached Dover Sole with Bacon and Chervil

SERVES 4

4 × 225 g/8 oz Dover sole
Salt and freshly ground white pepper
120 ml/4 fl oz dry white wine
350 ml/12 fl oz fish stock
8 rashers streaky bacon
50 ml/2 fl oz double cream
225 g/8 oz unsalted butter
15 g/½ oz fresh chervil leaves

Picture: page 161

This summery dish is great for lunch with a little tossed green salad. It is nice and simple to prepare and also quite cheap.

Method

Preheat the oven to 190°C/375°F/Gas Mark 5.

Skin the Dover sole. Cut off the heads and remove any roe and the blood clot from behind the heads and rinse well. Trim off the fins and the ends of the tails using a pair of kitchen scissors. Take a deep tray and butter the bottom. Lay the fish in and season with a little freshly ground white pepper and a sprinkle of salt. Pour in the white wine and the fish stock. Cover the fish with buttered paper or foil and set the tray over a medium heat until the liquid just starts to tremble, then transfer to the oven and cook for about 5 minutes. The fish will be cooked when the fillets just start to separate at the head end. Meanwhile, remove the rind from the rashers of bacon and lightly grill them.

When the fish are cooked, remove from the stock and drain, but keep them covered as they will soon dry out. Transfer the stock to a saucepan and reduce over a high heat until syrupy.

While the sauce is reducing, lay the fish on a flat surface and carefully remove the top fillets using a palette knife. Remove the bone, trim the fillets, and put the fillets back together to re-form the shape of the fish. Lay 2 rashers of the bacon over each of the fish and return them to the oven for a minute to reheat.

When the sauce has reduced, add the cream, bring back to the boil, then remove the pan from the heat. Gradually add the butter, whisking all the time, until it has all melted, then add the chervil and stir in.

To Serve

Pour a little of the sauce on to the centre of each plate and lay a sole on top of the sauce. Pour the rest of the sauce around the fish allowing a little to trickle over the rashers of bacon.

4 × 275-350 g/10-12 oz Dover sole

2 tomatoes

10 g/¼ oz parsley

Salt and freshly ground white pepper

25 g/1 oz shallots, finely chopped

300 ml/½ pint fish stock

Juice of ½ lemon

120 ml/4 fl oz white wine

225 ml/8 fl oz double cream

50 g/2 oz unsalted butter

Sole Dugléré

This classic dish can, in fact, be made using any number of different fish – brill, turbot, lemon sole, plaice, halibut, etc. – and it is nice and simple.

Method

Preheat the oven to 180°C/350°F/Gas Mark 4.

Blanch the tomatoes, skin and deseed them, and cut into dice of about 5 mm/¼ inch. Pick over the parsley, wash and roughly chop.

Skin the fish, remove the heads and blood clot behind the heads and rinse well. Trim off the fins and the ends of the tails with a pair of scissors. Butter an ovenproof pan or dish large enough to take the sole and scatter with the shallots. Lay the fish in, season, add the fish stock, lemon juice and the white wine, and cover with a lid or buttered paper or foil. Heat on top of the stove until the liquid starts to tremble, then transfer to the oven and cook for 7-10 minutes. When cooked, remove the fish from the stock, cover and allow to cool slightly. Turn up the oven to 220°C/425°F/Gas Mark 7.

Meanwhile, reduce the cooking liquor by three-quarters. When the sole have cooled slightly, lay them on a flat surface, and carefully remove the top two fillets using a palette knife. Remove the bone, trim the fillets, and return the top two fillets to re-form the shape of the sole. When the stock has reduced, add the cream, bring back to the boil and reduce slightly until it starts to thicken.

To Serve

Reheat the fish in the hot oven for a few minutes. Add the diced tomato and the chopped parsley to the sauce and return to the boil. Turn the heat down to low and gradually add the butter a little at a time, shaking the pan continuously until all the butter has melted. Once the butter has been added, do not allow the sauce to boil or it will separate. Place a sole on each plate and pour over the sauce.

NOTE Although this classical dish should always, strictly speaking, be made using whole fish, fillets of sole can be used instead if you find it easier.

Fillets of Dover Sole with Herb Mousse on a Bed of Wild Rice

SERVES 4

2 × 450 g / 1 lb Dover sole
40 g / 1 ½ oz wild rice (see note)
115 g / 4 oz mixed fresh herbs (parsley, tarragon, chives, dill)
½ recipe for basic fish mousse (see page 41)
Salt and freshly ground white pepper
250 ml / 9 fl oz fish stock
120 ml / 4 fl oz dry white wine
225 ml / 8 fl oz tomato sauce (see page 32)
125 g / 4 ½ oz butter

Method

Preheat the oven to 200°C/400°F/Gas Mark 6.

Cover the rice with cold water and soak for 10 minutes. Skin and fillet the fish and, using a cutlet bat or the side of a heavy knife, lightly flatten each fillet.

Pick and finely chop the herbs and mix into the fish mousse. Lightly season each fillet on the skin side, then spread the mousse onto four of the fillets to give a depth of about 1 cm/½ inch, but do not take the mousse quite to the edge – fall short by 3 mm/⅛ inch. Cover each of these fillets with a plain fillet and roll the stuffed pairs of fillets in greaseproof paper – this will help to keep their shape while they cook.

Drain the water from the rice, place the rice in a saucepan, add 150 ml/¼ pint of the fish stock and season. Bring to the boil and allow to simmer gently for 30 minutes.

Lay the fillets of sole in a deep tray just large enough to take them without overlapping and add the remaining fish stock and the white wine. Cover and heat the liquid until it just starts to tremble, then transfer to the oven and cook for 10 minutes. After 5 minutes, turn the fillets over so that they cook more evenly. When cooked, remove the fish parcels from the pan, cover and keep warm. Pour the stock into a saucepan and reduce over a high heat until syrupy.

To Serve

Once the stock has reduced sufficiently, pour in the tomato sauce and bring back to the boil. Drain the rice, melt 15 g/½ oz of the butter in a frying pan and toss the rice in this. Place a line of wild rice in the centre of each plate.

Remove the sauce from the heat and gradually add the remaining butter, whisking continuously until it has all melted. Strain the sauce and pour around the rice. Remove the wrappings from the sole, and cut each fillet across at a 45 degree angle into four thick slices. Arrange the slices propped against the line of rice on each plate. Serve immediately.

NOTE There are a few different varieties and qualities of wild rice, all of which take differing times to cook, so the 30 minutes is only a guideline. When cooked, the rice should still remain a little nutty and some of the grains will have started to split – if they have all split open, it is overcooked.

Halibut, Chicken halibut
(FRENCH: *fletan* GERMAN: *heilbutt*)

Halibut is the largest of all the flat fish with recorded landings of fish up to a staggering 252 kg/560 lb. This size of fish is, however, quite rare; the normal size ranges from about 2.25 kg/5 lb through to 5.5-7 kg/12-15 lb.

The halibut is a rather sleek-looking fish, its elongated diamond-shaped body being a dark, black-green colour on its back and pearl white on its underside. With its rather pointed head, it cannot be mistaken for any other fish, except perhaps for the Greenland halibut, or mock halibut, which is a much inferior fish, but the colour of its skin is not so dark and it is also quite a bit cheaper.

I must confess that halibut is not one of my favourite fish. Although it is held in great esteem around the world, it does have a tendency to be a little on the dry side. Halibut can be used in any other recipe for flat fish, but do try to buy the middle cut as the tail meat, which is pointed and thin, does not lend itself to much.

SERVES 4

2 × 400-450 g/14-16 oz fillets of halibut
2 limes
Salt and freshly ground white pepper
300 ml/½ pint fish stock
85 ml/3 fl oz dry white wine
300 ml/½ pint double cream
4 bouchée cases (2.5 cm/1 inch in diameter)
50 g/2 oz caviar
50 g/2 oz unsalted butter

Slices of Halibut with Lime and Caviar Cream Sauce

Omit the caviar if you must, but it certainly will not be the stunning dish that it is meant to be. Whatever you do, do not use lumpfish roe; it is dyed and when heated the colour will come out of the roe and spoil the whole dish. I know that caviar is expensive, but there is always a day when you need to treat yourself! Turbot, brill or even monkfish can be used for this dish instead of halibut.

Method

Preheat the oven to 200°C/400°F/Gas Mark 6.

Skin and trim the fillets, then with the knife at a slight angle cut widthwise across the fillets to obtain 6 50 g/2 oz slices from each fillet. Remove the zest from the limes and cut into fine strips. Extract the juice and put to one side. Lay the slices of halibut in a lightly buttered, shallow tray, but do not overlap them or they will stick together. Lightly season, add the fish stock and white wine, cover with buttered paper or foil and place in the oven for about 5 minutes. Remove the fish, cover and keep in a warm place. Turn the oven up to 220°C/425°F/Gas Mark 7.

Pour the stock into a saucepan, add the lime juice and set over a high heat. Boil rapidly until reduced by three-quarters, then add the cream and bring back to the boil. Add the lime zest and continue boiling for a minute or two until the sauce starts to thicken.

To Serve

Return the fish along with the bouchée cases to the hot oven for about 1 minute to heat through. Once the sauce has started to thicken, add half of the caviar, then remove the pan from the heat and gradually add the butter, shaking the pan with a swirling motion until all of the butter has melted.

Fill the bouchée cases with the remaining caviar, arrange the slices of halibut on the plates in a fan, pour the sauce around and place a bouchée case at the point of each fan.

Fillet of Halibut with Glazed Sabayon

SERVES 4

| 4 × 175 g/6 oz fillets of halibut |
| A little butter |
| 15 g/ ½ oz shallots, very finely chopped |
| 450 ml/¾ pint fish stock |
| 3 egg yolks |
| 50 ml/2 fl oz dry sherry |

Method

Preheat the oven to 200°C/400°F/Gas Mark 6.

Skin the fillets of halibut. Butter an ovenproof pan and strew with the shallots. Place the fillets of fish on top, add the fish stock and cover with a lid or buttered paper or foil. Heat the stock until it just starts to tremble, then transfer to the oven and poach for about 4 minutes. When the fish is cooked, remove it from the stock, cover and keep warm.

Reduce the stock by two-thirds over a high heat. Put it with the egg yolks and sherry into a round-based bowl and place over a pan of simmering water but do not allow the water to touch the bottom of the bowl. Whisk this mixture continuously until it froths up and thickens. The sabayon is ready when it leaves a trail across itself that does not run back in (ribbon stage).

To Serve

Place the fillets of halibut on the serving dishes, pour over the sauce and brown under a very hot grill. (The browning will only take a matter of seconds so do not walk away and leave it.) Serve immediately.

SERVES 2-4

1 × 350-400 g/ 12-14 oz fillet of halibut
15 g/ ½ oz parsley
25 g/ 1 oz white breadcrumbs
40 g/ 1 ½ oz sesame seeds
Salt and freshly ground white pepper
25 g/ 1 oz sorrel
25 g/ 1 oz Dijon mustard
150 ml/ ¼ pint fish stock
Juice of ½ lemon
50 ml/ 2 fl oz double cream
115 g/4 oz unsalted butter, chilled
1 tbsp oil

Picture: page 19

Halibut rolled in Sesame Seeds with Sorrel Butter Sauce

This is very quick and easy to prepare as well as quick to cook. Like so many dishes, it is suitable either as a first course or as a light main course.

Method

Pick over, wash and finely chop the parsley, then mix it together with the breadcrumbs and the sesame seeds. Remove the stalks from the sorrel, wash well, then tear the leaves into small pieces; do not cut with a knife.

Skin the fillet of halibut and, holding the knife at a slight angle, cut 6 slices diagonally across the fish. Place the slices skin side down and lightly season each slice, then spread a thin layer of mustard over each piece using a palette knife. Place each piece, mustard side down, onto the sesame mixture and pat each slice to ensure that it is well coated. Gently shake to remove any loose seeds.

To make the sauce, reduce the fish stock over a high heat with the lemon juice, then add the cream and the sorrel and return to the boil. Remove from the heat and gradually add 85 g/3 oz of the butter, continuously shaking the pan until all of the butter has melted. Keep the sauce warm by putting the saucepan in a bain-marie over a very low heat.

To Serve

Heat the oil in a frying pan, add the remaining butter and when it sizzles, gently lay the slices of halibut into the fat, seed side down. When lightly browned, turn the slices of fish and finish cooking. The whole cooking time should not take any more than 3 minutes. Remove the fish from the pan and drain on kitchen paper to remove any excess fat. Fan 3 slices onto each plate and pour the sauce around the slices.

Halibut with Oyster Mushrooms and Crayfish Sauce

SERVES 4

4 × 175 g/6 oz fillets of halibut
Salt and freshly ground white pepper
120 ml/4 fl oz fish stock
50 ml/2 fl oz dry white wine
8 live crayfish
50 ml/2 fl oz crayfish sauce (see page 34)
120 ml/4 fl oz double cream
25 g/1 oz butter
225 g/8 oz oyster mushrooms

Garnish

4 sprigs fresh dill or fennel

This recipe is suitable for almost any white fish.

Method

Preheat the oven to 200°C/400°F/Gas Mark 6.

Skin the fillets of halibut. Butter a shallow ovenproof pan, lay in the fish and lightly season. Add the fish stock and the white wine, cover with buttered paper or foil and heat until the liquid starts to tremble. Transfer to the oven and cook for about 4 minutes, then remove the fish from the stock, cover and keep warm. Turn the oven up to 220°C/425°F/Gas Mark 7.

Set the stock over a high heat and bring to the boil. Remove the intestinal tract from the crayfish by pinching the centre part of the tail between your thumb and forefinger, then twist and pull. Plunge the crayfish into the boiling stock for 3 minutes, then remove and allow to cool. When cold, shell the tails but keep the heads on. Continue boiling the stock and reduce until it is syrupy. Add the crayfish sauce, return to the boil, then pour in the cream and reduce until the sauce has thickened.

To Serve

Heat the butter in a frying pan until it starts to sizzle and fry the oyster mushrooms on both sides until lightly browned. When cooked, remove the mushrooms from the pan and drain on kitchen paper to remove the fat. Place the halibut and the crayfish in the hot oven for 1 minute to reheat.

Arrange the oyster mushrooms in a circle on the plates and place a fillet of halibut in the centre of each circle. Pour a circle of sauce around and prop two crayfish side by side against the edge of each fillet. Top with a sprig of dill.

John Dory, St Peter's fish
(FRENCH: *St Pierre, dorée* GERMAN: *heringskonig)*

Although this is certainly not famed for its good looks – John Dory is probably one of the ugliest of food fish – it has, over the years, enjoyed a good reputation both for its delicate flavour and fine texture, which is, of course, reflected in the price as it is quite expensive. In addition, John Dory is made more expensive by the amount of waste on it – the head, innards and bones probably account for at least two-thirds of the total weight. Each of the two fillets break into three natural pieces – the only fish I know of to do this. Any of the recipes using a firmer white fish, such as sole or turbot, could be used to good effect with John Dory. It also seems to lend itself very well to salads, whether warm or cold.

One thing to always remember when handling John Dory is that it is well armed. There are two rows of rather lethal spines on both sides of its body, around its back and along its belly that can easily inflict more than a little damage on an unsuspecting pair of hands. Even for a seasoned professional like myself they can be difficult to avoid.

John Dory is found mainly around the seas of Europe and not off the coast of America, where here the Atlantic fish porgy or scup can be used instead.

SERVES 4

2 × 900 g/2 lb John Dory

300 ml/ ½ pint fish stock

120 ml/4 fl oz dry white wine

300 ml/ ½ pint double cream

2 fresh vanilla pods

1 tbsp oil

15 g/ ½ oz unsalted butter

Salt and freshly ground white pepper

Juice of ½ lemon

Good pinch of sugar

Garnish

Sprigs of fresh chervil

Sautéed John Dory with Vanilla

This may sound like an unusual combination, and possibly not a very nice one. The answer is not to judge before trying it – John Dory and vanilla really do go very well together indeed. It is also quite a simple dish to prepare and cook and is well worth a try.

Method

Fillet and skin the John Dory. Each fillet breaks naturally into 3 pieces, then split each piece in half lengthwise, so you have 12 strips.

Reduce the fish stock and white wine in a pan until about only 2 tablespoons remain, then add the cream. Split the vanilla pods in two lengthwise, scrape out the centre and add to the sauce. Cut the pods again in two and add to the sauce. Reduce this a little until it just starts to thicken.

Heat the oil in a frying pan and add the butter. Season the strips of fish and fry gently, turning only once, until cooked and slightly browned. The fish should take no more than 1 minute each side to cook. Season the sauce using the lemon juice and the sugar. Remove the vanilla pods from the sauce and reserve.

To Serve

Pour the sauce onto the plates, top with the strips of fish and garnish with the split vanilla pods and a few sprigs of fresh chervil.

Sautéed John Dory with Ginger and Chive Cream Sauce

SERVES 4

2 × 900 g / 2 lb John Dory
2 medium tomatoes
25 g / 1 oz fresh chives
300 ml / ½ pint fish stock
85 ml / 3 fl oz dry white wine
120 ml / 4 fl oz double cream
1 tsp grated fresh ginger
1 tbsp oil
25 g / 1 oz butter
Salt and freshly ground white pepper

Method

Fillet, skin and trim the John Dory. Separate each fillet into its three natural sections. Blanch the tomatoes, skin and deseed them. Cut the flesh into 5 mm / ¼ inch dice and reserve. Finely snip the chives, reserving 8–12 nice lengths as garnish.

Bring the fish stock and the white wine to the boil in a saucepan and reduce the liquid by at least three-quarters. Add the cream and the grated ginger, return to the boil and reduce until it starts to thicken.

To Serve

Heat the oil and butter in a frying pan until they start to sizzle. Season the strips of John Dory and carefully place them into the hot fat. Cook for about 30 seconds to brown slightly and then turn them over and cook for a further 30 seconds. Remove from the pan and drain on kitchen paper to remove any excess fat. Return the sauce to the boil, add the chives and the diced tomato and allow the sauce to simmer for 30 seconds to bring out the flavour of the chives.

Divide the sauce out between the plates and arrange the fillets of Dory attractively on top of the sauce. Garnish with the reserved chives.

SERVES 4

2 × 900 g/ 2 lb John Dory
4 finger-sized courgettes with their flowers
¼ tsp salt
1 egg white
150 ml/ ¼ pint double cream
25 ml/ 1 fl oz dry sherry
Freshly ground white pepper
Pinch of freshly grated nutmeg
A little oil for frying
125 g/ 4 ½ oz butter
450 ml/ ¾ pint tomato sauce (see page 32)

Sautéed John Dory with Stuffed Courgette Flowers

This makes a really pretty dish full of the colours of summer; the red of the tomato sauce against the yellow of the flowers makes a wonderful picture.

Method

Carefully wash the courgettes and flowers. Very gently remove all the flowers from the courgettes.

Fillet the John Dory. Skin each fillet and break them into their 3 natural pieces each side. Cut each of the long pieces, 4 to each fish, in half at an acute angle, and put to one side. The 4 small pieces are to be used for the mousse.

Cut the small fillets into small pieces and place in a blender or food processor along with the salt and process until a smooth paste. Add the egg white and mix in thoroughly until it stiffens. Remove from the blender and rub through a sieve. Place in a bowl set on crushed ice and gradually add two-thirds of the cream, followed by the sherry and seasoning. Test the mousse (see page 41). If the mousse is a little firm, add more cream; the mousse needs to be really soft for this recipe.

Place the mousse in a piping bag with a fairly fine nozzle. Carefully fill each flower about half full with the mixture. Fold the ends of the petals over to form a seal. Place each flower, folded end down, in a steaming basket along with the courgettes and steam for 4 minutes.

While these are cooking, heat the oil in a frying pan and, when the oil is hot, add 15 g/½ oz of the butter. Season the fillets and carefully lay them in the pan. Fry on one side for about 30 seconds, then turn and fry on the other side for a further 30 seconds. Remove the fillets from the pan and drain on kitchen paper to remove any excess oil. Keep in a warm place. Bring the tomato sauce to the boil, remove from the heat and gradually whisk in the remaining butter until it has all melted.

To Serve

When the flowers and courgettes are cooked, remove them from the steamer. Slice each courgette lengthwise into 4 slices. Pour the sauce on to the plates and place a flower on each plate against the rim. Lay 4 fillets of fish on each plate, fanning them out from the flower, and then add the slices of courgette, one between each piece of fish. Serve immediately.

Fricassée of John Dory with Florets of Calabrese

2 × 900 g-1.25 kg/2-2½ lb John Dory
175 g/6 oz calabrese
Salt and freshly ground white pepper
300 ml/½ pint fish stock
150 ml/¼ pint dry white wine
225 ml/8 fl oz double cream

Method

Fillet the John Dory. Skin each fillet and separate into 3 pieces on each side. Cut each fillet into thick strips to give at least 24 pieces of equal size.

Cut the calabrese into small florets and 'turn' the stalks into small barrel shapes using a small knife. If there are any leaves save these and use them to garnish the finished dish. Lightly blanch both the florets and the 'turned' stalks in boiling salted water – the florets for 30 seconds, the stalks for 1 minute. Refresh in iced water, drain and dry them off in a cloth.

Place the strips of fish in a poaching tray, season and add the fish stock and white wine. Cover with buttered paper or foil and place over a high heat until the liquid starts to tremble. Hold it at this point and allow to cook for 1 minute. Carefully drain the fish from the stock, cover and keep warm.

Return the stock to a high heat and reduce until syrupy. Pour in the cream and reduce again over a high heat until it starts to thicken.

To Serve

When the sauce is ready, add the calabrese and simmer for about 30 seconds – the calabrese should retain a little crunch. Add the strips of Dory, remove from the heat and allow them to soak in the sauce for 30 seconds.

Divide the fish and calabrese florets out between the dishes – soup plates are the best to use for this type of dish. Pour over the sauce and neatly arrange the florets throughout the sauce. If you have any, garnish with calabrese leaves, which should be dropped into boiling salted water for 15 seconds then drained before using.

SERVES 4

2 × 450-550 g/1 - 1 ¼ lb John Dory

2 oranges

Juice of 1 orange

1 tbsp white wine vinegar

1 tbsp olive oil

½ head curly endive

24 fresh basil leaves

Salt and freshly ground white pepper

15 g/ ½ oz butter

A little oil for frying

Orange and Basil Salad with Sautéed Strips of John Dory

John Dory seems to lend itself to a warm salad very well indeed. This dish really is very simple and makes a light and attractive first course.

Method

Fillet and skin the John Dory, and break each fillet into its 3 natural strips. Cut the 2 larger strips in half lengthwise, leave the smaller strips as they are. You should now have 20 pieces.

Peel and segment the oranges. Put the orange juice in a saucepan and reduce until half its original volume is left. Allow it to go cold and then mix it with the vinegar and the olive oil.

Wash the curly endive well and break up the leaves. Add the orange segments and the dressing and reserving 4 nice basil leaves to garnish, tear the rest into the salad. Lightly season with a little salt and pepper.

Heat a little oil in a frying pan, then add the butter and heat until it starts to sizzle. Lightly season the strips of fish and gently fry them in the fat for no more than 1 minute; 30 seconds on one side and then 30 seconds on the other side. Remove the fish from the pan and drain on a sheet of kitchen paper to remove any excess fat.

To Serve

Divide the salad out between the plates or bowls and carefully arrange the pieces of fish through it. Pour any extra dressing into the frying pan, swill around and then pass through muslin or a coffee filter and pour over the salad. Garnish with the whole leaves of basil.

Salad of John Dory with Blackcurrant Vinaigrette

SERVES 4

I can hardly ever wait for the arrival of the first blackcurrants of the season. They are a fruit of tremendous versatility, and I do tend to get a little carried away using them. They always appear on my menus in at least three forms at the same time. This is just one of them; a salad full of the colours of summer, and with it a fish that is always at its best during the summer months.

Method

Preheat oven to 200°C/400°F/Gas Mark 6.

Fillet and skin the John Dory. Each fillet should then separate naturally into 3 pieces. Cut these into strips – you should be able to get 6 good strips out of each side. Butter a shallow tray, lay the strips of fish in, add the fish stock and cover with buttered paper or foil. Poach in the oven for about 5 minutes – be careful not to overcook or the fish will be very dry; it should remain quite moist. When cooked, remove the paper or foil and let the fish cool in the stock. When cold, drain the fillets and cover them with a damp cloth, but do not put them in the refrigerator.

Put 25 g/1 oz of the blackcurrants to one side and purée the rest in a blender or food processor. Pass the purée through muslin or a fine sieve to remove any seeds and skin. Combine the purée, vinegar and the mustard in a bowl, mixing well. Gradually whisk in the oils and season the dressing with a little sugar and salt and freshly ground pepper if needed. If you feel that the dressing is a little too heavy, add the 50 ml/2 fl oz of warm water. Break up the lettuces, keeping the leaves whole where possible, and wash and drain well.

To Serve

Pour a little of the vinaigrette onto each plate or bowl to form a colourful border. Toss the leaves of salad in the remaining dressing and lightly season. Divide the salad out between the plates, carefully placing the leaves in the centre of the plates with the sauce around the edge. Arrange the strips of fish through the salad along with the reserved blackcurrants.

2 × 550 g/1 ¼ lb John Dory
A little butter
120 ml/4 fl oz fish stock
115 g/4 oz blackcurrants
2 tbsp blackcurrant vinegar
½ dessertsp Dijon mustard
2 tbsp hazelnut oil
85 ml/3 fl oz salad oil
Pinch of sugar
Salt and freshly ground white pepper
50 ml/2 fl oz warm water
1 small radicchio
2 bunches corn salad
¼ head curly endive
1 small head red oak leaf lettuce
1 small lettuce heart

Picture: page 99

Monkfish
(FRENCH: *lotte, baudroie* GERMAN: *seeteufel* USA: *anglerfish, goosefish*)

It seems to be only recently that the monkfish has been used for food. At one time it would have been thrown back or used as bait, but not now. Monkfish has gained quite considerably in popularity, probably because it was so cheap, but, as with everything else, now that it has become more sought after, up goes the price. Having said that, however, it is still a cheap fish with very little wastage.

Apparently, monkfish is or once was used by the frozen food industry in place of scampi; the theory being that the texture is similar to that of scampi and once in those dreaded breadcrumbs no one can tell the difference. So beware if you buy what seems to be cheap scampi!

Monkfish, although lacking in flavour slightly, is a very fine fish and is excellent for mousselines. Firm of flesh and with only a single bone (its backbone) it is extremely easy to fillet. Make sure you remove all of the dark meat as this tends to look unsightly once cooked.

This is not a fish to buy during the summer months as its flesh takes on a jelly-like texture.

Monkfish with Cucumber and Vermouth Sauce

SERVES 3-6

1 × 675-750 g / 1 ½-1 ¾ lb monkfish tail
85 ml / 3 fl oz dry vermouth
150 ml / ¼ pint fish stock
Salt and freshly ground white pepper
23 cm / 9 inch piece of cucumber, weighing about 275 g / 10 oz
300 ml / ½ pint double cream

Garnish

Sprigs of fresh dill

This recipe is designed as a first course, but will serve equally well as a light main course for three. It is a particular favourite of mine and tends to reappear quite regularly on our lunch menu.

Method

Preheat the oven to 200°C/400°F/Gas Mark 6.

Fillet and skin the monkfish tail and remove and discard any dark meat. Cut the flesh into 2.5 cm/1 inch cubes, allowing 4 pieces to a portion. Place the cubes of fish in an ovenproof pan along with the vermouth and the fish stock, and season with salt and freshly ground white pepper. Cover with buttered paper or foil and poach in the oven for 3-4 minutes.

Meanwhile, cut the cucumber widthwise into 4 cm/1½ inch lengths and then each piece in 6 lengthwise. 'Turn' each piece of cucumber into a small barrel shape.

116

(continued on page 125)

Poached Red Mullet with Spring Onions
(see page 133)

LEFT *Salad of Lobster with Raspberry Vinaigrette*
(see page 177)

RIGHT *Monkfish Braised with Bacon in Red Wine*
(see page 126)

BELOW *Roast Lobster in a Rich Red Wine Sauce*
(see page 179)

BELOW RIGHT *Roast Baby Lobster on a Bed of Artichokes*
(see page 176)

119

Warm Salad of Scallops and Mangetout
(see page 199)

Sautéed Scallops with Rhubarb Butter Sauce
(see page 202)

FAR LEFT *Crayfish with Strips of Dover Sole*
and Creamy Saffron Sauce
(see page 160)

ABOVE LEFT *Fillets of Dover Sole*
Veronique
(see page 93)

LEFT *Dublin Bay Prawns Poached with*
Cucumber
(see page 167)

ABOVE *Turban of Fish Mousse with Crayfish*
(see page 166)

Consommé of Dublin Bay Prawns with
Coriander
(see page 170)

When the fish is cooked, remove from the liquor, drain, cover and keep warm. Reduce the liquor until syrupy and then add the cream and the cucumber barrels. Reduce again until the sauce has thickened, by which time the cucumber should be just cooked.

To Serve

Reheat the monkfish in the sauce for 1 minute. Place the fish and the cucumber on the plates (I find a soup plate is best for this), pour over the sauce and garnish with sprigs of fresh dill.

Warm Salad of Monkfish and Toasted Pine Kernels

SERVES 4

1 × 675 g/1½ lb monkfish tail
25 g/1 oz pine kernels
2 tbsp olive oil
1 tbsp sherry vinegar
¾ tsp Dijon mustard
Salt and freshly ground white pepper
2 heads lambs lettuce
½ small radicchio
½ head frizzy lettuce
½ head oak leaf lettuce
50 g/2 oz watercress
1-2 tbsp oil
15 g/½ oz butter

Garnish

A few sprigs of fresh chervil

Picture: page 192

Method

Preheat the oven to 230°C/450°F/Gas Mark 8.

Skin and fillet the monkfish and remove all of the dark meat and discard. Holding the knife at a slight angle, cut each fillet across into thin slices so that you have 12 slices from each fillet.

Toast the pine kernels under a hot grill or in the oven until golden. Mix together the olive oil, vinegar and the mustard to make a vinaigrette and season to taste. Break up the salads, wash well and shake dry.

Heat a little oil in a frying pan, then add the butter. Season the slices of fish and as soon as the butter starts to sizzle quickly fry them in the fat for about 15 seconds each side, turning only once. Remove the fish from the pan and keep warm.

To Serve

Place the salad leaves in a metal bowl along with the pine kernels. Pour in the vinaigrette and toss, than place in the oven for about 30 seconds to warm through. Once warm, toss the salad again and divide it out between the plates. Arrange the slices of fish through it, sprinkle with chervil leaves, and serve immediately. NOTE It is important to serve the salad as quickly as possible once it has been warmed through as it will not stand for very long and cannot be reheated.

SERVES 4

2 × 900 g/2 lb monkfish tails
20 large spring onions or button onions
20 small button mushrooms
2 rashers smoked back bacon
Salt and freshly ground white pepper
Oil for frying
175 ml/6 fl oz red wine
175 ml/6 fl oz fish stock
300 ml/½ pint veal stock

Garnish

4 sprigs fresh dill

Picture: page 119

Monkfish Braised with Bacon in Red Wine

This is possibly not a combination that one would readily think of, but it really does work. It is one of those occasions where red wine is called for with fish, and quite a robust one at that.

Method

Preheat the oven to 200°C/400°F/Gas Mark 6.

Fillet and skin the monkfish tail. Remove all of the dark-coloured meat and discard. Cut each fillet into squares roughly 2.5 cm/1 inch square – each fillet should yield about 8 pieces. Peel the outside layer from the spring onions and cut off the tops to within 1 cm/½ inch of the bulb. Discard the tops. If possible 'turn' each of the button mushrooms and cut off the stalks. Cut the bacon into strips about 4 cm × 5 mm/1½ × ¼ inches. Blanch these in boiling water for a couple of seconds and drain well, then fry them in a little oil until nicely browned.

Combine the red wine and fish stock in an ovenproof pan, add the cubes of monkfish and season. Heat the pan until the liquid just starts to tremble, then place it in the oven until cooked – this will only take about 5 minutes. When the fish is cooked, remove it from the pan, cover and keep warm.

Reduce the liquid over a high heat until only a quarter of its original volume remains. Add the veal stock, bring back to the boil, then add the spring onions and mushrooms. Continue boiling until the onions are cooked and the sauce has reduced slightly and thickened a little. The onions should remain a bit crisp. If they have cooked before the sauce has thickened, remove them from the pan – they can always be added later.

To Serve

When the sauce is ready, add the pieces of fish and the strips of bacon and allow to 'soak' for a minute; check the seasoning. Divide the fish, mushrooms, onions and bacon out equally between the plates, making sure that they are all arranged attractively. Pour over the sauce and top each with a sprig of fresh dill.

Sautéed Monkfish with Asparagus and Chervil Sauce

SERVES 4

1 × 900 g/2 lb monkfish tail
16 thin asparagus tips
15 g/½ oz fresh chervil
450 ml/¾ pint fish stock
175 ml/6 fl oz dry sherry
1 tbsp oil
250 g/9 oz unsalted butter
120 ml/4 fl oz double cream

Method

Fillet the monkfish tail and remove all of the dark meat and discard. Cut each fillet with the knife slightly angled into 10 slices about 5 mm/¼ inch thick. Peel the asparagus tips if necessary, tie them into bundles and cook in boiling salted water until still slightly crisp, then refresh in iced water. When cold, cut each tip into 3 or 4 pieces about 4 cm/1½ inches long at a slight angle. Remove the chervil leaves from their stalks.

Combine the fish stock with the dry sherry, set over a high heat and reduce until syrupy. While the stock is reducing, heat the oil in a frying pan, add about 25 g/1 oz of the butter and gently fry the slices of monkfish until lightly browned. Remove from the pan and keep warm. Cut the remaining butter into cubes of about 1 cm/½ inch and leave them in the refrigerator until needed.

When the stock has reduced to the desired level, add the cream and bring to the boil. Remove the pan from the heat and gradually add the butter, shaking the pan or whisking continuously until it has all melted. If you need to keep the sauce warm, stand the pan in a bain-marie over a very low heat; do not allow to boil.

To Serve

Place the cooked fish into a hot oven (200°C/400°F/Gas Mark 6) for about 1 minute to reheat. At the last moment add the asparagus and the chervil to the sauce. Pour the sauce with the asparagus and the chervil onto the plates, being careful to divide out the asparagus evenly. Arrange the slices of monkfish on top. If you have any spare chervil, sprinkle some over the top of the finished dish.

NOTE The asparagus and the reduction can be done some time in advance but the cooking of the fish and the finishing of the sauce must be done at the last minute as the sauce will not stand reheating once made.

SERVES 4

1 × 1.5 kg/3-3½ lb monkfish tail
225 g/8 oz fillet of salmon
175 g/6 oz cold unsalted butter
350 ml/12 fl oz fish stock
120 ml/4 fl oz dry sherry
25 g/1 oz mixed fresh herbs (chervil, dill, chives, basil, parsley, tarragon)
50 ml/2 fl oz double cream

Monkfish and Salmon with Herb Butter Sauce

This dish can also be made substituting the monkfish for turbot or brill, or you can even use salmon on its own. The sauce is very simple and will complement any fish.

Method

Preheat the oven to 200°C/400°F/Gas Mark 6.

Fillet the monkfish tail and remove and discard any dark meat. Cut each fillet into six slices about 5 mm/¼ inch wide, cutting at an angle to give slices about 10 cm/4 inches long. Then cut the salmon into similar-sized pieces, but cutting at an angle straight across the fillet. Butter a tray large enough to take the fish without overlapping and lay the slices in. Add the fish stock and the sherry. Cover with buttered paper or foil and bring the liquid up to trembling point. Transfer to the oven and poach gently for 2 minutes or until the fish is cooked. When it is cooked, remove the slices from the stock and cover and keep warm.

Set the stock over a high heat and reduce until syrupy. Roughly chop the herbs and mix them together.

To Serve

When the stock is syrupy, add the cream and bring back to the boil. Turn down the heat to very low and gradually add the butter in small pieces, whisking continuously until it has all melted. Do not allow the sauce to boil again once the butter has been added. Stir in the herbs and then stand the sauce in a warm place for 1 minute to allow the herbs to infuse. Arrange the slices of fish on the plates, alternating them and allowing 3 pieces of monkfish and 2 of salmon per portion. Pour the sauce around and serve immediately.

Red Mullet
(FRENCH: *rouget* GERMAN: *rotbarbe*
USA: *goatfish*)

Often known as the 'woodcock of the sea', because it can be cooked and eaten without gutting – its liver being much prized – this is a striking fish to look at. Its back is a beautiful pinky-red colour with strips of yellow, fading to almost white across the belly. Its scales are large and must be removed before cooking.

The French name 'rouget' is often applied to a few different types of fish because of their red colouring; one is the red gurnard, which is not of the same quality as mullet but can be used in any mullet recipe. Red gurnard is an under-rated fish in my opinion, and it is much cheaper in price, for the time being anyway.

Sauté of Red Mullet with Pepper and Vinegar Sauce

SERVES 4

4 × 175 g / 6 oz red mullet
I small red pepper
I small green pepper
I medium carrot
I medium courgette
Salt and freshly ground white pepper
25 ml / I fl oz peanut oil
50 g / 3 oz butter
2 shallots, finely chopped
50 ml / 2 fl oz sherry vinegar
50 ml / 2 fl oz fish stock
10 g / ¼ oz fresh chives, finely chopped

This light, summery dish requires the minimum of effort.

Method

Scale and fillet the mullet, and remove the line of small bones that runs down the middle of the fillets using a pair of pliers.

Remove the seeds from the peppers and cut them into 3 mm/ ⅛ inch dice. Peel the carrot and dice the same size as the peppers. Dice the courgettes to a similar size but do not peel.

Heat half the oil in a frying pan, then add about 25 g / 1 oz of the butter and allow it to sizzle but not brown (do not allow the pan to get so hot that it burns the butter). Season the fillets of mullet on the meat side only, and gently place them in the pan, skin side down, for about 20 seconds, then turn and slowly cook on the other side for about 2 minutes or until cooked. Remove them from the pan and drain on kitchen paper. Cover and keep warm.

Tip the fat out of the pan, add the remaining oil and gently fry all the vegetables for about 10 seconds. Add the vinegar and the fish stock, return to the boil, then remove the pan from the heat and gradually add the remaining butter, shaking the pan until all the butter has melted.

To Serve

Place the fish on the plates. At the last minute, stir the chives into the sauce and then spoon it over the mullet. Serve immediately.

Mousseline of Red Mullet with Basil Cream Sauce

SERVES 2-4

Mousseline

4 × 110 g / 4 oz or 2 × 225 g / 8 oz red mullet
½ tsp salt
1 egg white
300 ml / ½ pint double cream
40 ml / 1 ½ fl oz dry sherry
2 egg yolks
Freshly ground white pepper
Pinch of nutmeg
15 g / ½ oz butter

Sauce

175 ml / 6 fl oz fish stock
85 ml / 3 fl oz dry vermouth
120 ml / 4 fl oz double cream
50 g / 2 oz unsalted butter
12 fresh basil leaves, shredded

This recipe is suitable either as a first or a main course. It will make eight 85 ml/3 fl oz or four 175 ml/6 fl oz moulds. The sauce should be sufficient for both. By not skinning the fish, the mousse will take on a slightly pink tinge. In its raw state, the mousse should last perfectly well for two days if kept refrigerated, but it must be served immediately once cooked.

Method

Preheat the oven to 180°C/350°F/Gas Mark 4.

Scale and fillet the fish but do not skin, and remove the line of small bones that runs down the middle of each fillet using a pair of pliers. Cut the fillets into small pieces, place in a blender or food processor with the salt and process until a smooth paste. Add the egg white and blend again to mix in thoroughly. Remove from the blender and rub through a sieve. Place in a bowl set on crushed ice and gradually add two-thirds of the cream, then the sherry, egg yolks and seasoning. Test the texture of the mousse (see page 41). If it is too rubbery, add a little more cream and test again. Use the butter to grease the moulds and fill with the mousse, pressing it in well to get rid of any air bubbles. Cover with foil and cook in a bain-marie in the oven for 14-18 minutes for the larger moulds, or 10-12 minutes for the small ones.

To make the sauce, reduce the fish stock and vermouth until syrupy, add the cream and reduce until it starts to thicken. This will not take long.

To Serve

Tip the cooked mousses out on to the plates (if the moulds were well-buttered this should be very easy). At the last minute, add the butter to the sauce in small pieces, whisking until it has all melted – this will give the sauce the texture of velvet – then add the basil leaves and pour the sauce over the mousses. If you have some of the leaves from the tops of the basil plants, garnish with these. Serve immediately.

Warm Salad of Red Mullet with Vegetables

This light, colourful first course is very quick and easy to prepare and cook.

Method

Scale and fillet the mullet, and remove the line of small bones that runs down the middle using a pair of pliers. Peel the carrots and wash all the vegetables. Cut into batons about 25 cm/1 inch long by 5 mm/⅛ inch wide, then blanch in boiling water for a few seconds and refresh in iced water. Drain. Butter a flameproof pan and, holding the knife at a slight angle, cut each fillet of mullet into 4 pieces across the fillet. Place these in the pan, add the fish stock and white wine and cover with buttered paper or foil. Bring the liquid to a tremble, reduce the heat to very low and very gently poach for 30 seconds. When cooked, remove the fish from the liquid and keep warm.

To Serve

Preheat the oven to 230°C/450°F/Gas Mark 8.

Wash the lettuces and put in a bowl. Mix together the mustard, walnut oil, salad oil and vinegar and season to taste with the sugar, salt and freshly ground pepper. Pour the vinaigrette over the salad and toss well. Put the salad and vegetables in an ovenproof dish and place in the oven for about 1 minute and then remove.

Toss the salad and vegetables again and arrange on the plates with the pieces of mullet. Sprinkle on a few parsley leaves.

2 × 175 g/6 oz red mullet
115 g/4 oz carrots
175 g/6 oz courgettes
115 g/4 oz celery
A little butter
50 ml/2 fl oz fish stock
25 ml/1 fl oz dry white wine
1 small head radicchio
¼ head curly endive
½ head red oak leaf lettuce
½ tsp Dijon mustard
25 ml/1 fl oz walnut oil
50 ml/2 fl oz salad oil
2 tbsp red wine vinegar
Pinch of sugar
Salt and coarsely ground black pepper

Garnish

Parsley leaves

SERVES 4

4 × 225 g/8 oz red mullet
Salt and freshly ground white pepper
175 g/6 oz unsalted butter, well chilled
3 oranges
120 ml/4 fl oz fish stock
55 ml/2 fl oz dry vermouth
55 ml/2 fl oz double cream
10-12 fresh basil leaves

Grilled Red Mullet with Orange and Basil Butter Sauce

This sensational summer dish is so easy to prepare, and with such vivid colours it will never fail to impress.

Method

As red mullet can be cooked either with or without being gutted the choice is yours. Scale the fish and either leave whole or fillet. Place the fish on a grilling tray and season. Melt 25 g/1 oz of the butter, baste the fish and grill under a hot grill for 3 minutes for a fillet and 8-10 minutes for a whole fish. The whole fish will have to be turned, but be careful as the skin is very thin indeed, so try not to break it. If, however, you are cooking only the fillets, grill them skin side up without turning. Whichever way you choose, baste frequently with the melted butter.

To make the sauce, peel 1 orange, cut the zest into very fine strips or julienne and squeeze out the juice. Segment the remaining oranges. Bring the fish stock, vermouth and the orange juice to the boil and reduce until syrupy. Add the zest and the cream and bring back to the boil.

To Serve

At the last minute, add the remaining butter to the sauce a little at a time, whisking continuously until all the butter has melted – on no account allow the sauce to boil after starting to add the butter. When the butter has melted, shred the basil, reserving a few small leaves for garnish, and add to the sauce along with the orange segments. Check the seasoning and divide the sauce between the plates immediately. Top with the fish and sprinkle with a few small basil leaves as garnish.

Poached Red Mullet with Spring Onions

SERVES 2-4

1 × 115 g/4 oz red mullet

175 g/6 oz spring onions

175 g/6 oz cold unsalted butter

50 ml/2 fl oz dry sherry

175 ml/6 fl fish stock

50 ml/2 fl oz double cream

Picture: page 117

This is a very quick dish both to prepare and cook and is ideal as a first course, but it is also good as a main course for two people. The colour combinations of this dish do make it look quite stunning.

Method

Preheat the oven to 190°C/375°F/Gas Mark 5.

Scale and fillet the red mullet. Remove the line of small bones that runs down the middle of each fillet with a pair of pliers.

Trim the onions as necessary. Save 12 small ones as garnish and finely chop the rest. Heat about 15 g/½ oz of the butter in a saucepan, add the chopped onions, cover with a tightly-fitting lid and cook over a fairly high heat, stirring to prevent burning, for about 1 minute or until they are soft but still retain a little bite. When cooked, transfer them to a blender or food processor and chop until they are fairly smooth but not a purée.

Lay the fillets of red mullet, skin side up, in a buttered ovenproof pan, add the sherry and the fish stock and cover with buttered paper or foil. Heat the liquid gently until it just starts to tremble, then transfer to the oven and cook for about 1 minute. It really does not take very long to cook the fillets, so be careful not to overcook them. When cooked, remove the fish from the stock, cover and keep warm.

To make the sauce, return the stock to the heat, bring back to the boil and reduce until syrupy. Add the cream and the spring onions that were set to one side, return to the boil briefly, and then remove from the heat. Gradually add the remaining butter, whisking until it has all melted. If you need to reheat the sauce, do not let it get too hot or the butter will separate. Finally, reheat the finely chopped spring onions in a little butter.

To Serve

Place a spoonful of the chopped spring onion in the middle of each plate, and place a fillet of the mullet beside this. Spoon the sauce and the small, whole onions over and around the fish. Serve immediately.

SERVES 4

2 × 115 g/4 oz red mullet
175 g/6 oz gooseberries
25 ml/1 fl oz sugar syrup (see page 40)
50 ml/2 fl oz dry white wine
175 ml/6 fl oz fish stock
120 ml/4 fl oz veal stock
A little oil for frying
25 g/1 oz butter

Red Mullet with Gooseberry Purée

This is another unusual combination and one that you will probably find a little too rich as a main course, so use it as a first or fish course.

Method

Scale and fillet the red mullet. Remove the line of small bones that runs down the middle of the fillets.

Top and tail the gooseberries and cut them up small. Place in a pan with the syrup and half of the white wine, bring to the boil and simmer until soft. When soft, purée them in a blender or food processor, then pass through a sieve.

Bring the remaining wine and the fish stock to the boil in a saucepan and reduce until syrupy. Add the veal stock, bring back to the boil and reduce slightly until it starts to thicken.

Season the fillets only on the meat side. Heat a little oil and half the butter in a frying pan until it sizzles. Place the fish, skin side down, in the pan and fry gently for about 20 seconds, then turn and finish cooking on the meat side for 1 minute. When cooked, remove the fish and drain on kitchen paper to remove any excess fat. Cover and keep warm.

To Serve

Reheat the gooseberry purée over a very low heat. Return the sauce to the boil, then reduce the heat and whisk in the remaining butter until it has all melted. Strain the sauce through a sieve. Place a spoonful of the purée in the centre of each plate, surround with a ring of sauce and place a fillet on top.

Courgette Flowers Stuffed with Mousseline of Red Mullet

SERVES 8

The first courgettes of the season – picked young complete with flowers – stuffed with a red mullet mousse then lightly steamed and served on a tomato vinaigrette. What could be better?

16 finger-sized courgettes (with flowers)
2 × 115 g/4 oz red mullet
¼ tsp salt
1 egg, separated
200 ml/7 fl oz double cream
25 ml/1 fl oz dry sherry
Freshly ground white pepper, pinch of freshly grated nutmeg, pinch of cayenne pepper

Garnish

300 ml/½ pint tomato vinaigrette (see page 39)
8 cherry tomatoes
Flat parsley leaves

Picture: page 143

Method

Scale and fillet the fish, but do not skin, and remove the line of small bones that runs down the middle of the fillets using a pair of pliers. Cut the fillets into small pieces and place in a blender or food processor along with the salt and process until a smooth paste. Add the egg white and blend in thoroughly until it stiffens. Remove from the blender and rub through a sieve. Place in a bowl set on crushed ice and gradually add two-thirds of the cream (keep a little back to test with), then the sherry and the egg yolk and seasoning. Test the mousse (see page 41). If the mousse is a little firm, add more cream. The mousse needs to be really soft for this recipe, so continue adding cream and testing the mousse until you are happy with it.

Carefully wash the courgettes and flowers so that the flowers do not break off. Inspect the insides of the flowers well as they do tend to attract insects. Drain. Put the mousse into a piping bag with a fairly small tube. Carefully fill the flowers, which should still be attached to the courgettes, about half full with the mixture. Fold the ends of the petals over to form a seal. Place them into a steaming basket and steam for 4 minutes.

To Serve

Divide the vinaigrette out between the plates, forming a circle in the centre. Gently place 2 flowers on top of the vinaigrette. Garnish the plates with a leaf of flat parsley and top with a cherry tomato.

NOTE It is important to handle the courgettes and the flowers carefully at all times because they will easily separate. It is also important not to overfill the flowers – the mousse will expand as it cools, and if the flowers are too full, they will split. Remember to leave enough length in the flower to fold over and completely seal in the mousse.

Turbot, Chicken turbot
(FRENCH: *turbot* GERMAN: *steinbutt*)

Turbot is easily recognized because it has no scales, but bony 'stones' embedded across the dark skin of its back instead. Although turbot resembles brill in some ways it is much more round in shape than brill and also much better in quality.

The meat of the turbot is much deeper than that of the brill and has a much more pronounced flavour, making it, along with the sole, the best of the flat fish. It goes very well with both strong and delicate sauces, as well as making a fine-flavoured mousseline or terrine.

Again, like brill, the turbot is confined to European waters and mainly the North Sea, but because its flesh is so good, it is now being transported to fish markets around the world, especially America.

If turbot is unavailable, make these recipes using brill.

During part of June and July turbot are not really at their best as this is spawning time, so the fish tend to be full of roe and the flesh often has a slightly jelly-like texture.

Tronçon of Turbot Filled with Lobster Mousse

SERVES 4

4 × 175-200 g/6-7 oz tronçon of turbot

A little butter

225 ml/8 fl oz fish stock

300 ml/½ pint lobster sauce

175 ml/6 fl oz double cream

Mousse

1 × 450 g/1 lb live female lobster

300 ml/½ pint court bouillon (see page 31)

1 egg, separated

½ tsp salt

85 ml/3 fl oz dry sherry

150 ml/¼ pint double cream

Garnish

A few flat parsley leaves

Method

Preheat the oven to 180°C/350°F/Gas Mark 4.

Kill the lobster (either with a trussing needle between the eyes or by cutting through the head with a heavy, sharp knife) and pull off the claws and arms. Cook these in the court bouillon for about 6 minutes, then leave to cool in the bouillon.

Detach the tail from the body, cut lengthwise and remove all of the meat, making sure you discard the tract. Finish splitting the head open, remove the gritty sac and discard. Any coral should be added to the lobster meat. Use the shells to make the lobster sauce. Place the meat in a food processor or blender along with the egg white and salt and process until smooth. Rub the resulting mixture through a sieve into a bowl set on crushed ice. Add the sherry and the egg yolk, work it into the mousse, and then gradually pour in two-thirds of the cream, mixing into the mousse gently. Test the mousse (see page 41); if it is a little too rubbery, add a bit more cream and test again. Leave the mousse to stand in the refrigerator until required.

If you have a good fishmonger, ask him to cut the turbot into troncons for you. The troncons are cut from the middle of the thick, right-hand side of the fish and are about 2 cm/¾ inch thick. Remove the middle section of bone from each piece of fish; this is done by cutting down each side of the bone between the backbone and the fins, then, using a pair of strong scissors, snip this portion of bone away at both ends. You should then have an almost pear-shaped piece of turbot with a gap of 6–7.5 cm/2½–3 inches long in the middle.

Remove the lobster claws and arms from the bouillon, shell them and cut each piece of claw meat in half lengthwise. Dice the arm meat and mix this into the mousse. Butter an ovenproof pan large enough to hold the troncons and lay them in, making sure the hole in the middle of each troncon is about 2 cm/¾ inch wide. Fill each troncon with the lobster mousse, pressing it down well to exclude any air, and round the top off smoothly. Add the fish stock, cover with buttered paper or foil, and bring the liquid up to trembling point. Then transfer to the oven and cook for about 12 minutes or until the mousse has souffléd slightly and is firm to the touch. When cooked, remove the fish from the liquor and keep warm. Reheat the lobster sauce and add the double cream. Reduce until thickened. Reheat the lobster claws gently in the reserved cooking liquor.

To Serve

Peel off any dark skin from around the turbot and place the troncons on the plates. Pour the sauce around, and garnish with the lobster claws and the parsley.

NOTE If the lobster is carrying any eggs, remove these before splitting the tail and poach in a little fish stock until they turn bright red. They can be sprinkled over the dish for added colour.

Terrine of Turbot and Button Mushrooms

SERVES 18-20

1 kg/2 lb turbot meat (a 2.5-3 kg/5-6 lb turbot should yield this amount)
56-60 button mushrooms
Juice of ½ lemon
20 g/¾ oz butter
16-18 large spinach leaves
1 tsp salt
2 egg whites
450 ml/¾ pint double cream
4 egg yolks
85 ml/3 fl oz dry vermouth
Freshly ground white pepper
Pinch of nutmeg

Method

Preheat the oven to 180°C/350°F/Gas Mark 4.

Remove the stalks from the mushrooms and wash well. Put them in a saucepan with the lemon juice and 15 g/½ oz of the butter, bring to the boil, then remove from the heat, leave to cool and then drain. Blanch the spinach leaves in boiling salted water for a couple of seconds and refresh in iced water. Lay them out on a cloth to drain. Butter a 28 cm/11 inch terrine mould with the remaining butter, then line it with the spinach, saving about 4 leaves for later. Make sure there are no holes and allow a 7.5 cm/3 inch overhang all the way round.

Fillet and skin the turbot, cut a strip of about 4 cm/1½ inches wide lengthwise from each of the 2 large fillets. Season these strips, lay them end to end so that they are the length of the terrine and wrap in the saved spinach leaves. (This strip is placed down the middle of the terrine later.)

Cut the remaining turbot into small pieces and purée in a blender or food processor along with the salt until smooth. Add the egg whites and blend for a few seconds more or until well mixed in. Remove from the blender and rub the mixture through a sieve to remove any sinews – only by doing this can you be sure of a really fine texture. Set the bowl on crushed ice and gradually add two-thirds of the cream, followed by the egg yolks, vermouth and seasoning. Test the mousse (see page 41) and, if it is too rubbery, add a little more cream and test again. The texture should be soft, but should still hold together and not break up.

To assemble the terrine, put a 1 cm/½ inch layer of mousse in first, making sure there are no air bubbles. Put in 2 lines of mushrooms the length of the terrine and cover with another 1 cm/½ inch layer of mousse. Lay the turbot wrapped in the spinach down the centre and cover with mousse, making sure you fill in between the strip and the sides of the dish – this is best done using a piping bag. Lay in another 2 lines of mushrooms and cover with the remaining mousse. Fold over the spinach so that the top is completely covered. Cover the terrine with buttered foil and place in a bain-marie of simmering water. Cook in the oven for 35-45 minutes. To test whether the terrine is cooked, pierce the centre with a trussing needle – it should go in and through the centre of the turbot easily and come out clean and warm. Leave the terrine to rest in a cool place – it is best eaten about 24 hours later.

To Serve

Turn out the terrine by dipping the dish in hot water for a few seconds. Cut it into 1 cm/½ inch slices, serve on a green sauce (see page 36) and garnish the plate with 'turned' mushrooms. NOTE This terrine can be kept for up to one week in a refrigerator, but keep it covered as it will dry out. If kept like this, it is best to remove it to a warmer place for about 1 hour before eating.

Fillets of Turbot Topped with Grain Mustard

SERVES 4

4 × 150 g/5 oz fillets of turbot
175 g/6 oz cold unsalted butter
15 g/½ oz shallots, finely chopped
175 ml/6 fl oz dry sherry
475 ml/16 fl oz fish stock
50 g/2 oz whole grain mustard

Garnish

Flat parsley leaves

The delicate butter sauce for this dish contrasts well with the meaty texture of the turbot and the coarse-grained mustard topping, giving an easy to prepare and interesting main course dish. Be sure to use a grain mustard; it tends not to be so fiery as most others and also has a nicer texture. Brill or halibut would make good substitutes for the turbot.

Method

Preheat the oven to 190°C/375°F/Gas Mark 5.

Skin the fillets of turbot. Butter an ovenproof pan large enough to take the fillets without folding them. Sprinkle the pan with the shallots and lay the fish on top. Add the sherry and the fish stock, cover with buttered paper or foil, and poach in the oven for 4–5 minutes. When cooked, remove the fish from the pan, spread each fillet with a thin layer of mustard, and cover and keep warm.

Reduce the liquid until only about 4 tablespoons remain, then add the cream and bring back to the boil. Remove from the heat and add the butter gradually, whisking continuously until it has all melted.

To Serve

Pour the sauce onto the plates as soon as it is ready. Top with the fillets of turbot and sprinkle with fresh parsley leaves to enhance its appearance. Serve immediately.

SERVES 4

4 × 175 g/6 oz fillets of turbot

50 g/2 oz black chanterelles

15 g/½ oz shallots, finely chopped

25 g/1 oz butter

120 ml/4 fl oz dry white wine

350 ml/12 fl oz fish stock

½ red pepper

Salt and freshly ground white pepper

120 ml/4 fl oz double cream

Garnish

4 flat parsley leaves

Picture: page 17

Poached Fillet of Turbot with Black Chanterelle Sauce

This makes a really stunning dish with the white of the turbot against the dark grey, almost black, sauce, and is best served on a plain white plate for maximum effect. Of course, it also tastes good! Although the appearance of chanterelles may put you off – not to mention the price – do try them; they are worth it.

Method

Preheat the oven to 200°C/400°F/Gas Mark 6.

Put the 4 best-looking chanterelles to one side to use later as a garnish. Break up the rest into smaller pieces, wiping each one as you go to remove any dirt. Sweat the shallots in half of the butter in a small saucepan until they are soft, then add the chanterelles and continue to sweat for a further minute. Pour in the white wine and about 400 ml/14 fl oz of the fish stock, bring to the boil and simmer for 15 minutes. Place the resulting sauce in a food processor or blender and blend until it is a smooth paste.

Remove the seeds from the pepper and cut its flesh into long and very thin strips. Blanch these in boiling salted water for a few seconds, then refresh in iced water and drain.

Using the remaining butter, grease a shallow tray or ovenproof pan large enough to take the fillets of turbot without overlapping. Lay the fish in the pan, lightly season and add the remaining fish stock. Cover the fish with buttered paper or foil and heat the stock until it just starts to tremble, then transfer to the oven and cook for 4–6 minutes, depending on the thickness of the fillets. When cooked, drain the fillets from the stock, cover and keep warm. Turn up the oven to 220°C/425°F/Gas Mark 7.

Set the stock over a high heat and, when it boils, drop in the whole chanterelles and poach for 30 seconds. Drain them and keep warm. Continue to reduce the stock until syrupy.

To Serve

Just before serving, add the cream to the reduced stock and return to the boil, then stir in the chanterelle paste and gently reheat. Place the turbot in a hot oven for 1 minute to reheat. Pour the sauce onto the plates to form a puddle in the centre of each one. Lay the fillets of turbot on top and scatter strips of blanched pepper over the top of the fish only and not on the sauce. Lay a poached chanterelle on the edge of the sauce along with a parsley leaf.

Tartlet of Brill with Baby Leeks
(see page 88)

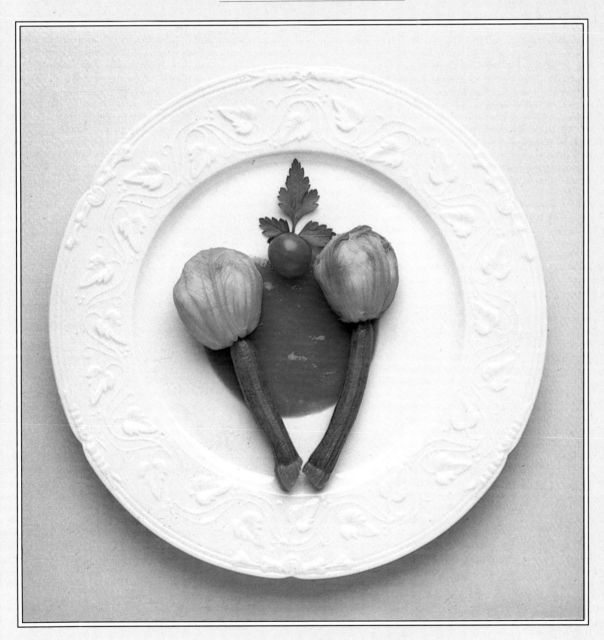

Grilled Sea Bass with Mint
(see page 82)

Turbot with Foie Gras and Truffle Cream Sauce

SERVES 4

4 × 175 g/6 oz fillets of turbot
Salt and freshly ground white pepper
175 ml/6 fl oz fish stock
85 ml/3 fl oz dry sherry
225 ml/8 fl oz double cream
4 × 25 g/1 oz thin slices of foie gras
10 g/¼ oz diced truffle
10 g/¼ oz unsalted butter

This is bursting with cholesterol, but what a way to go!

Method

Preheat the oven to 200°C/400°F/Gas Mark 6.

Skin the fillets of turbot, trim off any dark meat from the underside and discard. Butter an ovenproof pan, place the fillets in it, season, and add the fish stock and the sherry. Cover with buttered paper or foil and poach in the oven for 4–6 minutes. When cooked, remove the fish from the pan, cover and keep warm. Turn the oven up to 220°C/425°F/Gas Mark 7.

For the sauce, reduce the liquor by at least two-thirds over a high heat. Add the cream and reduce until it starts to thicken.

To Serve

Lay the slices of foie gras on top of the fillets and place in the oven for about 30 seconds or until the foie gras goes soft. Add the truffle to the sauce, place a fillet on each plate and pour the sauce over and around. Serve immediately.

SERVES 4

2 × 550 g / 1 ¼ lb fillets of turbot

25 g / 1 oz ground hazelnuts

150 g / 5 oz white fish, trimmed

¼ tsp salt

1 egg, separated

85 ml / 3 fl oz double cream

25 ml / 1 fl oz dry sherry

Freshly ground white pepper

225 ml / 8 fl oz dry white wine

275 g / 10 oz unsalted butter

Garnish

15 g / ½ oz whole hazelnuts

Picture: page 142

Fillets of Turbot Stuffed with a Hazelnut Mousseline

I know this seems an unusual combination, but it is a dish that has always proved to be very popular with our customers – maybe because it is so unusual. It does, however, work very well indeed. Although I have never tried it, I am sure it would work equally well with walnuts. Use the two large fillets from a 2 kg/ 4½ lb turbot to make this dish; the white fish can be any firm white meat, for example monkfish, sole or brill.

Method

Preheat the oven to 220°C/425°F/Gas Mark 5.

Lightly toast the ground hazelnuts in the oven or under the grill, then allow to go cold. Remove and discard any dark meat from the white fish, then cut it up finely. Purée this with the salt in a food processor until smooth. Add the egg white and mix in until stiff. Pass the fish through a sieve into a bowl set on crushed ice. Gradually add two-thirds of the cream, mix in well, then add the sherry and the egg yolk and season with a little freshly ground white pepper. When the hazelnuts are cold, add them to the mousse, again mixing in well. Test the mousse (see page 41) and if it is rubbery, add a little more cream and test again. Keep adding cream until you are happy with its texture and flavour.

Skin and trim the fillets. Using a sharp knife and starting at the head of each fillet, make a pocket in the fillet almost to the end, stopping about 1 cm/½ inch before the tail and falling short of the sides by 5 mm/¼ inch so they remain joined. Sprinkle the insides with a little salt and pepper. Fill a piping bag with the mousse mixture and pipe it into the pockets so that they fill up evenly but are not too full; remember that the mousse will expand while it cooks and if the fillets are too full they will burst.

Butter the base of an ovenproof pan, lay in the fillets and add the white wine. Cover with buttered paper or foil and heat the liquid until it starts to tremble, no more, then place in the oven for about 8 minutes. When cooked, drain the fish, cover and keep warm. Set the liquid over a high heat and reduce until syrupy.

To Serve

When the liquid is syrupy, reduce the heat to very low and gradually add the butter, whisking continuously until it has all melted. If you need to keep it warm, then place the saucepan in a bain-marie. Using a sharp carving knife, cut each fillet into 8

146

slices, discarding the first and last slices. Pour the sauce onto the plates, arrange 4 slices of fish on each plate and sprinkle the whole hazelnuts around the fish.

Poached Fillet of Turbot with Salmon Caviar Sauce

SERVES 4

Method

Preheat the oven to 190°C/375°F/Gas Mark 5.

Skin the fillets of turbot, trim off any dark meat from the underside and discard. Butter a flat ovenproof pan large enough to take the fillets without overlapping, lay them in and add the fish stock. Season, cover with buttered paper or foil and bring to trembling point. Transfer to the oven and gently poach for about 4-5 minutes. When cooked, remove the fillets from the stock, cover and keep warm.

Add the champagne to the stock, set over a high heat and reduce by three-quarters, then add the cream and reduce again until it starts to thicken.

To Serve

Place the fillets of turbot into the oven along with the bouchée cases for about 30 seconds to warm through, then remove from the oven and place a teaspoon of caviar into each case. Add the remaining caviar to the sauce and remove from the heat. Place a fillet of turbot in the middle of each plate and mask with the sauce, making sure not to leave any of the caviar behind. Place a bouchée on each plate and finish the garnishing with a few flat parsley leaves.

4 × 150 g/5 oz fillets of turbot
A little butter
450 ml/¾ pint fish stock
Salt and freshly ground white pepper
120 ml/4 fl oz champagne
300 ml/½ pint double cream
4 bouchée cases, 2.5 cm/1 inch in diameter
50-85 g/2-3 oz salmon caviar

Garnish

Flat parsley leaves

Picture: page 190

SERVES 4

4 × 150 g/5 oz fillets of turbot
2 medium courgettes
1 small leek
2 medium carrots
115 g/4 oz celeriac
115 g/4 oz shallots
Salt and freshly ground white pepper
350 ml/12 fl oz beer
175 ml/6 fl oz fish stock
225 ml/8 fl oz double cream

Turbot Braised in Beer with Vegetables

Using a light beer such as lager for this recipe will give a much better flavour than a full-bodied, traditional beer. At first it may sound rather a heavy dish, but it really is very light. Braising in beer is far from being a new way to cook, although not many fish seem to have been treated this way as it tends to be confined to heavier dishes using beef.

Method

Preheat the oven to 200°C/400°F/Gas Mark 6.

Skin and trim the fillets. Cut all of the vegetables into 5 mm/ ¼ inch dice. Butter a tray and scatter the vegetables over the bottom. Lightly season the fish and lay on top of the vegetables, then pour over the beer. Cover with buttered paper or a lid and place in the oven for about 12-15 minutes. When cooked, remove the fish and vegetables, cover and keep warm.

Pour the liquor into a saucepan, add the fish stock and reduce over a high heat by at least three-quarters. Pour in the cream, return to the boil and reduce until it just starts to thicken.

To Serve

Return the vegetables to the sauce and simmer for a further minute to heat through. Meanwhile, return the fish to the oven for about 1 minute to reheat.

Spoon about three-quarters of the vegetables across the serving dishes with a little of the sauce. Place the fish on top, then spoon the remaining sauce and vegetables over the fish.

Slices of Turbot Marinated in Tomato and Walnut Oil

SERVES 6

1 × 1.75 kg/4 lb turbot
8 medium tomatoes
50 ml/2 fl oz sherry vinegar
85 ml/3 fl oz walnut oil
Salt and freshly ground white pepper
30 fresh basil leaves

This dish is simple to produce and makes a wonderfully light and colourful first course. Once made, it needs to stand for at least 6 hours; however, if you are not too keen on the raw texture of fish, then leave it in the marinade for a few more hours – the longer it stands, the softer the fish will become. Brill or sea bass will work just as well in this recipe; if walnut oil is not available, then use olive oil instead.

Method

Fillet and skin the turbot and rinse the fillets in clean water. Roughly chop up 6 of the tomatoes (reserve 2 for garnish) and place them in a food processor or liquidizer. Add the sherry vinegar, walnut oil, a good pinch of salt and a few turns of the pepper mill and process until smooth. Pass through muslin or a fine strainer to remove any skin and seeds. Check the seasoning and, if required, add a little more. The marinade needs to be quite highly seasoned otherwise the fish will taste a bit bland.

Slice each fillet into thin slivers, lay them in the marinade, then leave in the refrigerator for at least 6 hours.

For the garnish, blanch and skin the remaining tomatoes, cut them into quarters and remove the seeds, then cut each quarter into thin strips.

To Serve

Lay the slices of turbot on the plates, whisk the marinade (it has probably started to separate by now), then pour a little over the fish. Sprinkle with the slices of tomato and scatter the basil leaves on top. What a picture!

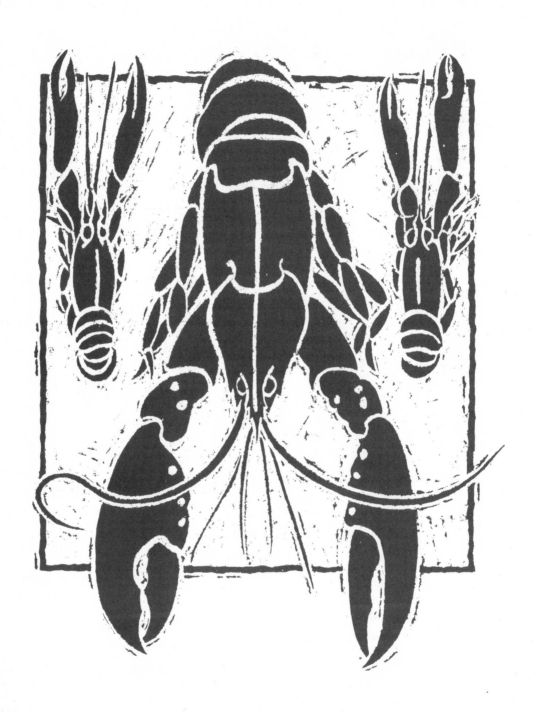

Crustaceans

What better way is there to eat a lobster or crab than straight out of the shell while still warm, or prawns dipped in a little garlic mayonnaise, peeling them as you go. These are the most common of the crustaceans, but there are, of course, others such as crawfish and shrimps. There is also the freshwater crayfish, which was once abundant in our rivers and streams, but, alas not now; pollution has seen to that. In this section, I have again tried to introduce a few new ideas for the dinner table; some are easy and some a little more difficult, but all of them are well worth a try.

All crustaceans are expensive to buy, so be careful to buy only the best – they will be no more expensive. Crustaceans should always be bought alive where possible, and do cook your own – they will always taste far better. I cannot recall even one occasion where I have served frozen shellfish. I tend to avoid them like the plague, especially frozen prawns, which are really not worth bothering with if fresh ones are available (and they are just as easy to prepare). In any case, the price difference, if any, is minimal.

Crab
(FRENCH: *crabe* GERMAN: *krabbe*)

There are a great number of types of crabs available throughout the world. The edible or common crab is the one normally used in Britain and Europe, but is not found in American waters. The rock crab, blue crab and snow crab are those normally found there, and of these the blue crab is the one that enjoys the most acclaim.

Again, like all shellfish, crabs must be bought alive and a sign of a good crab is that it will feel heavy for its size. The yield of meat from a good healthy crab will be about one-third of its total weight. Normally, the larger the crab, the better the yield, and the easier it is to clean. Preparing a crab can be very time consuming and fiddley, but it is, nevertheless, a job worth doing well. In my experience, many people remove only the dark meat from the main shell and the white meat from the claws. This is sinful! The white meat found in the smaller legs and the body carapace is quite delicious, far sweeter than the claw meat, although it is more difficult to remove. Cleaning a crab also frightens a lot of people off, because they are not sure what is edible and what is not. Well, it is quite easy really. The only inedible parts are the gills, or 'dead man's fingers' as they are more commonly known, which are finger-shaped and very grey in colour, and the part immediately behind the head. To remove this, first remove the body from the shell, then press down on the mouth part of the shell with your thumbs until it cracks off. As you pull this away, it will bring with it the inedible parts.

When buying a crab, go for one with larger claws, as this is where the majority of the meat is, and always try to choose a male – the males have a larger amount of meat than the females and a much better flavour. To sex a crab, turn it onto its back: the male has a very narrow tail, whereas the female's tail is broad and slightly heart-shaped.

Crab Consommé

Method

Crush the crab shells or break them up as small as possible. Wash, peel and roughly chop up the vegetables. Heat the oil in a large, heavy-based saucepan, add the vegetables and sweat for at least 5 minutes, then add the shells and continue sweating for a further 4 minutes. Pour in the brandy, reduce it slightly, then stir in the tomato purée followed by the fish stock, herbs, saffron and peppercorns. Bring to the boil and simmer for at least 3 hours. Alternatively, put the stock in an ovenproof pan and simmer for 3 hours in a moderate oven (180°C/350°F/Gas Mark 4); cooking this way will ensure that the stock does not burn. When cooked, strain the liquid through a strainer and allow it to go cold.

To clarify the consommé, wash and peel the vegetables and mince or chop very finely with the fish. Mix in the tomato purée and the egg whites followed by the cold stock; the stock must be cold at this stage or it will cook the egg white. Set the pan over a high heat and bring almost to the boil, stirring occasionally to prevent the consommé from sticking. Stop stirring the consommé when it has almost reached boiling point otherwise it will cloud. Allow to simmer for at least 1 hour, then gently strain the liquid through muslin and season to taste.

To Serve

The consommé, which should be crystal clear, can be served in a number of ways. If you have used fish stock in the basic stock, it should jelly slightly when chilled and can be served 'en gelée' on a hot day.

NOTE A 2.25 kg/5 lb crab should yield enough shell for this recipe. Alternatively, a 900 g/2 lb live crab can be used; follow the instructions as for crab soup (see page 154). Water can also be used to partly or even completely replace the fish stock, but the final flavour will suffer.

Stock

1.25 kg/2½ lb crab shells
175 g/6 oz carrots
175 g/6 oz celery
175 g/6 oz white of leek
175 g/6 oz onion
115 g/4 oz fennel
2 medium tomatoes
1 head garlic
25 ml/1 fl oz oil
120 ml/4 fl oz brandy
150 g/5 oz tomato purée
2.75 litres/5 pints fish stock
2 bay leaves
2 sprigs fresh rosemary
2 sprigs fresh thyme
Pinch of saffron (optional)
1 tsp black peppercorns

To clarify

50 g/2 oz celery
50 g/2 oz onion
50 g/2 oz leek
25 g/1 oz carrot
225 g/8 oz white fish or fish trimmings
50 g/2 oz tomato purée
3 egg whites
Salt and freshly ground white pepper

MAKES 2.25-2.7 litres/
4-5 pints to give 15 servings

1 × 1.5 kg/3-3½ lb live crab
225 g/8 oz onions
225 g/8 oz leeks
115 g/4 oz carrots
225 g/8 oz celery
1 head garlic
25 ml/1 fl oz oil
50 g/2 oz flour
175 g/6 oz tomato purée
175 ml/6 fl oz brandy
85 ml/3 fl oz Pernod
300 ml/½ pint dry white wine
3.5 litres/6 pints fish stock
Sprig of fresh thyme
2 bay leaves
Pinch of cayenne pepper
A few parsley stalks
10 g/¼ oz white peppercorns
½ tsp saffron

Crab Soup

I always prefer to use a live crab for this recipe, but a lot of people will find this offputting. A cooked crab can be used instead, although the flavour will not be as strong. Crab shells that have been saved from another day can also be used, but once again the flavour will not be as good – in fact, if you are only using saved shells, then either cut down on the amount of liquid added or use at least a third more shells.

Method

Preheat the oven to 230°C/450°F/Gas Mark 8.

Rinse the crab in fresh cold water. Using a large heavy knife or cleaver and one swift blow, cut the crab in two through the middle of its body between the eyes and parallel with its legs. Break the legs away from the body, remove the dead men's fingers and discard; everything else can be used, juices as well. Leave the claws and the arms of the crab whole, but break everything else up into small pieces. Wash, peel and roughly chop the vegetables and cut the garlic into small pieces. Heat the oil in an ovenproof pan, add the vegetables and garlic, cover with a lid and sweat until they start to go soft. Add the crab, cover and sweat for about 5 minutes, stirring occasionally to prevent burning. Sprinkle the flour over the contents of the pan, but do not stir in, then place the pan in the oven for 10 minutes to singe the flour. Dot the tomato purée across the top of the flour but do not stir in. Place the pan back in the oven for a further 5 minutes to singe the tomato purée. Turn the oven down to 180°C/350°F/ Gas Mark 4. Remove the pan from the oven, add the brandy and Pernod, ignite and burn off the alcohol. Add the white wine, fish stock and the rest of the ingredients and bring to the boil. Cover and return to the oven to barely simmer for 3 hours. After 15 minutes, remove the whole claws and leave to cool. When cold, crack and remove the meat, put to one side and return the shells to the soup.

After 3 hours strain the soup through a sieve, pressing with the back of a spoon to ensure that every drop is drained.

To Serve

Reheat the soup, add the reserved meat and pour into soup plates. Serve with toasted croûtons of French bread floating in the soup liberally spread with Rouille (see page 40).

Terrine of Crab Wrapped in Smoked Salmon

Method

Bring the court bouillon to the boil, plunge in the crabs and cook for 12-15 minutes. Allow the crabs to go cold in the court bouillon. When cold, shell the crabs keeping the brown and white meat separate. Save the shells and use for the consommé. Liquidize the brown meat until it is smooth. Blanch, skin and deseed the tomatoes, and cut into small dice. Stir into the brown meat and season with a dash of Worcester sauce and salt and pepper. Add the chives to the white meat along with the lemon juice and season with salt and pepper. Soak 5 leaves and 4 leaves of the gelatine separately in a little cold water. When soft, remove from the water and melt separately in a saucepan over a very gentle heat. Add the 5 leaves to the brown meat and the 4 leaves to the white meat, mixing in thoroughly and quickly before the jelly has a chance to set.

Line a 28 cm/11 inch terrine mould with the slices of smoked salmon, leaving enough overlapping the edges to fold over and finish off the terrine. Divide the white meat into 3 equal amounts and the brown into 2. Layer the crab into the terrine, starting with a layer of white meat, alternating with the brown meat and finishing with a layer of white. Allow each layer to set for 10 minutes in the refrigerator – this will make it easier to get the layers even. Finally, carefully fold over the smoked salmon to form a lid. Leave in the refrigerator for at least 1 hour before serving. The terrine will keep perfectly well in the refrigerator for up to 4 days.

To Serve

Soak the remaining 18 leaves of gelatine in a little cold water until soft, then melt in a small amount of hot crab consommé. Stir this into the rest of the consommé and allow to cool to form a jelly.

Serve about a tablespoon of jelly on each plate, place a slice of terrine on top of this, and garnish with a tomato rose.

2 × 1.75 kg/4-4½ lb live crabs
4.5 litres/8 pints court bouillon (see page 31)
2 tomatoes
Dash of Worcester sauce
Salt and freshly ground white pepper
15 g/½ oz chives, finely chopped
Juice of ½ lemon
27 leaves gelatine
350 g/12 oz smoked salmon, thinly sliced
1.7 litres/3 pints crab consommé (see page 153)

Garnish

18-20 tomatoes, cut into roses

Picture: page 61

SERVES 8

1 × 900 g/2 lb live crab

2.25 litres/4 pints court bouillon (see page 31)

½ recipe for basic fish mousse (see page 41)

Salt and freshly ground white pepper

40 asparagus tips

50 g/2 oz fresh chervil

450 g/1 lb unsalted butter

600 ml/1 pint fish stock

175 ml/6 fl oz dry sherry

175 ml/6 fl oz double cream

Picture: page 63

Crab Mousse with Asparagus and Chervil Butter Sauce

Method

Preheat the oven to 200°C/400°F/Gas Mark 6.

Bring the court bouillon to the boil, plunge in the crab and cook for 15 minutes. Allow the crab to go cold in the bouillon. When cold, remove all the meat – both the brown meat from the body and the white meat from the claws and legs. Save the shells for another recipe. Combine this all together and process in a blender or food processor until it is a little finer than it was, but do not reduce it to a fine paste. Mix the crab meat thoroughly with the fish mousse, season to taste (if necessary, add a little more dry sherry to the mixture), then test (see page 41).

Peel the asparagus tips if they need it, then tie them into bundles of fives. Trim the tips so that they are about 10 cm/4 inches long. Pick the chervil leaves from their stalks. Cut the butter into 1 cm/½ inch cubes and leave in the refrigerator. Combine the fish stock and dry sherry together, set over a high heat and reduce by three-quarters.

Lightly butter 8 oval or round 85 ml/3 fl oz moulds, divide the mousse between them and press in well to exclude any air. Top each one with buttered foil. Heat an ovenproof pan or tray large enough to take all the moulds with about 1 cm/½ inch water. When the water boils, put in the moulds and place in the oven for 15 minutes. When the mousses are cooked, remove them from the bain-marie and allow to rest.

Meanwhile, add the cream to the reduced stock, bring back to the boil and then remove from the heat. Gradually add the butter a piece at a time, whisking continuously until it has all melted. Plunge the asparagus tips into boiling water and cook until they still have a little bite, about 2 minutes. Remove and drain.

To Serve

Tip the mousses out of their moulds and place in the centre of each plate. At the last minute add the leaves of chervil to the sauce. Pour the sauce over and around the mousses. Remove the strings from the asparagus and arrange 5 tips around each mousse.

NOTE On no account allow the sauce to boil once it is made; it can be reheated but you must keep it moving all the time.

Crab and Grapefruit Cocktail in a Filo Pastry Basket

SERVES 6

1 × 1.25 kg/2 ½ lb live crag
175 g/6 oz filo pastry (see page 43)
2.5 litres/4 pints court bouillon (see page 31)
3 pink grapefruits
600 ml/1 pint fish stock
600 ml/1 pint double cream
85 ml/3 fl oz champagne, chilled
Salt and freshly ground white pepper

Garnish

A few sprigs of fresh chervil or dill

Method

Preheat the oven to 200°C/400°F/Gas Mark 6.

Divide the pastry in two and roll each piece out as thin as possible. Finish by stretching them over the backs of your hands (the pastry should now be so thin you can see through it) to give 2 sheets about 60 × 45 cm/24 × 18 inches. Allow the pastry to dry out a little, then cut each sheet into 12 squares of about 15 cm/6 inches. Take 6 round, high-sided tins, such as brioche tins, about 10 cm/4 inches across and about 5 cm/2 inches deep. Lay 4 pastry squares in each tin, one on top of the other so that the points of the squares form a petal formation. Bake in the oven for about 10 minutes or until golden brown.

Bring the bouillon to the boil, then plunge in the crab and simmer for 12 minutes. Remove the pan from the heat and allow the crab to go cold in the stock. When cold, remove all of the meat, both from the body and from the legs and claws. Put the white meat to one side, and place the dark meat in a food processor or blender and process until fine.

Skin and segment 2 of the grapefruits, and squeeze the juice from the third. Reserve 12 nice segments for garnish, cut the rest into 3 or 4 pieces and mix with the white crab meat. Bring the grapefruit juice and fish stock to the boil and reduce by three-quarters. Add the cream and the brown crab meat to the stock, return to the boil and reduce again by almost a half. Allow the sauce to go cold.

To Serve

Carefully stir the champagne into the sauce and, if required, season with a little salt and pepper. Lightly season the white crab meat, then add a few spoonfuls of the sauce to this, mixing in well. Arrange 2 grapefruit segments to one side of each plate, fill the filo cases with the white crab meat and place a case in the centre of each plate. Pour the sauce around and garnish with a sprig of chervil or dill.

Crayfish
(FRENCH: *ecrevisse* GERMAN: *krebs*)

The crayfish is a freshwater shellfish which once could be found in rivers everywhere, but, thanks to pollution, is now very rare in the wild. They are, however, extensively farmed in Europe as well as other parts of the world, although they are still expensive and difficult to get hold of.

There are two main varieties: the red claw *(pattes rouge)* which is a very rich red and has quite meaty claws; the other type is smaller but more common and is a greeny brown in colour. Both varieties turn bright red like lobsters when cooked.

Crayfish, just as all other types of shellfish, should be bought while still alive, but take care as they can give a nasty nip with their sharp little claws. They have a very delicate flavour and are marvellous for ganishing.

The crayfish season starts the first or second week of June and you will find crayfish most plentiful and cheaper between June and December.

Steamed Crayfish Mousse Wrapped in Lettuce

SERVES 6

30 live crayfish

225 g/8 oz fillet of monkfish, trimmed

¾ tsp salt

I egg, separated

350 ml/12 fl oz double cream

1.2 litres/2 pints court bouillon (see page 31)

300 ml/½ pint crayfish sauce (see page 34)

I large lettuce

50 g/2 oz cold unsalted butter

Garnish

6 sprigs fresh dill or fennel

Method

To make the mousse, cut the monkfish up into small pieces and blend in a food processor or blender until smooth. Add the salt and egg white and process again until it stiffens. Rub the mixture through a sieve into a bowl set on crushed ice. Gradually add half the cream then put the mixture in the refrigerator until needed.

Bring the court bouillon to the boil. Remove the intestinal tract from the crayfish by pinching the middle section of the tail between your forefinger and thumb, then twist and pull. Plunge the crayfish into the bouillon, cover with a lid and cook for 3 minutes. Drain and allow to cool. Shell the crayfish tails, but leave 6 with their heads still on and save for garnish. Make the crayfish sauce from the shells (see page 34). Cut the 24 tails into 5 mm/¼ inch dice and mix these into the mousse.

Reduce half of the crayfish sauce until only about a quarter of its original volume remains. Make sure that you stir the sauce while it is reducing or it will stick and burn. Allow the sauce to go cold, then mix into the mousse along with the egg yolk. Test the mousse (see page 41); it should hold together but not be too rubbery. If it is too rubbery, add a little more cream and test again until you are happy with both the texture and flavour. Store the mousse in the refrigerator until ready to use.

Gently remove each leaf of lettuce from the head, wash well, then blanch in boiling salted water for 10 seconds. Refresh in iced water, drain and dry well in a cloth.

To assemble the mousse moulds, either take a small, shallow, bowl-shaped coffee cup or an 85 ml/3 fl oz ladle and line with 2 layers of lettuce, leaving an overhang all the way round. Fill with mousse and fold the overhanging lettuce over to make a completely sealed ball. Repeat this 5 more times, using up all the mousse.

To cook, lay the balls in a steaming basket set over boiling water and steam for 10 minutes. Meanwhile, bring the remaining crayfish sauce to the boil, add the rest of the cream and return to the boil. Reduce until the sauce starts to thicken, then turn the heat down to very low and gradually whisk in the butter and continue whisking until it has all melted.

To Serve

When the mousses are cooked, they must be served immediately. Remove them from the steamer and drain on a cloth to remove any excess moisture. Place the reserved crayfish into the steamer to reheat for a few seconds. Pour a little of the sauce in the centre of each plate, and place a ball half on the sauce and half off. Lay a whole crayfish on the opposite edge of the sauce. Garnish with a sprig of fresh dill or fennel.

SERVES 4

2 × 450 g / 1 lb Dover sole

32 live crayfish

15 g / ½ oz butter

Salt and freshly ground white pepper

15 g / ½ oz shallots, chopped

400 ml / 14 fl oz fish stock

120 ml / 4 fl oz dry sherry

300 ml / ½ pint double cream

Good pinch of saffron

Garnish

Fresh parsley

Picture: page 122

Crayfish with Strips of Dover Sole and Creamy Saffron Sauce

This is another of my all-time favourites; not a new combination by any means, but a dish of such stunning colour and flavour – who could resist it? Dover sole is the best fish for this dish; there really is no substitute here.

Method

Skin, fillet and trim the sole. Cut each fillet into 5 diagonal strips about 1 cm / ½ inch wide.

Remove the intestinal tract from the crayfish by pinching the middle section of the tail between your thumb and forefinger, then twist and pull.

Heat the butter in a saucepan until it just starts to sizzle. Lightly season the strips of sole and gently but quickly fry them in the butter until the strips of sole turn white. Remove from the pan, cover and keep in a warm place. Add the shallots to the pan and cook for a few minutes until soft, then pour in 350 ml / 12 fl oz of the fish stock and all of the sherry and bring to the boil over a high heat. When boiling, plunge in the crayfish, cover and boil for 3 minutes. Drain the crayfish from the stock and allow them to cool. Continue boiling the stock and reduce by three-quarters. While the stock is reducing, shell the crayfish and leave 8 with their heads still attached. Save the shells and the rest of the heads for another recipe. Pour the remaining fish stock over the crayfish meat to keep it moist and cover.

When the stock has reduced sufficiently, pour in the cream and add the saffron. Return to the boil and reduce until it starts to thicken.

To Serve

When the sauce has just started to thicken, turn the heat down to low and add the sole and the crayfish tails, which have been drained, to the sauce. Allow to soak in the sauce for 1 minute to finish cooking. Reheat the whole crayfish separately in the fish stock over a gentle heat.

Divide the sole and crayfish out between the plates – soup plates are better for this than flat plates. Spoon over the sauce and garnish each plate with 2 whole crayfish and parsley.

Whole Poached Dover Sole with
Bacon and Chervil
(see page 103)

RIGHT   *Puff Pastry Cases Filled with Oysters and Green Peppercorns*
(see page 195)

BELOW   *Salmon Trout in a Buttery Court Bouillon*
(see page 69)

LEFT *Smoked Haddock Marinated in Cider* **(see page 214)**

BELOW *Mousse of White Asparagus with Pearls of Salmon Caviar* **(see page 58)**

163

Gravlax with Mustard and Dill Dressing
(see page 57)

Chilled Cucumber and Crayfish Soup

Wonderful on a hot summer's day, and easy to prepare, this soup is best eaten as soon as it is made.

Method

Bring the fish stock and white wine to the boil. Remove the intestinal tract from the crayfish by pinching the middle section of the tail between your fingers, then twist and pull. Plunge the crayfish into the boiling stock and cook for 3 minutes. Remove the crayfish and allow to cool. When cold, remove the meat from the tails and put to one side. Crush all the heads and shells, return these to the stock and continue to boil until only half of the stock remains. Strain the stock to remove the shells, then pass the stock through muslin. Return to the boil and reduce by half again – only a quarter of the original volume should remain.

Cut about 50 g/2 oz of the cucumber into very small dice and put to one side. Remove and discard the seeds from the remaining cucumber and roughly chop up the flesh. Place the cucumber, dill and the reduced stock in a food processor and blend until smooth. Rub the purée through a sieve.

Stir the cream and the yoghurt into the soup and season to taste with the lemon juice, salt and white pepper. Leave the soup to stand in the refrigerator for about 1 hour to chill.

To Serve

Divide the soup out between the soup bowls, place 5 crayfish tails into each one, and sprinkle with the diced cucumber. Top with a sprig of dill.

1 cucumber (weighing about 450g/1 lb)
20 live crayfish
600 ml/1 pint fish stock
150 ml/¼ pint dry white wine
10 g/¼ oz fresh dill, roughly chopped
150 ml/¼ pint double cream
1 tbsp natural yoghurt
Juice of ½ lemon
Salt and freshly ground white pepper

Garnish

4 sprigs dill

SERVES 6

225 g/8 oz fillet of monkfish, trimmed

¾ tsp salt

1 egg white

About 200 ml/7 fl oz double cream

25 ml/1 fl oz dry sherry

A little nutmeg

Freshly ground white pepper

6 large spinach leaves

Sauce

1.2 litres/2 pints court bouillon (see page 31)

24 live crayfish

300 ml/½ pint crayfish sauce (see page 34)

300 ml/½ pint double cream

Garnish

Sprigs of fresh dill

Picture: page 123

Turban of Fish Mousse with Crayfish

Although this recipe is quite time-consuming, these light rings of mousse provide a first course worthy of any table. Be careful when removing them from their moulds as they are quite fragile.

Method

Preheat the oven to 190°C/375°F/Gas Mark 5.

For the mousse, cut the monkfish up into small pieces, then place in a food processor or blender and process until smooth. Add the salt and egg white and process again until it stiffens. Rub the fish through a sieve into a bowl set on crushed ice. Gradually add two-thirds of the cream and, when well mixed in, add the sherry and season with nutmeg and a little pepper. Test the mousse (see page 41), then leave in the refrigerator until needed.

Wash the spinach leaves well and blanch for about 15 seconds in boiling salted water. Remove and refresh immediately in iced water. Drain the leaves, lay them out on a cloth and dry well. Lightly butter 6 small savarin moulds, measuring 9 cm/3½ inches in diameter. Line each mould with spinach leaves, making sure that there are no gaps. Allow an overhang all the way around to fold over and totally enclose the mousse. Place the mousse into a piping bag and fill each of the moulds. Fold over the spinach and tightly cover each mould with buttered foil.

For the sauce, bring the court bouillon to the boil. Remove the intestinal tract from the crayfish by pinching the middle section of the tail between your thumb and forefinger, then twist and pull. Plunge the crayfish into the boiling liquid, cover with a lid and cook for 3 minutes. Drain and allow to cool. Shell the crayfish, reserving 6 with their heads on as garnish. Make the crayfish sauce from the shells (see page 34).

Place the moulds into a bain-marie of simmering water, then transfer to the oven and cook for 8 minutes. Meanwhile, mix the crayfish sauce with the cream, and reduce until it thickens.

To Serve

Gently reheat the reserved whole crayfish in a little of the court bouillon. Add the crayfish tails to the sauce and allow to soak for a few seconds. Tip the mousses out of their moulds and place 1 on each plate. Spoon 3 tails into the centre of each ring, pour the sauce around and add a little to the centre of each ring. Garnish each plate with a sprig of fresh dill and a whole crayfish.

Dublin Bay Prawns
Norway lobster, scampi
(FRENCH: *langoustine* GERMAN: *kaisergranat*)

Prawn cocktail, scampi and chips in a basket – there have got to be better uses for this full-flavoured crustacean!

Well, there are. Most recipes using lobster or crayfish or crawfish will also work with prawns, so why is it that they are continually battered or crumbed? Try the consommé – prawns are so full of flavour and are delicious treated this way.

Dublin Bay Prawns Poached with Cucumber

SERVES 6

Method

Cut the cucumber across into 6 pieces each 2.5 cm/1 inch long. Cut each round lengthwise into 6 equal pieces, and 'turn' each piece into a barrel shape.

Wash the Dublin Bay prawns and remove their heads. Put the heads in the freezer for another recipe. If the claws are large, remove them and put with the tails into a large pan along with the fish stock and the vermouth. Cover this with a tightly-fitting lid, set over a high heat and bring to the boil. When boiling, turn down to simmer and continue simmering for 5 minutes. When cooked, remove them from the liquor and allow to cool.

Return the liquor to the stove and reduce until only a quarter of its original volume remains. While this is reducing and when the tails have cooled enough to handle, carefully remove the meat and discard the dark line that runs the length of the tail. If you have also cooked the claws, remove the meat from these too.

To Serve

When the stock has reduced, add the cream and the pieces of cucumber, bring back to the boil and reduce a little more. Cut the butter into small cubes and gradually add these to the sauce, whisking continuously until all the butter has melted. On no account allow the sauce to boil once you have started to add the butter as it will separate. Add the tails and claws of the prawns to the sauce and allow them to soak in the sauce for 1 minute.

Divide the prawns and the cucumber between the plates, pour over the sauce and top with the sprigs of fennel.

24 Dublin Bay prawns (weighing about 2.25 kg/5 lb)
15 cm/6 inch piece of cucumber
350 ml/12 fl oz fish stock
175 ml/6 fl oz dry vermouth
120 ml/4 fl oz double cream
225 g/8 oz cold unsalted butter

Garnish

12 sprigs fresh fennel

Picture: page 122

Tartlet of Dublin Bay Prawns with Asparagus

SERVES 4

20 Dublin Bay prawns (weighing about 1.5 kg/3 lb)

300 ml/½ pint fish stock

50 ml/2 fl oz dry white wine

8 tips thin, fresh asparagus

15 g/½ oz butter

1 small shallot, roughly chopped

½ small clove garlic, crushed

25 ml/1 fl oz brandy

1 sprig fresh thyme

120 ml/4 fl oz double cream

8 bunches corn salad

4 × 10 cm/4 inch shortcrust tartlet cases (see page 42)

Garnish

4 sprigs fresh dill

This dish makes an interesting starter and can be altered to use other ingredients, such as substituting freshwater crayfish for the prawns, or using water or wild asparagus.

Method

Remove the heads from the prawns and reserve. Place the tails in a pan with the fish stock and the white wine, heat until the liquid starts to tremble and then poach the tails gently for 4 minutes. When cooked, drain them from the stock and allow to cool. Roughly chop up the heads from the prawns, and peel the asparagus tips if necessary. Cut each tip into 3 at a slight angle so that each piece is about 2.5 cm/1 inch long. When the prawns have cooled, shell them and remove and discard the dark line that runs the length of the tail. Add the shells to the chopped heads.

Heat the butter in a heavy-based saucepan until it starts to sizzle, add the shallot and garlic and fry gently for about 1 minute without browning. Add the chopped shells and heads and fry for a further minute. Add the brandy and reduce by half. Add the cooking stock and the thyme, bring to the boil and reduce by half. Strain the stock through muslin or a fine sieve into a clean saucepan, return to a high heat and reduce by half again. Pour in the cream, return to the boil and then add the asparagus. Continue boiling until the sauce has thickened and the asparagus has cooked. At this point, add the prawns, leave on a very low heat and allow the prawns to reheat and soak in the sauce.

To Serve

Pick over the corn salad leaves and wash well. Arrange them in a circle on each plate. Reheat the tartlet cases in a hot oven (220°C/425°F/Gas Mark 7) for a few seconds, then place a case in the middle of each circle of corn salad. Pile in the prawns, asparagus and sauce, top each with a sprig of dill, and serve before the pastry becomes soggy.

Nage of Dublin Bay Prawns with Vinegar Butter Sauce

This is equally delightful either as a first course or a main meal. The prawns can be cooked in advance and kept in a little of the cooking liquor to prevent them drying out. However, the sauce must be made at the last moment as it will not stand any reheating.

32 Dublin Bay prawns (weighing about 2.75 kg/6 lb)
2 small carrots
4 large, bulbous spring onions or 6 button onions
1 small leek, white part only
85 ml/3 fl oz white wine vinegar
600 ml/1 pint fish stock
120 ml/4 fl oz double cream
225/8 oz cold unsalted butter, cut into small cubes

Garnish

16-20 flat parsley leaves

Method

Peel the carrots, cannelize them, then slice them across into thin discs. Peel the onions and slice them into rounds about the same thickness as the carrots. Trim the white part of the leek and cut this across as for the other vegetables.

Combine the vinegar and the fish stock in a large pan with a tightly-fitting lid and bring to the boil. When boiling, plunge in the prawns, cover with the lid and continue boiling for a further 5-6 minutes. Once the prawns are cooked, remove them from the liquor, drain and allow to cool. Strain the stock through muslin or a fine strainer into a saucepan and set over a high heat. Reduce the stock until just under a quarter of its original volume remains. While the stock is reducing, shell the prawns and remove and discard the dark line that runs the length of the tail.

To Serve

When the stock has reduced enough, add the cream and the sliced vegetables. Return to the boil, remove the pan from the heat and, shaking the pan continuously, gradually add the butter. Continue shaking the pan until all the butter has melted. Add the prawns and allow to soak in the sauce for about 1 minute – keep the sauce over a very low heat or in a bath of hot water, but do not allow to boil.

At the last minute, add the flat parsley leaves to the sauce. Divide the prawns out equally between the plates, arrange the slices of vegetables across the top and pour over the sauce.

Consommé of Dublin Bay Prawns with Coriander

MAKES 2.25 litres/4 pints

3 kg/7lb Dublin Bay prawns
25 ml/1 fl oz oil
900 g/2 lb mirepoix (leek, onion, celery, carrot)
1 head garlic, roughly chopped
350 ml/12 fl oz brandy
225 g/8 oz tomato purée
4.5 litres/8 pints fish stock
350 ml/12 fl oz dry white wine
10 g/¼ oz black peppercorns
2 bay leaves
Pinch of saffron

To clarify

175 g/6 oz mirepoix (leek, celery, onion)
15 g/½ oz fresh coriander
2 medium tomatoes
6 egg whites
25 g/1 oz tomato purée

Picture: page 124

The finished consommé will keep in the refrigerator for about 5-6 days or several weeks in the freezer. Make the stock the day before, as it needs to be cold to clarify. When clarifying the consommé, it is best done in a deep, narrow saucepan.

Method

Preheat the oven to 160°C/325°F/Gas Mark 3.

Remove the heads from all of the prawns and roughly chop them. Put 20 unshelled tails to one side, shell the rest and add the shells to the heads. Save the tail meat to clarify the consommé.

Heat the oil in a heavy-based ovenproof pan, add the mirepoix of vegetables and the garlic, cover with a lid or buttered foil and sweat for about 5 minutes, stirring occasionally to prevent browning. Add the shells and heads of the prawns and continue sweating for a further 5 minutes, stirring from time to time. Add the brandy, ignite and allow to burn out. Stir in the tomato purée followed by the fish stock and the white wine. Bring to the boil and skim off any scum that comes to the surface. Add the peppercorns, bay leaves and saffron and then place the pan, uncovered, in the oven for 2 hours. Strain the stock through muslin or a fine sieve; discard the shells. Allow stock to go cold.

To clarify the consommé, place the mirepoix of vegetables in a food processor along with the shelled tails, coriander, reserving a few leaves to garnish the finished dish, and the tomatoes until finely chopped. Put this mixture in a heavy-based saucepan and add the egg whites and tomato purée, mixing in well. Gradually add the cold stock, stirring all the time, and bring to just below boiling point over a high heat, stirring frequently to prevent it sticking. Once the consommé has just reached boiling point, stop stirring and turn down the heat so that it only simmers very gently; the consommé will cloud if it is allowed to boil. Simmer for 45 minutes, then strain through muslin. It should now be crystal clear and a bright, golden colour.

To Serve

Poach the 20 reserved tails in a little fish stock for 3 minutes. Shell the tails, remove and discard the dark line that runs the length of the tail, and cut each tail into four. Place 4 pieces of tail into each bowl. Pour the consommé over and garnish with leaves of fresh coriander.

Dublin Bay Prawns in a Filo Pastry Basket

SERVES 6

24 Dublin Bay prawns (weighing about 1.5 kg/3 lb)
175 kg/6 oz filo pastry (see page 43)
12 asparagus tips
25 ml/1 fl oz white wine vinegar
600 ml/1 pint fish stock
120 ml/4 fl oz white wine
115 g/4 oz shallots, finely chopped
120 ml/4 fl oz double cream
50 g/2 oz carrots, finely chopped
350 g/12 oz cold unsalted butter
1 tbsp fresh chervil, roughly chopped

Method

Preheat the oven to 200°C/400°F/Gas Mark 6.

Divide the pastry in two, roll each piece out as thin as possible, then stretch over the backs of your hands (the pastry should now be so thin you can see through it) to give 2 sheets about 60 × 45 cm/24 × 18 inches. Allow the pastry to dry out slightly, then cut each sheet into 12 squares of about 15 cm/6 inches. Take 6 tins, such as brioche tins, about 10 cm/4 inches across and 5 cm/2 inches deep. Lay 4 pastry squares in each tin, one on top of the other so that the points of the squares make a petal formation. Bake in the oven for about 10 minutes or until golden brown.

Peel the asparagus tips and plunge into boiling salted water for 2 minutes, then refresh in iced water and drain. Bring the vinegar and half of the fish stock to the boil. Remove the heads from the prawns (save them for another recipe) and plunge the tails into the boiling stock; cover and simmer for 3 minutes. Drain the tails from the stock and allow to cool.

To make the prawn sauce, return the stock to the boil and reduce by two-thirds. Meanwhile, for the second sauce, bring the white wine and remaining fish stock to the boil in a separate pan and reduce by two-thirds. Add about 85 g/3 oz of the shallots and 85 ml/3 fl oz of the cream, return to the boil and reduce slightly. When the prawn stock has reduced, add the remaining shallots and the carrots along with the rest of the cream, then return to the boil and reduce slightly.

To Serve

Shell and cut each prawn in half. Cut each asparagus tip slightly at an angle into 3 or 4 pieces. Bring the prawn sauce to the boil, then remove from the heat and gradually add 85 g/3 oz of the butter, shaking the pan continuously until all of the butter has melted. Add the prawns and asparagus, then leave over a very low heat until the other sauce is ready (do not allow the sauce to boil once the butter has been added).

Bring the second sauce to the boil, remove from the heat and gradually add the rest of the butter, again shaking the pan until it has all melted. Pour a little of the sauce onto each plate. Add the chervil to the prawn sauce and divide out between the filo cases. Place one case in the middle of each plate. Serve immediately.

Lobster
(FRENCH: *homard* GERMAN: *hummer*)

This is one shellfish that is probably known the world over. Lobsters are extensively fished; the American or Canadian being slightly different to the European variety but mainly only in colour. The European lobster is a rich blue-black in colour, turning to white underneath; the American lobster is more of a russet brown. Both turn a bright red once cooked. The one drawback of lobsters is that they have always been incredibly expensive and probably always will be.

The meat of the female just before she lays her eggs is meant to be the best. There are two main ways to sex a lobster. Firstly, the tail of the female is that much broader and straighter than that of the male, which tapers slightly. Secondly, and the easiest way, is to turn the lobster upside down – the first two legs on the tail of the female are very spindly, whereas those of the male are very heavy and thick.

Lobsters are now being farmed quite extensively, but this does not seem to have brought the price down, probably because it takes a lobster five years to reach about 450 g/1 lb in weight.

SERVES 6

3 × 450 g/1 lb live female lobsters
2.25 litres/4 pints court bouillon (see page 31
2 egg whites
1 tsp salt
50 ml/2 fl oz dry sherry
600 ml/1 pint double cream
6-8 large spinach leaves
2 stalks fresh mint (about 10 g/ ¼ oz
85 ml/3 fl oz dry white wine
350 ml/12 fl oz fish stock
115 g/4 oz unsalted butter

Lobster Mousse with a Creamy Mint Sauce

As this is an amazingly expensive dish, this recipe is meant only as a first or fish course. Lobster really does make a perfect and delicate mousse that cannot be compared with any other. Make sure you save the shells of the lobsters to use in another recipe, and try choosing lobsters that are carrying eggs as they can be used to garnish and finish the sauce.

Method

Preheat the oven to 200°C/400°F/Gas Mark 6.

Bring the court bouillon to the boil. Rinse the lobsters in cold water. Take one lobster, remove any eggs it may be carrying and keep to one side, then plunge the lobster into the boiling water. Cook for 8 minutes and allow to cool in the stock. When cold, shell the tail and cut the meat into 6 nice medallions. Shell the arms and claws and cut the meat into small dice.

Kill the remaining lobsters (either with a trussing needle plunged between the eyes or, with the lobster facing you, place the point of a large knife above its head, about 2.5 cm/1 inch away from the eyes, and with a swift movement bring the knife down through the shell and between the eyes). Remove any eggs and save with the others. Pull off the claws and arms and detach the tails. Using a pair of scissors or a large knife, cut the tails lengthwise and remove all the meat, making sure you discard the tract. Crack the claws and remove all the meat and add it to the tail meat – the best way to remove the meat is to use a teaspoon and scrape it out. Finish off splitting open the head, remove the gritty sac from behind the eyes and discard. Any coral should be added to the lobster meat. Save the shells to use in another recipe.

Put the meat into a food processor or blender along with the egg white and the salt and process until smooth. Rub the resulting mixture through a sieve into a bowl set on crushed ice. Add the sherry and work into the mousse, then gradually add 225 ml/8 fl oz of the cream, mixing it into the mousse gently. Stir the diced claw meat into the mousse, then test (see page 41). Leave it to stand in the refrigerator until needed.

To assemble the moulds, remove the stalks from the spinach leaves, wash the leaves well, then blanch in boiling salted water for a couple of seconds. Refresh in iced water, drain and dry the leaves by spreading them on a cloth. Butter the moulds – these should be 120 ml/4 fl oz oval moulds. Line these with the spinach, leaving a sufficient overhang all the way round to fold over the top and completely enclose the mousse. Fill the moulds with the lobster mousse, pressing it in well with a spoon to exclude any air. Cover each mould with a piece of buttered foil. Place the moulds in a bain-marie so that the water comes halfway up them and heat the water until it reaches boiling point. Transfer to the oven and cook for 16–18 minutes.

For the sauce, crush the lobster eggs, and roughly chop the mint. Bring the white wine and the fish stock to the boil in a saucepan and reduce by three-quarters. Add the cream, the crushed eggs and the mint, bring back to the boil and reduce again until it starts to thicken. The sauce will take on a pinky-orange colour from the eggs. Strain through muslin or a fine sieve into another pan. Return to the boil, then turn down the heat to very low and gradually whisk in the butter until it has all melted.

To Serve

Carefully tip out the mousses from their moulds. Pour the sauce onto the plates, place a mousse in the centre of each plate and top each one with a medallion of tail meat. If you have some good leaves of mint left over, place one under each slice of lobster.

SERVES 10

1 × 400-450 g/14-16 oz live lobster

900 ml/1½ pints court bouillon (see page 31)

400 ml/14 fl oz lobster sauce (see page 33)

1 × 450 g/1 lb monkfish tail

115 g/4 oz soft white bread

2 eggs

500 ml/18 fl oz double cream

15 g/½ oz chives, finely chopped

Salt and freshly ground white pepper

350 g/12 oz ravioli paste (see opposite)

40 g/1½ oz shallots, chopped

25 g/1 oz butter

225 g/8 oz button mushrooms, finely diced

½ small clove garlic, crushed

Juice of 1 lemon

150 ml/¼ pint oil

Garnish

30 small, firm button mushrooms (optional)

10 sprigs fresh dill

Lobster and Monkfish Ravioli with Mushroom Cream Sauce

This recipe may seem like a lot of portions, but it can in fact be made and frozen for later use, although I would not recommend leaving it in the freezer for more than a fortnight. Ten portions is working on two ravioli pieces each, but it can equally serve as a main course for five or six people. If a lobster the size specified below proves to be too expensive, it can always be substituted for crab. The ratio of monkfish to lobster or crab can also be increased to make the dish cheaper. It has always been a great favourite at the restaurant and people often ask whether it is on the menu before booking. If not, then I sometimes think they have second thoughts about coming at all!

Method

Bring the court bouillon to the boil, plunge in the lobster and cook for 5 minutes. Allow the lobster to go cold in the bouillon. When cold, remove all the meat from the shell and dice into 1 cm/½ inch cubes. Keep the shell pieces to make the lobster sauce (see page 33).

To prepare the monkfish, skin and fillet the tail, remove any dark meat and discard, and cut the remaining meat into 1 cm/½ inch cubes. If you have no fish stock for the lobster sauce, chop up the monkfish bones and add these to the lobster shells, then use water instead of fish stock.

For the filling, remove the crusts from the bread and discard. Break the bread up into small pieces and soak in 120 ml/4 fl oz of the lobster sauce until soft. Place the soaked bread in a blender along with 1 egg and 50 ml/2 fl oz of the cream and process until it is smooth. Remove from the blender and combine with the cubes of monkfish and lobster meat, mixing in well, then add the chives to the mixture and season to taste.

Divide the ravioli paste into two. Roll out both halves to a thickness of 2 mm/1/16 inch either by hand or using a pasta rolling machine. If using a pasta roller, you will have to roll it into strips about 7.5 cm/3 inches wide; if rolling by hand, then 2 large squares can be rolled. Now take the filling and make 20 even piles on the paste leaving a square of about 2.5–4 cm/1–1½ inches between each pile. Beat the remaining egg and egg wash the paste between the piles of filling, then cover with the other half of the rolled-out paste. Press the top layer of paste down well between the piles of ravioli filling to ensure a good seal and then cut out the ravioli using a 6.5 cm/2½ inch circular cutter.

To make the sauce, lightly fry the shallots in 15 g/½ oz of the butter for 30 seconds without colouring. Add the diced mushrooms, garlic and half the lemon juice and cook over a low heat until almost dry. Pour in 175 ml/6 fl oz of the cream and reduce until thickened.

'Turn' the 30 mushrooms for garnish and poach in the rest of the lemon juice, 15 g/½ oz of butter and about 2 tablespoons of water.

To Serve

Bring to the boil 7 litres/12 pints of salted water, add the oil, plunge in the ravioli and boil for 5-6 minutes, then remove and drain on a cloth. Bring the remaining 300 ml/½ pint of lobster sauce to the boil, add the rest of the cream and reduce slightly to thicken. Reheat the 'turned' mushrooms in their stock, then drain. Divide the mushroom sauce out equally between the plates to form an oval in the centre of each plate. Place 2 raviolis on top of the sauce and pour the lobster sauce around the mushroom sauce to fill the plates. Garnish each plate with 3 mushrooms and top with a sprig of dill.

NOTE If you do not have a saucepan large enough to take 7 litres/12 pints of water, cook the ravioli in two separate pans. Don't forget to divide the oil out equally between them.

Ravioli Paste

MAKES 350 g/12 oz

350 g/12 oz strong plain flour
Pinch of salt
1 egg
50 ml/2 fl oz oil

Method

Sieve together the flour and the salt. Knead in the egg and the oil, then add sufficient water to make a dough without it being too sticky or too dry. Mix in well to make a smooth paste.

Cover with a damp cloth and leave to rest in a refrigerator for at least 2 hours before using.

SERVES 4

4 × 350 g / 12 oz live lobsters
4 globe artichokes
Juice of 1 lemon
Salt and freshly ground white pepper
50 ml / 2 fl oz oil
175 ml / 6 fl oz dry sherry
225 ml / 8 fl oz fish stock
175 ml / 6 fl oz double cream
15 g / ½ oz butter
8 small spinach leaves
2 tbsp spinach purée

Picture: page 119

Roast Baby Lobster on a Bed of Artichokes

Method

Preheat the oven to 220°C/425°F/Gas Mark 7.

To prepare the artichokes, carefully pull away the outer leaves and then cut off the tops of the leaves about 2 cm/¾ inch from the bottom with a sharp knife. Break off the stalks, trim away all the green, leaving only the white bases (which are all you need for this dish). Place the bases into a pan of water containing the lemon juice, salt to taste and 25 ml/1 fl oz of the oil. this to the boil, then simmer until the artichokes are cooked, about 15 minutes (when you test with a knife, it should enter without too much resistance). Leave the bases to cool in the cooking liquor.

Using a heavy knife, cut through the head of each lobster in one swift movement. Pull away the tails and claws from the bodies and remove and discard the gritty sac from just behind the eyes. Roughly chop the body meat and any coral and set to one side. Heat the oil in a roasting pan and add the tails and claws along with the heads. Roll these in the hot oil for 1 minute, then place the pan in the oven and cook for 10 minutes. Turn the pieces of lobster in the pan every few minutes. When cooked, remove the tails and claws from the pan, leaving behind the heads. Add the dry sherry to the pan, reduce slightly and then add the fish stock. Bring to the boil and reduce the liquid by half. When reduced, strain the stock through a fine strainer or muslin into another pan. Continue reducing the stock until there is only a quarter of its original volume left.

While the stock is reducing and when the lobster has cooled sufficiently to handle, carefully shell the pieces of lobster. Keep the tail meat whole and leave the last section of shell still attached to the tail meat. Remove the claws from their shells; try and keep them as whole as possible. Cut the arm meat into small pieces and set to one side.

To Serve

Drain the artichokes, which should now be cold, and remove the chokes, or furry middles. Cut the bases into batons about 2.5 cm/1 inch long and 5 mm/¼ inch wide. When the stock has reduced far enough, add the cream, bring back to the boil and reduce until it starts to thicken. Cover and reheat the lobster tails and claws in the oven for 1 minute. Heat the butter in a frying pan and toss the batons of artichokes and the chopped lobster in this until hot, then season.

Arrange 2 small spinach leaves on each of the plates and spoon the artichokes on top. Lay a tail of lobster across each pile of artichokes and a claw on each side of the tail. At the last minute, add the spinach purée to the sauce, season if required and pour the sauce around the plate.

Salad of Lobster with Raspberry Vinaigrette

SERVES 4

The humble salad – this is one thing it should never be but so often is. The varied textures and colours of this salad are enough to excite any palate.

Method

Bring the court bouillon to the boil, then plunge in the lobster and continue to boil for 10 minutes. Remove the pan from the heat and allow the lobster to cool in the stock.

Purée 115 g/4 oz of the raspberries in a blender or food processor. Pass the purée through muslin or a fine sieve to remove the pips. Combine the raspberry purée, vinegar and mustard in a bowl and mix together well. Gradually whisk in the oils and season the vinaigrette with a little sea salt, sugar and, if needed, a little freshly ground white pepper. If you feel the dressing is a little too heavy, then add the warm water.

Break up the lettuces, keeping the leaves whole where possible, and wash and drain well. Remove all of the lobster meat from its shell. Cut the tail into 8 medallions. Remove the meat from the claws carefully so that it remains whole, and cut each claw in half across to give 2 equal pieces. Finely dice any small pieces of meat that remain.

To Serve

Pour a little of the vinaigrette onto each plate to form a colourful border. Toss the salad leaves in the remaining dressing along with any diced meat and lightly season. Carefully place the salad leaves in the centre of the plates with the sauce around the edge. Arrange the medallions and the claws through the salad, along with the reserved raspberries.

NOTE Do not store the salads or the cooked lobster in the refrigerator as they will be too cold.

1 × 675 g/1 ½ lb lobster
2.25 litres/4 pints court bouillon (see page 31)
150 g/5 oz fresh raspberries
2 tbsp raspberry vinegar
½ dessertsp Dijon mustard
3 tbsp walnut oil
85 ml/3 fl oz salad oil
Sea salt, sugar and freshly ground white pepper
50 ml/2 fl oz warm water (optional)
1 small radicchio
2 bunches corn salad
¼ head curly endive
1 small head red oak leaf lettuce
1 small lettuce heart

Picture: page 118

SERVES 4

4 × 350-450 g / 12 oz-1 lb live
lobsters

3.5 litres / 6 pints court bouillon
(see page 31)

25 g / 1 oz white of leek

25 g / 1 oz celery

25 g / 1 oz mixed fresh herbs
(tarragon, dill, parsley, chervil,
chives)

15 g / ½ oz butter

1 small clove garlic, crushed

50 ml / 2 fl oz brandy

50 ml / 2 fl oz dry sherry

600 ml / 1 pint fish stock

300 ml / ½ pint double cream

Salt and freshly ground white
pepper

Whole Poached Lobster with Herb and Cream Sauce

A light crisp green salad and a few new potatoes are all that are needed to accompany this colourful, albeit expensive, dish.

Method

Bring the court bouillon to the boil, plunge in the lobsters and cook for 10 minutes. When cooked, remove them from the court bouillon and allow to drain and cool slightly. Wash the leek and celery and cut into small, rough dice. Remove the leaves of herbs from their stalks, reserving the stalks. Mix the leaves and put to one side. When the lobsters have cooled, break off their tails and claws. Remove the tail meat; keep the end of the tail in one piece to use as a garnish. Crack the claws and arms and carefully remove the meat, keeping it all as whole as possible. Cut each tail into 2 lengthwise and remove the tract. Cover and keep warm.

To make the sauce, break away the underside of the head section, where the legs join the body – this should bring out the insides. Just behind the head is a groove in the shell that runs across and round underneath. Using a pair of heavy scissors, cut along this groove, wash the head well and save for garnishing. Chop up all of the legs, the coral and the intestines, discarding the gritty sac. Heat the butter in a saucepan and add the roughly cut vegetables and garlic. Fry gently, without colouring, for a couple of minutes, then add the chopped lobster. Continue frying for about another minute, again without colouring. Add the brandy, ignite and burn off the alcohol, then add the sherry and the fish stock. Bring to the boil, add the stalks from the herbs and reduce by three-quarters. When reduced, strain the stock through a strainer into another pan. Bring the stock back to the boil, add the cream, and reduce until it starts to thicken.

To Serve

Place the lobster meat into a hot oven (220°C/425°F/Gas Mark 7) for about 1 minute to reheat.

Arrange the meat on the plates; put the 2 halves of tail almost central side by side; place the 2 claws of each lobster in front of the tail; and place the arm meat between the tail and the claws. Remove the sauce from the heat, add the mixed herbs, stir them in and check the seasoning. Pour the sauce over and around the lobster meat. Place a head at the claw end of the plate and a tail piece at the tail end and serve immediately.

Roast Lobster in a Rich Red Wine Sauce

At first sight this may appear to be an unusual combination, but the richness of the sauce enhances the strong flavour of the lobster. It is best to use a good quality red Burgundy for the sauce rather than any old cooking wine; the better the quality of wine, the better the finished sauce will be.

Method

Preheat the oven to 230°C/450°F/Gas Mark 8.

Using a heavy knife, cut through the heads of the lobsters in one swift movement. Pull away their tails and claws, and remove and discard the gritty sac from just behind the eyes. Roughly chop up the bodies and any coral and set to one side. Cut each tail into 4 pieces through the joints of the shell and crack the claws with the back of the knife.

Heat the oil in a roasting tray or ovenproof pan. When hot, add the mirepoix of vegetables and quickly fry for about 30 seconds. Add all the pieces of lobster, including the bodies, and continue frying and turning the lobster in the oil for a further minute, then transfer to the oven and cook for 10 minutes, turning occasionally. Remove from the oven and take out the tails and claws and allow them to cool; leave the chopped bodies in the pan. Add the red wine and the garlic to the pan and reduce by two-thirds. Then add the fish stock and reduce again by two-thirds.

When cold enough to handle, remove the lobster meat from the claws and tails, cover and keep warm. Roughly chop the shells and add these to the reduction. When the fish stock has reduced far enough, add the veal stock and continue boiling until it starts to thicken.

To Serve

Once the sauce has almost reached the correct consistency – it should be thick enough to coat the back of a spoon evenly – strain it through a fine strainer or muslin into a clean pan; discard the solids. Add the pieces of lobster meat and allow them to soak in the sauce for 1 minute to reheat. It is best not to allow the sauce to boil at this point – all that is required is for it to remain hot.

Arrange the pieces of lobster attractively in the serving dishes. Whisk the butter into the sauce in small pieces and continue whisking until it has all melted. Pour the sauce over the lobster and finish with a sprig of fresh dill or fennel, if liked.

---

4 × 350 g/12 oz live lobsters

1 tbsp oil

85 g/3 oz mirepoix (carrot, onion, white of leek)

225 ml/8 fl oz red Burgundy

1 clove garlic, crushed

225 ml/8 fl oz fish stock

350 ml/12 fl oz veal stock (see page 30)

25 g/1 oz cold unsalted butter

Garnish

Sprigs of fresh fennel or dill (optional)

Picture: page 118

180

Molluscs

Although the oyster is probably held in high esteem among those lovers of edible molluscs, I personally much prefer the scallop. Whichever is your favourite, try some of the recipes that follow and broaden your culinary horizons.

Oysters and mussels have probably been the cause of more upset stomachs than anything else. To avoid this, buy them only while they are still alive; their shells should be tightly closed or snap shut on handling. In earlier times shellfish would only be bought during the months of the year with an 'r' in them, in other words during the colder months. This need not apply nowadays; because of sophisticated refrigeration and faster means of transport, it is now possible and safe to eat molluscs all year round.

Clams
(FRENCH: *palourde, clovisses*
GERMAN: *venusmuscheln*)

There are many different types of clam, all under the same name. I tend to stick to the one called Venus clam. Clams are very under-used in Britain, but the French and Americans do use them a lot. I have listed three different recipes here. If you can get fresh cockles, then use them in the recipes instead – to my mind they are superior to clams but difficult to get fresh.

When buying any of the molluscs, always make sure they are still alive; the shells should be tightly closed or they should snap shut as soon as they are handled. They should also be thoroughly washed before cooking. Sit the clams in clean fresh water for about 15 minutes, then change the water, allow them to sit for another 15 minutes, and then repeat the process one more time. If you have been fortunate enough to get hold of fresh cockles, they should be cleaned in the same way.

SERVES 4

225 g/8 oz clams

85 g/3 oz mirepoix (celery, leek, onion)

A little oil

150 ml/¼ pint fish stock

50 ml/2 fl oz dry white wine

1 stalk parsley

450 g/1 lb carrots, roughly chopped

½ orange, juice and zest

2 eggs

225 ml/8 fl oz double cream

A little butter

1 tsp chopped parsley

Carrot Mousse with Clam Sauce

Method

Preheat the oven to 200°C/400°F/Gas Mark 6.

Clean the clams thoroughly (see above). Heat the oil in a saucepan, then add the mirepoix of vegetables and sweat until they are soft. Add the fish stock, white wine and parsley stalks, and bring to the boil. When boiling, add the clams, cover and cook over a high heat until they open, stirring occasionally; this will only take 4 or 5 minutes. When cooked, tip the clams out into a colander, allow to drain until cold, then remove the meat from the shells. Strain the liquor through muslin and reserve.

Cook the carrots in the orange juice, zest and a little water to cover until soft. Drain and place into a food processor or liquidizer until a smooth purée. If the resulting purée is quite wet, dry it out by placing the purée in a heavy-based saucepan over a low heat, stirring occasionally, until some of the moisture has evaporated. Allow to go cold. Beat the eggs, and, when the carrot purée is cold, mix in the eggs together with 50 ml/2 fl oz of the cream. Season to taste. Butter four 85 ml/3 fl oz round or oval moulds and fill each with the carrot mixture. Top each mould with buttered tin foil and poach in a bain marie in the oven for 20 minutes.

While the carrot mousses are cooking, set the clam liquor in a saucepan over a high heat and reduce until it has almost all gone. Then add the remaining cream, return to the boil and reduce until it starts to thicken.

To Serve

Once the carrot mousses are cooked, tip them out of their moulds onto the plates, placing one in the centre of each plate. Add the clams to the sauce and allow to soak for 1 minute over a very low heat. At the last minute, add the chopped parsley to the sauce, then pour over the mousses. Serve at once.

Clam and Nettle Soup

SERVES 6

450g/1 lb Venus clams
1 small onion, roughly chopped
1 white of a small leek, roughly chopped
1 stick celery, roughly chopped
¼ tsp black peppercorns
2 stalks parsley
1.2 litres/2 pints fish stock
225g/8 oz young stinging nettle leaves
50g/2 oz streaky bacon
25g/1 oz butter
115g/4 oz shallots, roughly chopped
1 small clove garlic, crushed
Salt
150ml/¼ pint double cream

Picture: page 142

If you are like me, you will probably regard stinging nettles as somewhat of a pain, or perhaps I should say that I used to. I don't any more, not since I tried making soup from them – now I cannot get enough. This really is a wonderful soup – that is, if you can bring yourself to try it. Nettles are at their best during April and the early part of May. Use only the young leaves.

Method

Thoroughly clean the clams (see opposite).

Place the vegetables, peppercorns, parsley and fish stock in a saucepan that has a tightly-fitting lid and bring to the boil. Once boiling, add the clams, cover with the lid and boil until they open, about 4–5 minutes. Drain and save the liquor, allow the clams to cool, then remove them from their shells.

Wash the nettle leaves well and put 18 nice leaves to one side. Roughly cut the bacon into pieces. Melt the butter in a saucepan, add the shallots, garlic and bacon and sweat until the shallots start to soften. Add the nettles, continue sweating for a further 2 minutes, then pour in the clam liquor. Bring to the boil and simmer gently for 15 minutes. Strain the soup, put the liquid to one side and blend the solids in a food processor or blender until smooth. Return them to the liquid and then strain again.

To Serve

Reheat the soup. Blanch the saved nettle leaves in a little salted water for about 30 seconds, refresh in iced water, drain and decorate the edge of the soup plates with them. Whip the cream. Add the clams to the soup just before serving. Pour the soup into the plates and float the cream on top.

SERVES 6

1 kg/2 lb Venus clams
50 g/2 oz celery, roughly chopped
85 g/3 oz onions, roughly chopped
85 g/3 oz white of leek, roughly chopped
1 tbsp oil
150 ml/¼ pint fish stock
85 ml/3 fl oz dry white wine
A few parsley stalks
175 g/6 oz French beans, topped and tailed
50 g/2 oz lambs lettuce or watercress
1 tbsp mayonnaise
1 tbsp yoghurt
Salt and freshly ground white pepper
25 g/1 oz shallots, finely diced
3 tbsp French dressing

Garnish

6 sprigs fresh dill or chervil

Salad of Clams with French Beans

The clam seems to be a very under-rated mollusc. It resembles a cockle and can be used in any recipe that requires cockles or mussels. Clams can also be bought alive, whereas cockles are only available cooked. Here is a simple way to use this tasty shellfish.

Method

Clean the clams thoroughly (see page 182). Heat the oil in a large pan – the pan needs to be big enough to take about 3 times the amount of clams that you have. (If you do not have a pan this large, do not worry; cook them in smaller batches but start with all of the stock, wine and vegetables.) Add the celery, onions and leek to the oil and sweat until they are soft. Add the fish stock, white wine and parsley stalks and bring to the boil. Once boiling, add the clams, cover and cook over a high heat until they open – this will only take 4 or 5 minutes. When cooked, tip them out into a colander and allow to drain until cold, then remove the meat from the shells.

Cook the French beans in boiling salted water until still crisp, refresh in iced water, then drain. Thoroughly wash the lambs lettuce as it does tend to hold a lot of grit. Mix the mayonnaise with the yoghurt and season if necessary, then mix in the clams.

To Serve

Toss the French beans and shallots in the vinaigrette and season with a little salt and freshly ground white pepper. Form a nest of lambs lettuce in the centre of each plate and place a bed of the French bean salad on top. Finally, add the clams in their sauce and garnish with a sprig of dill or chervil.

NOTE The clams will keep perfectly well for a few days in the refrigerator if you strain the cooking liquor through muslin over them when shelled.

Clams with Creamy Dill Sauce Served in a Pastry Case

SERVES 6

1 kg/2 lb Venus clams
A little oil for frying
225 g/8 oz mirepoix (onion, leek, celery)
300 ml/½ pint fish stock
120 ml/4 fl oz dry white wine
2 stalks parsley
450 g/1 lb puff pastry (see page 42)
1 egg yolk, beaten
A little milk
15 cm/6 inch cucumber
20 g/¾ oz fresh dill
225 ml/8 fl oz double cream

Method

Preheat the oven to 220°C/425°F/Gas Mark 7.

Clean the clams thoroughly (see page 182). Heat the oil in a pan large enough to take 3 times the amount of clams that you have. If you do not have a pan this large, do not worry; cook the clams in smaller batches, but start with all the stock, wine and vegetables. Add the vegetables to the oil and sweat until soft, then add the fish stock, white wine and parsley stalks and bring to the boil. When boiling, add the clams, cover and cook over a high heat until they open, stirring occasionally. This will only take 4 or 5 minutes. When cooked, tip the clams into a colander, and strain the stock through fine muslin. Allow the clams to drain until cold and then remove the meat from the shells.

Roll out the puff pastry on a floured surface to a thickness of about 5 mm/¼ inch. Using a 10 cm/4 inch circular cutter, cut out 6 pieces. Place them on a baking tray and lightly score a criss-cross pattern on them using the point of a sharp knife, then brush them with a mixture of egg yolk and a little milk. Allow them to rest for at least 20 minutes in the refrigerator or a cool place before cooking. Bake the pastry circles for about 12 minutes in the oven.

Cut the cucumber into fine strips about 4 cm×3 mm/1½×⅛ inch, using only the flesh and discarding the seeds in the middle. Pick the dill, reserve 6 nice sprigs as garnish, and roughly chop the rest.

Bring the stock to the boil, reduce by at least three-quarters, then add the cream and reduce until it thickens.

To Serve

Add the clams and the cucumber to the sauce and simmer for about 1 minute until all the ingredients are heated through. Reheat the pastry cases in the oven and then split them across into 2. At the last minute, add the chopped dill to the sauce and stir in. Divide the mixture out between the cases and put their tops back on. Garnish with the sprigs of dill and serve.

Mussels
(FRENCH: *moules* GERMAN: *muschel*)

Everyone must be familiar with the dark blue shells of the mussel and probably think of them mainly in connection with the classic dish Moules Marinières. They can, of course, be used in many other ways, both hot and cold.

The mussels found for sale are a cultivated variety – most European countries are producers, from Spain in the south to Denmark in the north. Wild mussels can, of course, be gathered from seashores everywhere, but these do tend to be small and quite leathery as well as being susceptible to contamination, rendering them dangerous for consumption.

When buying mussels, go for the washed or purified ones, which are the most common, simply because it takes a lot of work out of cleaning them. This does not mean, however, that they do not need any further treatment. They will still need to be checked to ensure that their beards and barnacles are removed, and they will also still need to be washed thoroughly at least three times in fresh clean water, letting them sit in the water for about 5 minutes each time, and changing the water after each wash. As with any other shellfish, mussels must be purchased live, that is when their shells are tightly closed – if any are open, they should snap shut on being handled. If the shell is damaged or broken in any way, it is safer to discard the mussel, using only those in perfect condition.

Although traditionally used only when there is an 'r' in the month, they are available all the year round.

SERVES 4

1 kg/2¼ lb mussels
2 sprigs fresh parsley
1 sprig fresh thyme
1 bay leaf
150 ml/¼ pint dry white wine
50 g/2 oz shallots, roughly chopped
150 ml/¼ pint double cream (optional)
115 g/4 oz cold unsalted butter

Garnish

1 dessertsp finely chopped parsley

Mussels à la Marinière

Method

Prepare the mussels (see above).

Place the herbs, white wine and shallots in a large saucepan and bring to the boil. When boiling, add the mussels, cover with a tightly-fitting lid and cook over a high heat until all the mussels have opened (discard any that remain closed). When ready, remove the mussels from the liquor and discard one half of each shell. Pass the liquor through muslin or a very fine strainer and bring back to the boil. Add the cream, turn down the heat to low and gradually whisk in the butter until it has all melted.

To Serve

Divide the mussels between 4 deep bowls or soup plates and pour over the sauce. Sprinkle with the chopped parsley and serve immediately.

Fresh Mussel Salad on a Bed of Lambs' Lettuce

SERVES 4

1 kg/2¼ lb mussels
1 sprig fresh thyme
2 sprigs fresh parsley
50 g/2 oz shallots, chopped
300 ml/½ pint fish stock
150 ml/¼ pint dry white wine
115 g/4 oz lambs' lettuce

Sauce

150 ml/¼ pint double cream
1 dessertsp Dijon mustard
150 ml/¼ pint yoghurt

Garnish

1 carrot, cut into julienne
25 g/1 oz fresh chives, finely chopped

Picture: page 191

Method

Prepare the mussels (see opposite).

Place the herbs, shallots, fish stock and white wine in a large saucepan and bring to the boil. When boiling, add the mussels, cover with a tightly-fitting lid and cook over a high heat until the mussels have opened. When ready, remove the mussels from the liquor and allow to cool. Discard any that are not open.

To make the sauce, pass the liquid through muslin or a fine strainer into a clean pan and then reduce until syrupy. Add the cream and the mustard and reduce until thick. Leave to cool.

To Serve

When the sauce is cold, add the yoghurt. Remove the meat from the shells and mix the mussels into two-thirds of the sauce. Arrange a bed of lambs lettuce on each plate, pile the mussels coated in the sauce on top, and pour a spoonful of the remaining sauce over each pile. Garnish with the julienne of carrot and sprinkle with the chopped chives.

Oysters
(FRENCH: *huitres* GERMAN: *austern*)

Oysters were once so plentiful they were the food of the poor, but with the decrease in availability they have now become an expensive delicacy. They are probably best eaten raw from the freshly-opened shell with just a squeeze of lemon, but as an alternative try some of the dishes that follow using this delicate mollusc.

The three most common varieties of oyster are Natives, Pacifics, and Portuguese. Natives are often referred to by the region from which they come, for example, Whitstable, Colchester, and Helford. They are normally graded into four different sizes, grade 1 being the largest. Grade 2 is the one I would choose as it offers the best value for money.

Like all shellfish, oysters should be bought while still alive, their shells tightly closed and, traditionally, only during the months with an 'r' in them, although they are, in fact, available all the year round. If you find that you need to keep them for a few days, then cover them with damp newspaper, place a heavy weight on top and keep them in the refrigerator.

Be careful when cooking oysters as they only take a matter of seconds; cook them just that bit too long and all you will have is a ball of rubber.

SERVES 6

1 large round lettuce
18 small oysters
15 g/ ½ oz butter
25 g/ 1 oz shallots, finely chopped
900 ml/ 1 ½ pints fish stock
Juice of ½ lemon
175 ml/ 6 fl oz double cream
4 egg yolks
Salt and freshly ground white pepper

Picture: page 97

Lettuce and Oyster Soup

Like many other soups, this is very simple to make. The first part of the recipe can be prepared on the morning of the day it is required; the oysters, cream and egg yolks should be added at the last minute.

Method

Break up the lettuce, wash the leaves thoroughly and drain. Remove the central rib from each leaf and discard, then finely shred the leaves. Melt the butter in a heavy-based saucepan, add the shallots and gently soften for about 1 minute. Add the shredded lettuce and continue to soften for a further minute. Pour in the fish stock and the lemon juice, bring to the boil and reduce the liquid by about a quarter – this will take about 10 minutes. Once the soup has reached this stage, it can be stored in the refrigerator until needed.

(continued on page 193)

Boudin of Scallops Rolled in Herbs with
Tomato Vinaigrette
(see page 198)

LEFT   *Poached Fillet of Turbot with Salmon Caviar Sauce*
(see page 147)

BELOW   *Fillet of Scottish Salmon on a Bed of Spring Vegetables*
(see page 53)

LEFT *Scallop and Saffron Soup*
(see page 197)

BELOW *Fresh Mussel Salad on a Bed of Lamb's Lettuce*
(see page 187)

Warm Salad of Monkfish and
Toasted Pine Kernels
(see page 125)

To Serve

Shell the oysters over a bowl to catch the juices and strain these through muslin into the soup. Whip 50 ml / 2 fl oz of the double cream until it is stiff and set to one side. Mix the remaining cream with the egg yolks and strain through a fine strainer. Drop the oysters into the hot soup and simmer for 30–45 seconds, then remove and divide the oysters between the soup plates. Reduce the heat to very low, pour in the cream and egg yolk mixture and stir continuously for about 1 minute. The soup will noticeably thicken, but on no account let it boil or the eggs will scramble. Season to taste.

Pour the finished soup over the oysters, top with whipped cream and serve immediately.

Emincé of Oysters with Calabrese and Chanterelles

SERVES 4

12 oysters
115 g/4 fresh chanterelles
350 g/12 oz calabrese
175 ml/6 fl oz fish stock
85 ml/3 fl oz dry white wine
50 g/2 oz shallots, finely chopped
175 ml/6 fl oz double cream
15 g/½ oz butter
Salt and freshly ground white pepper

Method

Carefully shell the oysters, making sure that you save their juice, and cut them into 1 cm/½ inch dice.

Pick through the chanterelles, removing any dirt and root, and wipe but do not wash. Break the heads of the calabrese into small florets and blanch these in boiling salted water for about 15 seconds, then refresh in iced water and drain.

Strain the juice of the oysters through muslin or a fine sieve into the fish stock and combine this with the white wine and half the shallots. Set over a high heat and reduce until syrupy. Pour in the cream, return to the boil and reduce until it starts to thicken.

Heat the butter in a frying pan until it starts to sizzle, then add the remaining shallots and fry for a few seconds without colouring. Add the chanterelles and continue to fry gently. After about 15 seconds, add the calabrese and toss together until they have heated through. Season as necessary.

To Serve

Pile the calabrese and chanterelle mixture in the centre of the plates or bowls. Add the diced oyster meat to the hot sauce and allow it to soak for about 15 seconds. Finally, spoon the oysters over the calabrese and pour the sauce around.

NOTE If using dried chanterelles, use half the amount and soak in cold water for 20 minutes before using.

SERVES 4

16 oysters
1 × 675 g/1 ½ lb monkfish tail
2 medium courgettes
A little butter
225 ml/8 fl oz fish stock
175 ml/6 fl oz champagne
Salt and freshly ground white pepper
350 ml/12 fl oz double cream
3 egg yolks

Oysters and Monkfish in Glazed Champagne Sauce

Method

Preheat the oven to 190°C/375°F/Gas Mark 5.

Fillet and skin the monkfish tail. Remove any dark meat, discard, and then cut the fillets into 3-4 cm/1¼-1½ inch cubes. Shell the oysters over a bowl to catch the juices and briefly wash them in fresh water. To prepare the courgettes, cannelize them and cut across into rounds about 3 mm/⅛ inch thick.

Butter an ovenproof pan, put in the monkfish, fish stock, 120 ml/4 fl oz of the champagne and the reserved oyster juices (strain through muslin first). Season, cover with buttered paper or foil, and transfer to the oven and poach for 3-4 minutes. When cooked, remove the fish from the liquor, cover and keep warm. Bring the liquor back to the boil and plunge in the oysters for 30 seconds. Remove and keep warm.

To Serve

Reduce the stock until syrupy, then add 300 ml/½ pint of the cream and reduce until thickened – this should only take about 2 minutes. Whip the remaining cream so that it peaks but is not stiff. Add the monkfish, oysters and the remaining champagne to the sauce, remove the sauce from the heat and stir in the egg yolks and the whipped cream. Check the seasoning. Divide the mixture between the plates – if you use deep plates a better result will be achieved. Place under a hot grill to brown evenly and serve immediately.

NOTE If serving as a main course, a simple rice pilaff with possibly a touch of saffron will be the best accompaniment; if a first course, then serve it just as it is. Sparkling white wine can be used instead of champagne but it must be a dry wine.

Puff Pastry Cases Filled with Oysters and Green Peppercorns

SERVES 4

This delicate and exciting dish requires very little cooking; once the pastry is made, the rest is easy. The addition of the vegetables gives the dish a little 'crunch'.

Method

Preheat the oven to 220°C/425°F/Gas Mark 7.

Cut the carrot, leek and celery into fine julienne about 5 cm/2 inches long. Roll out the puff pastry to a thickness of 5 mm/¼ inch. Using a small, sharp knife, cut out 4 oval shapes, about 10×7.5 cm/4×3 inches. Lay these on a baking sheet and brush with the egg yolk mixed with the milk. Lightly mark a line 5 mm/¼ inch in from the edge all the way round for the lid. Leave in the refrigerator for about 30 minutes to rest, then bake in the oven for 10–12 minutes or until golden brown. When cooked, cut along the line you marked in the pastry and remove the lids. Keep the cases warm.

Carefully open the oysters over a bowl to catch any juice. Strain the juice through muslin into a saucepan and add the fish stock. Reduce over a high heat until syrupy. Add the cream and the lemon juice, return to the boil, then reduce the heat to very low and gradually add the butter, saving about 10 g/¼ oz to heat the spinach. Whisk continuously until all the butter has melted. Stir in the vegetables, oysters and green peppercorns and soak these in the sauce for a minute over a very low heat; do not allow the sauce to boil or even simmer.

To Serve

Reheat the cases in the oven for 30 seconds. Melt the remaining butter in a frying pan and add the spinach, lightly season with salt and pepper and toss in the butter until hot.

Place a little spinach in the bottom of each case. Spoon 3 oysters into each case on top of the spinach and spoon 3 more onto the plate next to the case. Top both the oysters in the cases and the oysters on the plates with a few vegetables, pour the sauce around the plate, put the lids in place and serve quickly.

---

24 oysters

1 carrot

½ small leek

2 sticks celery

350 g/12 oz puff pastry (see page 42)

1 egg yolk, beaten

1 tbsp milk

300 ml/½ pint fish stock

120 ml/4 fl oz double cream

Juice of ½ lemon

225 g/8 oz butter

2 tsp green peppercorns

115 g/4 oz cooked leaf spinach

Salt and freshly ground white pepper

Picture: page 162

Scallops
(FRENCH: *coquille St Jacques*
GERMAN: *jacobsmuscheln* USA: *bay scallops)*

To me these are the best shellfish available – they are so versatile, and what a flavour! Poach or fry them, use in a mousseline, either hot or cold – there is no end to their uses. There is also no substitute. Scallops can be bought in so many ways: fresh straight from the sea; cleaned but left in one half of the shell; completely clean (without the shell); or, of course, frozen, which if you have read the introduction to this book you will avoid buying.

Normally sold in the shell by number, or shelled by weight, like any shellfish they should be bought only if they are still alive – that is with their shells closed, or if not closed they should snap shut as soon as they are handled. Obviously, if buying ready-cleaned ones, there is no telling how fresh they are without using your nose.

The scallop is easily recognizable, having a semi-circular, ribbed, fan-shaped shell (you know the one, just think of a well-known petrol station). The upper shell is flat and the lower one convex, and inside the meat is white and there is an orange roe (which is the best bit).

Nowadays, scallops seem to be available all the year round, which is sinful and can only lead to them being over-fished. The best time to buy them is during the winter months and early spring when they have large roes; the rest of the year the roe is virtually non-existent.

SERVES 4-8

16 scallops
150 ml/ ¼ pint fish stock
32 fresh basil leaves
5 tomatoes
1 head radicchio
2 ripe avocadoes

Scallop and Avocado Salad

Method

Shell, trim and wash the scallops. Remove the roes but leave them whole, and cut all of the white meat across into 3. Poach the scallops in the fish stock for about 10 seconds, drain and leave to cool, covered. When cool, cut half of the roes into 3 and put the others to one side.

To make the sauce, mix the egg yolks and the mustard together. Gradually add the 2 oils, whisking all the time, then add the sherry vinegar. Half whip the cream and fold it into the sauce, season to taste with the sugar, salt and pepper.

Finely shred the basil leaves, reserving 8 leaves whole for garnish. Blanch, skin and deseed the tomatoes. Cut 4 tomatoes into 5 mm/¼ inch dice, and cut the remaining tomatoes into fingers and put to one side for the garnish.

To Serve

Combine together the slices of scallop meat, the diced tomato and the shredded basil. Add the sauce and gently fold it in. Cut the avocado into quarters lengthwise and skin them. Cut each quarter into a fan and arrange on the plates. Make a little nest of the radicchio next to this and divide the scallop mixture out onto the lettuce. Spoon any spare sauce over the top of the scallops. Finish off with a basil leaf and a scallop roe on top of each salad and sprinkle with the tomato fingers.

Sauce

2 egg yolks
½ dessertsp Dijon mustard
25 ml/1 fl oz walnut oil
75 ml/3 fl oz salad oil
50 ml/2 fl oz sherry vinegar
150 ml/¼ pint double cream
Pinch of sugar
Salt and freshly ground white pepper

Scallop and Saffron Soup

SERVES 4

This simple but expensive soup combines the flavour of the scallops with the scent of saffron and a hint of Pernod, and is also an extremely colourful dish.

Method

Shell, clean and wash the scallops; dry well. Remove the roes from 4 of the scallops and put the white part to one side. Cut the rest of the scallop meat, including the roes, into small pieces and season. Place the scallop meat in a saucepan with the fish stock and garlic and poach for 2 minutes. When cooked, put it all into a food processor or blender and blend until it is smooth, then pass through a strainer.

Heat the butter in a frying pan until it sizzles, add the diced vegetables and fry gently without colouring for about 30 seconds. Add the Pernod, followed by the fish mixture and saffron and mix well. Bring to the boil and simmer for about 4 minutes; the vegetables should still be a little crisp.

To Serve

Thinly slice the white meat you put to one side; each piece should yield about 5 slices. Place the slices of scallop into the soup plates and pour over the soup. The heat of the soup should be enough to cook the slices as they are very thin. Garnish with sprigs of freshly picked chervil.

12 scallops
Salt and freshly ground white pepper
600 ml/1 pint fish stock
1 small clove garlic, crushed
15 g/½ oz unsalted butter
1 medium carrot, finely diced
1 small leek, finely diced
1 stick celery, finely diced
25 g/1 oz shallot, finely diced
1 tbsp Pernod
Pinch of saffron

Garnish

Sprigs of fresh chervil

Picture: page 191

SERVES 8

Boudin

8 scallops (weighing about 450 g/ 1 lb)
1 tsp salt
1 egg white
Pinch of paprika
150 ml/ ¼ pint double cream
50 ml/ 2 fl oz dry vermouth
25 g/ 1 oz mixed fresh herbs (chervil, dill, parsley, chives)

Vinaigrette

5 medium tomatoes
25 g/ 1 oz shallots, finely chopped
1 small clove garlic, crushed
2 tbsp walnut oil
15 g/ ½ oz tomato purée
50 ml/ 2 fl oz dry white wine
100 ml/ 4 fl oz white wine vinegar
1 bay leaf

Garnish

Sprigs of fresh chervil

Picture: page 189

Boudin of Scallops Rolled in Herbs with Tomato Vinaigrette

This makes a wonderful first course but does take quite some time to make, but the end result is well worth the effort. Once described by a happy customer as 'utter bliss', try it and see for yourself.

Method

To make the boudin, shell, trim and thoroughly wash the scallops. Dry well. Place in a blender or food processor along with the salt and the egg white and blend for a few minutes until you have a smooth paste. Rub the mixture through a sieve into a bowl set on crushed ice and mix in the paprika. Gradually add two-thirds of the cream, mixing in well. Add the vermouth and season. Test the mousse (see page 41) and if it is too firm, add a little more cream. Set aside in the refrigerator until needed.

Discard the stalks of the herbs, wash the leaves well, drain and finely chop. Using a 30 cm/12 inch roll of cling film, draw out about a 30-35 cm/12-14 inch sheet but do not cut it off. Sprinkle half of the chopped herbs over the cling film in an area about 20 cm/8 inches square. Divide the scallop mousse into 2 and gently place one half in an even line about 4 cm/1½ inches high, building a rough cylinder on top of the herbs along the edge nearest to you. Taking the end of the cling film, roll the mixture away from you across the herbs so that the mousse is completely coated. As you roll the mousse, leave the film on and continue rolling for another 30 cm/12 inches. Cut the roll off and tie up the ends tightly with string. You should now have a cylinder about 18-20 cm/7-8 inches long and 4.5-5 cm/1¾-2 inches across. Repeat the process with the remaining herbs and mousse. Bring a pan of water to the boil – the pan should be large enough to hold both rolls and deep enough for them to float freely. When boiling, plunge in the rolls, cover and simmer for 10 minutes. When cooked, remove from the pan and cool in iced water, still in the cling film, ensuring that they float clear so that they remain circular. Leave floating in iced water until needed.

To make the vinaigrette, blanch, skin and deseed the tomatoes, then cut them into 5 mm/¼ inch dice. Heat the oil in a saucepan, add the shallots and garlic and gently fry without colouring for about 1 minute. Add the tomatoes, tomato pureé, white wine, wine vinegar and bay leaf. Simmer over a low heat for 20 minutes. Remove from the heat and allow to go cold.

To Serve

When the boudin is cold, remove it from the cling film and slice each roll into 16 even slices discarding the end slices. Divide the vinaigrette out equally between the plates, forming an oval in the centre of each plate. Lay 4 slices on top of the sauce, and garnish around the edges of each oval with sprigs of chervil.

NOTE Both the vinaigrette and the cooked boudin will keep for 2 or 3 days in a refrigerator, so there is no need to do all of the work on the day that it is required.

Warm Salad of Scallops and Mangetout

SERVES 2-4

12 scallops (weighing 275-300 g/10-12 oz)
50 g/2 oz mangetout
15 g/½ oz pine kernels
¼ head frizzy lettuce
1 tbsp sherry vinegar
3 tbsp walnut oil
Salt and freshly ground white pepper
15 g/½ oz butter

Where good food is important but time is of the essence, this makes a wonderfully simple first course that will complement any meal. It is also perfect for a light main course at lunchtime, and is quick and easy to prepare and even quicker to finish. I always select smaller scallops for this dish as they cook more quickly and I think they also look more attractive, particularly for a starter.

Picture: page 120

Method

Preheat the oven to 230°C/450°F/Gas Mark 8.

Shell, trim and wash the scallops. Dry well. Cut the white meat across into 2 pieces, leaving the roe attached to one half.

Top and tail the mangetout and blanch in boiling salted water for about 30 seconds or until they are still slightly crunchy. Refresh in iced water and drain. Spread the pine kernels on a baking sheet and toast either in a hot oven (230°C/450°F/Gas Mark 8) or under a hot grill until golden brown.

To Serve

Wash the lettuce and break up into quite small pieces, add the sherry vinegar and 2 tablespoons of the walnut oil, season and toss together. Heat the remaining oil in a frying pan with the butter until it starts to sizzle. Season the scallops and add them to the hot fat. Sauté for about 30 seconds, tossing occasionally, then add the mangetout and pine kernels and continue cooking until the mangetout and the pine kernels are heated through. Tip the scallop mixture onto the lettuce, give a final toss, and serve.

Mousseline of Scallops with Ginger

SERVES 4-8

Mousseline

12 scallops
1 tsp salt
1 egg white
300 ml/ ½ pint double cream
40 ml/ 1 ½ fl oz dry vermouth
Pinch of cayenne pepper
Freshly ground white pepper

Sauce

50 g/ 2 oz fresh root ginger
225 ml/ 8 fl oz fish stock
120 ml/ 4 fl oz dry white wine
300 ml/ ½ pint double cream

Garnish

4 slices truffle (optional)
Sprigs of fresh chervil or dill

Picture: page 62

This dish works equally well as a first course and as a main course. As with mussels, many people do not like the texture of scallops but like the flavour. Used in a mousseline, the texture is lost but the intense flavour remains. I must confess to preferring scallops this way. This will make four 175 ml/6 fl oz moulds to serve as a main course, or eight 85 ml/3 fl oz moulds for a first course.

Method

Preheat the oven to 180°C/350°F/Gas Mark 4.

To make the mousseline, ensure that the scallops are well cleaned and washed, then dry them thoroughly on kitchen paper or a cloth. Remove 4 roes and set to one side; these will be used to garnish the finished dish. Place the remaining scallops in a blender or food processor along with the salt and blend until you have a smooth paste. Add the egg white and blend again to mix in thoroughly. Rub the mixture through a sieve into a bowl set on crushed ice. Gradually add two-thirds of the cream, then stir in the vermouth, the cayenne and a little freshly ground white pepper. Now test the mousse (see page 41). If the texture is a little too rubbery, add a bit more cream and test again until you are satisfied with the texture. Divide the mousse out between the moulds, which should be well buttered, cover with buttered foil and cook in a bain-marie in the oven for 10-12 minutes for small moulds or 15-18 minutes for a large one.

For the sauce, peel the ginger and cut into very fine strips about 2 cm/¾ inch long. Poach the reserved roes in a little of the fish stock for about 15 seconds. When cooked, remove from the liquor, cover and keep warm. Add the liquor to the rest of the fish stock along with the white wine and ginger peelings and reduce until it is syrupy. Add the cream and reduce again until it starts to thicken.

To Serve

Strain the sauce through a conical strainer, add the strips of ginger and whisk in the butter gradually until it has all melted. Tip the mousselines out of their moulds and onto the serving plates. Pour over the sauce and top with the poached roes and slices of truffle.

Mousseline of Scallops with Orange

This is a variation on the scallop mousse with ginger. Orange complements scallops very well. Once the art of making a mousse has been mastered, the variations are limitless. This quantity will give you four 175 ml/6 fl oz moulds to serve as a main course, or eight 85 ml/3 fl oz moulds for a first course.

Method

Preheat the oven to 180°C/350°F/Gas Mark 4.

To make the mousseline, ensure that the scallops are well cleaned and washed, and dry them thoroughly on kitchen paper or a cloth. Place the scallops into a blender or food processor along with the salt and blend until you have a smooth paste. Add the egg white and blend again until it is mixed in thoroughly. Rub the mixture through a sieve into a bowl set over crushed ice. Gradually mix in two-thirds of the cream, then add the vermouth, the zest of the orange, the cayenne and a little pepper. Test the mousse (see page 41) and add more cream if necessary.

Divide the mousse out between the moulds, which should be well buttered, cover with buttered foil and cook in a bain-marie in the oven for 10-12 minutes for the small moulds and 15-18 minutes for the large ones.

For the sauce, remove the zest and juice from the orange. Combine the orange juice with the fish stock and the white wine and bring to the boil. Reduce until syrupy, then add the zest and cream and return to the boil. Gradually add the butter, shaking the pan with a swirling motion until all the butter has melted. Once made, do not allow the sauce to boil. If you need to keep the sauce warm, place the pan in another saucepan of warm water over a very low heat.

To Serve

Tip the mousses out of the moulds, place a mousse just off-centre on each plate and pour a little of the sauce over one corner of the mousse and a little more onto the plate. Garnish each plate with 2 orange segments and a sprig of dill.

Mousseline

12 scallops
1 tsp salt
1 egg white
300 ml/ ½ pint double cream
40 ml/ 1 ½ fl oz dry vermouth
Zest of 1 orange
Pinch of cayenne pepper
Freshly ground white pepper

Sauce

1 orange
225 ml/8 fl oz fish stock
120 ml/4 fl oz dry white wine
120 ml/4 fl oz double cream
225 g/8 oz cold unsalted butter, cut into 1 cm/ ½ inch cubes

Garnish

1 orange, segmented
Sprigs of fresh dill

SERVES 4

20 scallops (weighing about
675 g/1 lb 8 oz)

225 g/8 oz rhubarb

50 ml/2 fl oz sugar syrup

25 ml/1 fl oz oil

125 g/4½ oz unsalted butter

Salt and freshly ground white
pepper

175 ml/6 fl oz fish stock

Garnish

Fresh chervil leaves

Picture: page 121

Sautéed Scallops with Rhubarb Butter Sauce

This is an unusual and interesting combination; the scallops and the rhubarb perfectly complement each other. The early forced rhubarb is best for this dish as it has a milder flavour and retains its delicate pink colour when cooked. This dish has always been a favourite at the restaurant with our customers, as well as with myself.

Method

Cut 64 4 cm/1½ inch long by 5 mm/¼ inch thick batons of rhubarb. Bring the syrup to the boil, drop in the batons and stir in well, then remove from the heat and allow to cool. Drain the batons and save the syrup. Roughly cut up the remaining rhubarb and poach in the saved syrup until cooked. Purée this and pass through muslin or a fine strainer – the resulting juice should be quite thick and still pink.

Shell, trim and wash the scallops, and dry well. Cut the white meat across into halves, leaving the roe attached to one half. Gently heat the oil and 15 g/½ oz of the butter in a frying pan, season the scallops and sauté in the fat for about 1½ minutes each side. Remove, drain and keep warm. Reduce the fish stock until syrupy, then add the rhubarb purée and bring to the boil. When boiling, remove from the heat and gradually add the butter in 1 cm/½ inch pieces to the sauce, whisking until all the butter has melted.

To Serve

Reheat the scallops by placing them in a hot oven (200°C/400°F/Gas Mark 6) for about 1 minute with the batons of rhubarb. Divide the sauce out equally between the plates and arrange the scallops and batons of rhubarb on the sauce, saving 8 batons as garnish for each plate. Arrange these attractively around the sauce and sprinkle with the chervil.

NOTE Be careful not to overcook the scallops, which is extremely easy to do as they require very little cooking. If they are overcooked, they will shrink and become quite tough. The cooking of the rhubarb batons is also quite crucial as these do need very little cooking and will easily overcook.

Scallops in Basil Butter Sauce

20-24 scallops
Salt and freshly ground white pepper
300 ml/ ½ pint fish stock
25 ml/ 1 fl oz dry sherry
12 fresh basil leaves, shredded
150g/5 oz cold unsalted butter

Garnish

4 small scallop-shaped pastry shells (optional) (see page 42)

This dish is a particular favourite of mine – the fresh basil sauce really complements the delicate flavour of the scallops. It is also very simple and easy to prepare and requires very little cooking.

Method

Shell, trim and wash the scallops, then dry well. Season and poach them gently in the fish stock and sherry for 2–3 minutes. Do not allow the liquid to boil as the scallops will overcook and become dry very quickly. When they are cooked, cover and keep warm.

To make the sauce, reduce the liquor to a quarter of its original volume and add the basil leaves. Bring the sauce to the boil, then immediately reduce the heat to very low and gradually add the butter, whisking continuously until it has all melted. Be careful not to let the sauce boil once the butter goes in or it will separate; the butter will thicken the sauce and give it a smooth velvety texture. Season the sauce to taste.

To Serve

Arrange the scallops in the soup plates and pour over the sauce. If wished, garnish with small pastry shells cut from shortcrust pastry (see page 42).

Terrine of Scallops with Green Peppers

24 (900 g/2 lb) fresh scallops with good-sized roes
2 × 175 g/6 oz green peppers
Oil for frying
2 tsp salt
2 egg whites
450 ml/¾ pint double cream
1 egg yolk
85 ml/3 fl oz dry sherry
Pinch of grated nutmeg
Freshly ground white pepper
A little butter

The good thing about terrines is that they feed so many people. They can also be made a couple of days in advance. In fact, they are much better eaten the day after making. Serve this with a green pepper vinaigrette and fresh herbs scattered around.

Cleaning and shelling the scallops is the time-consuming part of this recipe, so try and get your fishmonger to do it for you.

Method

Preheat the oven to 200°C/400°F/Gas Mark 6.

Shell and clean the scallops. Wash well to remove any traces of sand and grit. After washing, dry them really well as they tend to hold a great deal of water; if they are too wet, this will affect the finished mousse.

Drop the whole peppers into hot fat for a couple of minutes until their skins begin to blister. Allow to cool, then remove the skins and cut the flesh into quarters. Remove the seeds and cut again into 3 mm/⅛ inch dice.

Remove the roes from the scallops and cut into dice of about 5 mm/¼ inch; set to one side. Roughly cut up the white meat and purée in a blender or food processor along with the salt until smooth. Add the egg whites and beat in the machine until the mixture stiffens, then remove from the bowl and pass it through a sieve into a bowl set on crushed ice. Gradually and gently add the cream, mixing in well. When two-thirds of the cream has been added, add the egg yolk, sherry, nutmeg and a few turns of freshly ground white pepper. It is always best to test the mousse before adding all of the cream (see page 41), it may not need it all and it may need a little more seasoning. The mixture should hold together but should be light and soft to the touch. If it is still a little rubbery, then add more cream and test again.

Mix the diced peppers and roes through the mousse mixture. Butter a 28 cm/11 inch terrine mould, place about a third of the mixture in it and press in well to exclude any air. Repeat this process until the dish is full. Cover with buttered foil and place the lid on top. Allow the terrine to stand for 30 minutes to rest before cooking.

Cook the terrine in the oven for 35-45 minutes in a water bath or bain-marie containing sufficient water to come halfway up the dish. After 25 minutes, remove the lid, leaving on the foil. To test whether the terrine is cooked, place a trussing needle through the middle of it and hold it there for a couple of seconds. If it comes out warm in the centre, then it is ready. Allow to cool at room temperature overnight.

To Serve

Tip the terrine out onto a cutting board and cut slices about 1 cm/½ inch thick, discarding the end slices.

Poached Scallops with a Purée of Leeks

SERVES 6

30 scallops
450 g/1 lb leeks
225 g/8 oz unsalted butter
450 ml/¾ pint fish stock
150 ml/¼ pint dry vermouth
175 ml/6 fl oz double cream
6 scallop-shaped pastry shells (see page 42)
Salt and freshly ground pepper

Method

Trim and wash the leeks, cut about 25 g/1 oz of them into fine strips 4 cm/1½ inches long and set to one side. Roughly cut up the rest into quite small pieces. Using 15 g/½ oz of the butter, sweat the leeks in a covered pan over a low heat until cooked. When cooked, drain them well and then purée them in a blender or food processor until smooth.

Shell, trim and wash the scallops; dry well. Leave the roes attached and slice the white meat across into 2 rounds, leaving the whole roe attached to one round. Butter a pan, add the scallops, fish stock and vermouth, and cover with buttered paper or foil. Poach gently for 1 minute. Drain the scallops, cover and leave in a warm place. Bring the stock back to the boil, plunge in the strips of leek for about 15 seconds, remove and keep warm. Reduce the stock over a high heat until syrupy.

Add 50 ml/2 fl oz of the cream to the leek purée, check the seasoning and gently reheat. Add the remaining cream to the sauce and reboil, remove the pan from the heat and whisk in the butter in small amounts until it has all melted.

To Serve

Place a dessertspoon of leek purée on each plate, arrange the scallops on top and sprinkle with the strips of leek. Pour the sauce over and around and top each plate with a scallop-shaped pastry shell.

NOTE Once you have started to add the butter, do not allow the sauce to boil or it will separate. Make sure that everything else is ready before finishing the sauce and then serve immediately.

Fish Medley

In this section, I have included all those dishes that do not easily fall under a heading for a particular fish, where there are three or more different fish involved. Most types of fish will complement each other very well, so there really is immense scope for invention here. The combination of a few different fish, each with their own characteristics, can bring a variety of colour, flavour and textures to the palate and the eye. Try mixing different shellfish together, or shellfish and seawater fish, or seawater and freshwater fish. Whether it is for a first course or a main course, for lunch or for dinner, the permutations must be endless. Go on, have fun, create some dishes!

Three-fish Layered Terrine with Avocado Sauce

SERVES 20-22

18 large spinach leaves	
A little butter	
600 ml/1 pint avocado sauce (see page 31)	

Salmon mousse

300 g/11 oz fresh salmon, off the bone	
¾ tsp salt	
1 egg white	
150 ml/¼ pint double cream	
85 ml/3 fl oz dry vermouth	

Turbot mousse

300 g/11 oz turbot meat, off the bone	
¾ tsp salt	
1 egg, separated	
150 ml/¼ pint double cream	
85 ml/3 fl oz dry sherry	

Herb mousse

300 g/11 oz monkfish, off the bone	
¾ tsp salt	
1 egg white	
150 ml/¼ pint double cream	
85 ml/3 fl oz dry sherry	
50 g/2 oz mixed fresh herbs (parsley, chervil, dill, tarragon), finely chopped	

Garnish

1 ripe avocado	
Sprigs of fresh dill or chervil	

Picture: page 64

Terrines always seem to be an awful lot of work, but really they are not; they can be made a couple of days in advance and always cater for a lot of people – ideal for that family gathering. Not to worry if you have too much, they do keep very well in a refrigerator. However, do remember to leave them at room temperature for at least 1 hour before eating as, if served straight from the refrigerator, they will be too cold and therefore lose their flavour, which is often delicate.

Method

Preheat the oven to 200°C/400°F/Gas Mark 6.

For the salmon mousse, cut the salmon into small pieces and purée in a blender or food processor together with the salt until smooth. Add the egg white and blend for a few seconds more or until it is well mixed in. Remove from the blender and rub the mixture through a sieve to remove any sinews – only by doing this can you be sure of a really fine texture. Set the bowl on crushed ice and gradually add two-thirds of the cream, followed by the vermouth and seasoning. Test the mousse (see page 41). It should be soft and not rubbery, but should still hold together and not break up. Keep adding cream and testing until you obtain the right consistency.

To make the turbot mousse, follow the same steps as for the salmon mousse, adding the egg yolk and sherry together at the end.

The herb mousse is again made in exactly the same way as the other two mousses. When the mousse is made, add the mixed herbs.

To assemble the terrine, blanch the spinach leaves in boiling salted water for a couple of seconds and then refresh in iced water. Lay them out on a cloth to drain. Butter a 28 cm/11 inch terrine mould and line it with the spinach. Make sure there are no holes and allow a 7.5 cm/3 inch overhang all the way around.

Place each mousse into a separate piping bag. Taking the salmon mousse, pipe a line of mousse along one edge of the terrine; this should go the full length and be about 2 cm/¾ inch wide. Next pipe in the turbot mousse, laying 1 line of mousse on top of the salmon mousse and 2 lines on top of each other next to it (the idea is to create a rainbow effect, with about 5 mm/¼ inch deep layers of the different mousses radiating out from one corner, when the terrine is sliced). Pipe in a layer of herb mousse and continue building up the terrine until you reach the top – by then all of the mousses should be completely used. Fold over the overhanging spinach and finish off neatly by tucking any excess down the sides. Cover the terrine with a sheet of buttered foil and place the lid on top.

The terrine needs to be cooked in a bath of water or bain-marie to prevent it burning around the sides. Bring to the boil a tray containing sufficient water to come three-quarters of the way up the terrine. Put in the terrine and place in the oven for 45 minutes. After 25 minutes, remove the lid but leave the foil on. To test whether or not the terrine is cooked, pierce through the centre of the terrine with a trussing or darning needle. Hold it there for a couple of seconds, remove and hold it to your top lip. If it is warm in the centre, it is ready; if not, give it another 5 minutes and then try again. When cooked, remove the terrine from the tray and allow to go cold at room temperature.

To Serve

When the terrine is cold, cut it into slices about 5 mm/¼ inch thick. Place a slice on the plate and spoon a little avocado sauce onto the plate next to it. Peel the avocado and cut it into very thin slices. Garnish each plate with a couple of slices of avocado and finish each one with a sprig of fresh dill or chervil.

Layered Fish Terrine Wrapped in Spinach

SERVES 18-20

550 g/ 1 ¼ lb salmon, filleted
675 g/ 1 ½ lb turbot, filleted
550 g/ 1 ¼ lb skate, filleted
A little butter
175ml/6 fl oz fish stock
85 ml/3 fl oz dry white wine
15-18 large spinach leaves
3 tomatoes
3 limes
8 leaves gelatine
600 ml/ 1 pint fish consommé (see page 213)
85 g/3 oz cucumber, finely diced
15 g/ ½ oz chives, finely chopped
15 g/ ½ oz green peppercorns

Sauce

300 ml/ ½ pint natural yoghurt
300 ml/ ½ pint double cream
Juice of 2 lemons
Salt and freshly ground white pepper
1-2 tsp sugar

Garnish

Fresh chervil leaves

Method

Skin and trim the fillets of fish and cut across the turbot and salmon to make long slices about 5 mm/¼ inch thick; the skate fillets will be about this depth anyway. Poach the fish separately in a buttered shallow tray with the fish stock and white wine for about 1 minute. When cooked, remove from the liquor and allow to cool. (The stock can be used again in another recipe.)

Blanch the spinach leaves and refresh in ice-cold water, then pat dry between two cloths. Blanch, skin and deseed the tomatoes and cut into small dice. Peel and segment the limes and dice. Soak the leaves of gelatine in cold water until soft. Heat the consommé and, when the gelatine is ready, add it to the consommé and stir until dissolved. Allow to go cold.

Line the terrine mould with the spinach leaves, leaving at least a 5 cm/2 inch overhang all the way round and making sure not to leave any gaps. Pour a 3 mm/⅛ inch layer of the cold consommé into the mould, sprinkle in a little of the tomato, cucumber, chives, limes and peppercorns and allow to set in the refrigerator. When set, pour in a little more consommé and lay in half of the turbot to form an even layer. Leave this to set and then sprinkle it with the tomato, cucumber, chives, limes and peppercorns and add another 3 mm/⅛ inch layer of consommé. Return to the refrigerator and allow to set again. Continue building up the layers like this, alternating the fish and garnish, starting with the turbot followed by garnish, then salmon, garnish, skate, garnish, salmon, and so on. The quantities are enough for 2 layers of turbot and skate and 3 of salmon. Finish off by folding the overhanging spinach over the top of the terrine. Allow at least 6 hours for the terrine to set completely.

For the sauce, mix together the yoghurt and cream, add the lemon juice, seasoning and a little sugar if required; mix well.

To Serve

Turn out the terrine – if it does not come out easily, then warm the outside of the terrine gently to just soften the outer jelly. Cut the terrine into slices. Run a spoonful of the sauce onto each of the plates, leaving a gap of about 2.5 cm/1 inch between the sauce and the edge of the plate. Place a slice of terrine in the centre of each plate; garnish the edge of the sauce with chervil leaves.

Fricassée of Seafood with Spring Onions and Tomato

The quantities given here are for a first course, but this can be served equally well as a main course for three people. If a particular fish is not available, substitute it for something similar.

Method

Preheat the oven to 190°C/375°F/Gas Mark 5.

Fillet all of the fish; the skin should also be removed from the salmon and John Dory. Cut each fillet of fish into 6 pieces. Shell, trim and wash the scallops; dry well. Leaving the roe attached to 1 piece, cut the white meat into 2 pieces. Wash the prawns, remove the heads and put them in the freezer for another sauce recipe. Blanch, skin and deseed the tomatoes, and cut the flesh into fingers.

Butter the base of an ovenproof pan and lay the pieces of fish in except for the prawns. Lightly season, add the fish stock and sherry and cover with buttered greaseproof paper or foil. Heat the pan until the liquid starts to tremble, then transfer to the oven and cook for 1 minute. Remove all of the fish from the liquor, cover and keep warm. Bring the liquid to the boil, plunge in the prawns, cover and cook for 3 minutes. When cooked, remove them from the liquid and allow to cool.

Bring the liquid back to the boil and reduce until it is syrupy. Meanwhile, shell the prawns and remove the dark line that runs along the length of the tail. When the liquor has reduced, add the cream and return to the boil, then add the spring onions and reduce until the sauce just starts to thicken. Remove the pan from the heat and gradually add the butter, shaking the pan with a swirling motion until all the butter has melted. To keep the sauce warm, stand it in another saucepan of warm water over a very low heat.

To Serve

Return the fish to the sauce along with the tomato fingers and allow to soak for 1 minute. Divide the pieces of fish equally beween the plates, making sure everyone gets a piece of each. Pour over the sauce and top with a few leaves of parsley.

1 × 115 g/4 oz red mullet
1 × 175 g/6 oz fillet of John Dory
1 × 175 g/6 oz fillet of salmon
1 × 175 g/6 oz fillet of sea bass
6 scallops
6 Dublin Bay prawns
2 tomatoes
Sea salt and freshly ground white pepper
300 ml/½ pint fish stock
150 ml/¼ pint dry sherry
225 ml/8 fl oz double cream
6 large spring onions, finely sliced
85 g/3 oz butter

Garnish

Flat parsley leaves

Creamy Fish Soup Topped with a Puff Pastry Lid

SERVES 16

2 × 115 g / 4 oz red mullet
1 × 350 g / 12 oz sea bass
16 Dublin Bay prawns (weighing about 675 g / 1 ½ lb)
275 g / 10 oz Dover sole
1 × 350 g / 12 oz John Dory
1 × 225 g / 8 oz monkfish tail
1 tbsp oil
350 g / 12 oz white mirepoix (celery, onion, leek)
2 cloves garlic, crushed
115 g / 4 oz flour
300 ml / ½ pint dry white wine
2.25 litres / 4 pints fish stock
1 sprig fresh thyme
2 stalks fresh parsley
Pinch of saffron
450 ml / ¾ pint double cream
450 g / 1 lb puff pastry mix (see page 42)
25 g / 1 oz fresh chives, finely chopped
1 egg

Once made, this soup will keep perfectly well in the refrigerator for 3 or 4 days, topping and cooking it as required. Of course, it is a perfectly good soup without the pastry topping. All the fish must be bought whole as the bones are needed to make the soup.

Method

Preheat the oven to 240°C/475°F/Gas Mark 9.

Scale the red mullet and sea bass, and scale and skin the Dover sole; the John Dory and monkfish tail should also be skinned. Shell the Dublin Bay prawns and save the shells and heads. Fillet all the fish and trim each of the fillets, saving the trimmings. Cut the fillets into pieces to get 16 from each fish. Roughly chop up the fish bones, including the heads, and the shells and heads of the prawns together with the trimmings. Wash everything well, then drain.

Heat the oil in a large pan and when hot add the vegetables and garlic. Cover and gently sweat, without colouring, until they start to soften. Add the fish bones, heads and trimmings, and the shells and the heads of the prawns and continue sweating for about 2 minutes, again without colouring. Sprinkle the flour over the top of the bones and place the pan into the oven for about 5 minutes. Turn the oven down to 220°C/425°F/Gas Mark 7. Remove the pan from the oven and stir in the flour. Add the white wine and the fish stock, followed by the thyme, parsley stalks and saffron. Bring to the boil and then simmer for 30 minutes, stirring occasionally.

After 30 minutes strain the soup through a strainer, pressing the bones dry, then strain again through muslin into a clean pan. Return this to the heat and bring back to the boil. When boiling, add the cream, bring back to the boil again and allow to reduce slightly. Remove from the heat and allow to go cold.

To Serve

Roll out the puff pastry to about 3 mm/⅛ inch thick, and, using a plain cutter, cut out circles about 1 cm/½ inch wider than the soup cups so that they overlap the edges of the cups by 5 mm/¼ inch all round. Leave the circles to rest for 30 minutes in the refrigerator. Place a piece of each fish and a whole prawn in each cup. Pour in the soup so that it comes no higher than 1cm/½ inch from the top of the cup. Sprinkle a few chives on top.

Beat the egg with a little water and brush a strip about 1 cm/ ½ inch wide around the edges of the pastry circles. Place the circles over the soup cups, pulling them tight but without stretching, and fold the sides down. Allow to rest again in the refrigerator for about 15 minutes. When ready to cook, brush the tops of the pastry with the egg wash and place into the oven for 15 minutes.

Remove the soup from the oven and serve immediately. Watch their faces as your guests break into the pastry crust, releasing the aroma of the soup.

Fish Consommé

Method

Place the fish in a food processor along with the mirepoix and process until finely chopped. Transfer this to a saucepan, add the egg whites and peppercorns and stir in well. Gradually add the cold stock and the white wine, stirring continuously.

Bring to the boil over a high heat, stirring frequently to prevent it from sticking. Stop stirring just before the consommé boils. Once it has started to boil, turn down the heat so that it is barely simmering, and allow to simmer for 30–40 minutes.

Carefully strain the consommé through muslin or a fine strainer – the finished consommé should be absolutely crystal clear. Use within a few days.

NOTE By adding a little leaf gelatine to this (8 leaves to 600 ml/ 1 pint), you can create a light fish aspic to serve chopped as a garnish to a cold dish like the Galantine of Trout (see page 72), or the Layered Terrine (see page 210).

MAKES ABOUT
1.2 litres/2 pints

115 g/4 oz white fish
115 g/4 oz mirepoix (leek, onion, celery)
3 egg whites
¼ tsp white peppercorns
1.2 litres/2 pints cold fish stock
300 ml/½ pint dry white wine

Smoked Fish

What better meals are there than the simple ones: thinly-sliced smoked salmon; grilled kippers with a knob of butter and a few slices of brown bread; smoked haddock poached in milk. No, they cannot be beaten, but they may be equalled. Here I have included a few recipes to make your meal a little more special. Possibly you would not have thought of some of these yourself.

SERVES 6

4 × 115 g/4 oz fillets of smoked haddock

25 g/1 oz fresh chives

225 g/8 oz eating apples

Freshly ground black pepper

120 ml/4 fl oz olive oil

225 ml/8 fl oz dry cider

¼ head frizzy lettuce

Picture: page 163

Smoked Haddock Marinated in Cider

This is probably the only time that I would suggest using frozen fish instead of fresh, simply because it is virtually impossible to buy fresh smoked haddock these days. Never mind, in this instance frozen is not too bad.

Method

Snip the chives into lengths of about 5 mm/¼ inch and set to one side. Peel, core and quarter the eating apples and cut them into thin slices. Cover the bottom of a shallow tray with the apple, then sprinkle the chives over the top. Thinly slice the haddock as if carving smoked salmon and lay the slices over the apple and chives so that the fish does not overlap. Season liberally with the freshly ground black pepper. Mix together the oil and cider and pour over the fish. Allow to stand for 24 hours.

To Serve

Break up the frizzy lettuce, wash well and dry on a cloth. Scatter the leaves over the plates and carefully arrange the slices of fish and apple attractively through and over the lettuce. Spoon some of the marinade and all of the chives over and serve.

Smoked Haddock Mousse with Avocado

2 × 115 g/4 oz fillets of smoked haddock
A little butter
Freshly ground white pepper
150 ml/¼ pint milk
1 avocado
Juice of ½ lemon
2 leaves gelatine
1 tbsp dry white wine
85 ml/3 fl oz double cream
1 egg white
Pinch of nutmeg
300 ml/½ pint avocado sauce (see page 31)

Garnish

Sprigs of fresh dill (optional)

Method

Skin the fillets of haddock. Butter the base of a pan large enough to take the fish without overlapping, lay the fish in and season with pepper. Pour in the milk and gently poach over a low heat for about 5 minutes or until cooked. Remove the fish from the milk and allow to cool. Return the milk to a high heat and reduce by two-thirds.

Once reduced, strain through a fine strainer or muslin onto the fish, then purée in a blender or food processor until smooth. Dice half the avocado into 5 mm/¼ inch pieces and fold into the fish. Coat the remaining half with lemon juice to prevent discolouration and keep to garnish the dish.

Soak the leaves of gelatine in cold water to cover until soft, then remove and melt in the white wine over a very low heat. Pour into the fish purée and mix in well.

Half whip the cream and stiffly beat half of the egg white (use the other half for another recipe). Fold the cream and the egg white into the fish and season with a little fresh nutmeg to taste. Pour the mixture into six 85 ml/3 fl oz moulds and allow to set in the refrigerator – this will take about 1 hour.

To Serve

Once set, turn the mousse out of the moulds. Do this by dipping each mould into hot water for just a second and with a little sharp tap on the bottom the mousse should fall out. Cut 2 slices at a slight angle from each mousse and arrange on the plates with the cut slices spreading from the cut end. Spoon the avocado sauce onto the plates in a small puddle by the mousse. Cut the remaining avocado into thin slices and fan these onto the plates. If you have any fresh dill, finish each plate with a nice sprig.

SERVES 6

Pâté

350 g/12 oz fresh kippers
115 g/4 oz trimmed white fish (for example, monkfish)
½ tsp salt
2 eggs
25 ml/1 fl oz dry white wine
85 ml/3 fl oz double cream
A little butter

Sauce

300 ml/½ pint fish stock
50 g/2 oz shallots, finely chopped
Juice of ½ lemon
50 ml/2 fl oz double cream
225 g/8 oz unsalted butter, chilled

Garnish

Sprigs of fresh chervil

Hot Kipper Pâté with Shallot Butter Sauce

Here is a recipe that offers a slightly different use for the humble kipper – no longer just simply grilled for breakfast perhaps?

Method

Preheat the oven to 200°C/400°F/Gas Mark 6.

To make the pâté, remove as many of the bones as possible from the kippers and skin each fillet (the skin will pull off easily). Cut the meat into small pieces along with the white fish and blend in a food processor or blender until smooth. Add the salt and the white of 1 egg, and process again to beat in well. Rub the mixture through a sieve into a bowl set over crushed ice. Stir in the remaining egg and the egg yolk together with the white wine and mix in well. Gradually add the cream but do not overwork the mixture. Butter 6 oval or round moulds (7.5×4 cm/3×1½ inches), half fill each mould with the mixture, then firmly bang each mould a few times on a firm surface to remove any air bubbles. Finish filling each mould with the pâté, and again bang each one on a firm surface. Cover the moulds with buttered foil and cook in the oven for 18 minutes.

For the sauce, bring the fish stock to the boil and reduce over a high heat until it is thick and syrupy. Add the shallots, the lemon juice and the cream, and return to the boil. Once the sauce is boiling, reduce the heat to very low and gradually whisk in the butter. Continue whisking until all the butter has melted. Do not allow the sauce to boil once you have started to add the butter. If you need to keep the sauce hot for a few minutes, put the sauce in a bain-marie over a very low heat.

To Serve

Gently tip the pâtés out of their moulds and onto the plates. Spoon the sauce over and around them, and top with the sprigs of fresh chervil.

Smoked Salmon Filled with a Mousse of Broad Beans

SERVES 8

275 g/10 oz smoked salmon, thinly sliced

Mousse

1.25 kg/2½ lb shelled broad beans

3 leaves gelatine

1 tbsp dry white wine

85 ml/3 fl oz double cream

1 egg white

Salt and freshly ground white pepper

Salad

1 shallot, finely chopped

3 tbsp yoghurt vinaigrette (see page 39)

¼ head curly endive

Garnish

8 sprigs fresh chervil

This light mousse complements the salmon really well. You might also try the same recipe using Parma ham instead of the salmon, which is also very good. I know broad beans are a lot of work for what always seems very little, but I think they are worth it.

Method

To make the mousse, cook the beans in boiling salted water for about 1 minute. Refresh in iced water, drain, then remove their skins (this is the time-consuming part). You should now have about 625 g/1 lb 6 oz of beans. Put 175 g/6 oz of the beans to one side and place the remaining beans into a food processor or blender. Blend to a smooth purée, then rub through a sieve.

Immerse the gelatine in cold water and soak until soft, then remove and melt it in the white wine over a low heat. Whisk this into the bean purée so that it is well mixed in. Half whip the cream and stiffly beat the egg white. Fold the cream into the mixture, then fold in the egg white and season to taste.

Line 8 oval moulds, 7.5×4 cm/3×1½ inches, with the slices of smoked salmon, allowing an overhang all the way around of about 1 cm/½ inch. Fill each mould with the mousse and allow to set in the refrigerator for about 20 minutes. When set, fold over the overhanging salmon to completely seal.

To make the salad, mix together the shallot, the reserved broad beans and the yoghurt dressing. Pick the leaves of curly endive so that they are quite small, wash well and toss into the dressed broad beans. Season to taste.

To Serve

Turn the mousses out of their moulds and cut 2 slices from the end of each mousse. Place a mousse towards the edge of each plate and lay the cut slices so that they spread out from the mousse. Make a small pile of the broad bean salad on the opposite side of the plates. Garnish with a sprig of fresh chervil.

SERVES 8

450 g / 1 lb smoked salmon
25 ml / 1 fl oz dry sherry
3 egg whites
Pinch of paprika
Juice of ½ lemon
Nutmeg
300 ml / ½ pint double cream
115 g / 4 oz watercress
175 ml / 6 fl oz watercress yoghurt sauce (see page 32)

Picture: page 142

Smoked Salmon Mousse with Watercress Sauce

Yes, I know smoked salmon is expensive, but isn't it worth it? Here is a different way of using this expensive delicacy.

Method

Remove all of the skin, any bones and all of the dark meat from the salmon and discard. Cut about 50 g/2 oz of the salmon into strips 4 cm/1½ inches long by 3 mm/⅛ inch wide to use as garnish, allowing 18-20 pieces per portion. Place the remaining salmon in a food processor or blender along with the sherry, 1 egg white, the paprika, lemon juice and a little grated nutmeg and blend until it is a smooth paste. Remove and rub through a sieve. Half whip the cream (that is, until it will form a line on its surface and hold it). Beat the remaining egg whites until stiff. Fold the cream into the mixture, then carefully fold in the egg whites. Leave to stand in the refrigerator for at least 1 hour (it is possible to make the mousse 24 hours before it is needed).

To Serve

Wash the watercress and pick through it to remove any yellowing leaves. Divide the sauce out equally between the plates (there should be enough for 1 tablespoon each) to make an oval in the centre of each plate. Arrange the watercress in an oval on top of the sauce, to form a nest allowing a 2-2.5 cm/¾-1 inch border of sauce. Using 2 tablespoons dipped in hot water, form the mousse into egg-shaped mounds and place one in the middle of each nest of watercress. Decorate each plate with the strips of smoked salmon, placing the strips as attractively as possible around the sauce. To save you time, all the final preparation can be done before your guests arrive. Cover each plate with cling film and store in the refrigerator until needed.

Smoked Salmon with Asparagus Mousse

Method

Peel the asparagus and cook in boiling salted water. Refresh in iced water, then drain. Save 6 asparagus tips (about 4 cm/1½ inches long) for garnish and liquidize the rest. Soak the leaf gelatine in cold water to cover until soft, then add it to the sherry and heat gently until melted. Stir the sherry and gelatine into the asparagus and set the bowl on crushed ice to cool, stirring frequently. When almost set, lightly fold in the half-whipped cream, season to taste, and leave to set in the refrigerator.

Lay the smoked salmon slices out flat and place a spoonful of the mousse in the centre of each slice. Form into neat parcels.

For the sauce, combine the cream, yoghurt and lemon juice and add sugar and seasoning to taste.

To Serve

Pour the sauce equally between the plates and arrange the parcels on top. Garnish with the reserved asparagus tips, cut in half lengthwise, a sprig of dill and a tomato rose.

SERVES 4

8 thin slices smoked salmon, about 7.5-10 cm/3-4 inches square

Asparagus mousse

275 g/10 oz asparagus tips

1 leaf gelatine

1 tbsp dry sherry

150 ml/¼ pint double cream, half whipped

Salt and white pepper

Sauce

150 ml/¼ pint double cream

150 ml/¼ pint natural yoghurt

Juice of 1 lemon

Sugar and salt and white pepper

Garnish

4 tomatoes, cut into roses

4 sprigs fresh dill

Soft-Boiled Eggs Filled with Smoked Salmon

Not only will this make a good first course, but what about trying it for breakfast, or even as a light snack? Imagine starting the day with smoked salmon – go on, spoil yourself!

Method

Cut the smoked salmon into strips about 2 cm/¾ inch long by 3mm/⅛ inch wide. Boil the eggs for 4 minutes. When cooked, cut off the tops as neatly as possible and scoop the eggs out of the shells into a bowl. Break up the egg using a fork until it is in pieces but not mashed, then add the cream and the strips of salmon. Season and return the mixture to the shells.

To Serve

Serve in egg cups accompanied by a little tossed green salad if used as a snack.

SERVES 4

4 small eggs (size 5 will be sufficient for a first course)

50 g/2 oz smoked salmon

1 dessertsp double cream

Salt and freshly ground black pepper

219

220

Meat and Fish Dishes

The marrying of fish and meat is not a new combination; it has been practised for centuries. Sometimes it works and sometimes not, but a book on fish would not be complete if it did not include such dishes. If nothing else, they do show how versatile fish are.

All of the recipes in this section are ones that I have perfected over the years; they often feature on my menus and are always popular with our clients. My favourite? It must be the Lamb with Scallops, as this combines my favourite meat and fish, providing two contrasting flavours and textures that complement each other perfectly.

SERVES 4

4 × 115 g/4 oz chicken breasts
1 × 675 g/1 ½ lb live lobster
About 2.25 litres/4 pints court bouillon (see page 31)
8 small carrots
8 small turnips
12 mangetout
12 fine French beans
8 small heads calabrese
15 ml/½ fl oz oil
25 g/1 oz butter
Salt and freshly ground white pepper
120 ml/4 fl oz brandy
85 ml/3 fl oz dry sherry
350 ml/12 fl oz lobster sauce (see page 33)
300 ml/½ pint double cream

Garnish

Sprigs of fresh chervil or dill

Fricassée of Chicken and Lobster with Spring Vegetables

I think this is a really pretty dish when topped with brightly-coloured spring vegetables. However, it can be a little time-consuming if you do not have any lobster sauce in the refrigerator; whenever using lobsters, make sure you save the shells and make a drop of sauce for just such an occasion.

Method

Bring the bouillon to the boil, plunge the lobster in and poach for 4–5 minutes, then allow to go cold in the liquor. When cold, remove the meat from the shells. Cut each claw meat in half lengthwise and the tail meat into 12 slices across.

Remove any sinew and bones from the chicken breasts and cut the meat into slivers about 5 mm/¼ inch thick. Prepare the vegetables. Peel the carrots and the turnips to retain their natural shapes, top and tail the mangetout and beans. Break the calabrese into small florets. Blanch them all in boiling salted water for a few seconds and then refresh in ice cold water.

Heat the oil in a frying pan and, when hot, add half the butter. Season the chicken and quickly fry it in the fat without colouring until sealed. Tip off the fat, add the brandy and the sherry to the pan and reduce until the liquid has almost gone. Pour in the lobster sauce, bring to the boil and reduce a little, then add the cream and return to the boil. Allow the sauce to reduce slightly until it just starts to thicken, then add the chicken and simmer until the chicken is cooked, about 2 minutes.

To Serve

When ready to serve, add the lobster to the sauce and let it sit over a very gentle heat for a couple of minutes to let the lobster heat through; do not allow the sauce to boil at this stage. In the meantime, gently reheat the vegetables by tossing them in the remaining butter in a frying pan over a low heat. Season them if necessary. When ready, divide the chicken and lobster between the bowls, pour over the sauce and sprinkle the vegetables on top. Crown it all with a few sprigs of chervil or dill.

NOTE You could, of course, go quite mad, say hang the expense, and sprinkle a little black truffle cut into fine strips over the top of each dish.

222

Lobster and Chicken Sausage with Spring Onion Purée

MAKES ABOUT
8×85 g/3 oz sausages

Method

To make the mousseline, chop up the chicken breasts into small pieces, place these in a blender or food processor with the salt, and blend until it is a smooth paste. Add the egg white and process again until it stiffens. Rub the mixture through a sieve into a bowl set on crushed ice. Gradually add two-thirds of the cream, mix in well, then add the sherry and season with a little salt and pepper. Test the mousse (see page 41), and if it is too rubbery in texture, add a little more cream and test again. Put in the refrigerator until needed.

Bring the court bouillon to the boil, plunge the lobster in, bring back to the boil and continue boiling for 2 minutes. Remove the pan from the heat and allow the lobster to cool in the stock. When it is cold, remove the lobster meat from its shell (save the shells to make a lobster sauce for another recipe), and dice the meat into 5 mm/¼ inch cubes. Fold the meat and the chives into the mousseline. Using cling film as a sausage skin, form the mixture into 8 individual sausages and tie off the ends. Leave to rest in the refrigerator until needed; they will keep for about 4 hours.

To make the sauce, melt the butter in a saucepan, add the spring onions, season, cover with a lid and sweat them until cooked; about 3-4 minutes. Then place the cooked onions in a liquidizer and process so that they are chopped but not too finely. Return them to the saucepan, stir in the cream and reheat.

1 × 655 g/1 ½ lb live lobster
1.2 litres/2 pints court bouillon (see page 31)
15 g/½ oz chives, finely chopped
1 tbsp oil
25 g/1 oz butter

Mousseline

2 × 175 g/6 oz breasts of chicken
10 g/¼ oz salt
1 egg white
150 ml/¼ pint double cream
25 ml/1 fl oz dry sherry
Freshly ground white pepper

Sauce

25 g/1 oz butter
2 bunches of spring onions, roughly chopped
150 ml/¼ pint double cream

Garnish

Sprigs of fresh dill

Picture: page 18

To Serve

Drop the sausages, still in their cling film skin, into boiling water and poach for 10 minutes. When cooked, gently remove the cling film, heat the oil and the butter in a frying pan, and gently roll the sausages in the fat until brown.

Place a spoonful of the sauce in the middle of each plate and sit a sausage on top. Garnish with a few sprigs of dill.

NOTE The sausages can be cooked up to 3 days in advance and kept in the refrigerator until needed. After poaching them, drop the sausages into iced water to cool them rapidly, then store in the refrigerator. To reheat, drop the sausages into boiling water and simmer for 2-3 minutes.

SERVES 4

4 supremes of chicken
900 g/2 lb fresh clams in their shells
1 tbsp oil
85 g/3 oz white mirepoix (onion, leek, celery)
150 ml/¼ pint dry white wine
150 ml/¼ pint fish stock
1 tsp white peppercorns
115 g/4 oz fresh morels or 25 g/ 1 oz dried
15 g/½ oz unsalted butter
120 ml/4 fl oz dry sherry
Salt and freshly ground white pepper
300 ml/½ pint double cream

Garnish

2-3 sprigs fresh dill

Fricassée of Chicken and Clams with Morels

Use either fresh or dried morels for this recipe; if using dried, they must be soaked in cold water for at least 2 hours before using, which will bring them back to their original state. Dried are, however, not as good as fresh, although they cost about the same. Their flavour is a lot stronger and therefore you should reduce the quantity. Fresh morels will probably prove quite difficult to get but are well worth the effort. Also, if you do not wish to mess about with fresh clams, then cooked ones will do just as well. However, if using ready-cooked, then rinse them before adding them to the sauce as they are packed in brine and this will oversalt the finished sauce. Cockles can be used to achieve the same result.

Method

Clean the clams thoroughly (see page 182). Heat the oil in a pan with a tightly-fitting lid and sweat the vegetables, without colouring, until they start to soften. Add the white wine and the fish stock and bring to the boil. When boiling, add the clams and the white peppercorns, cover with a lid and cook until the clams open, about 5-8 minutes. When cooked, drain the clams and save the liquor. Once the clams are cold, remove them from their shells and set to one side.

Remove the wing bone from the supremes along with any skin and sinew. Remove the fillets and, angling the knife slightly, cut each one into 4. Cut each breast into 2 lengthwise, then cut each strip through at an angle to get about 5 pieces out of each.

If using fresh morels, discard the stalks and, if the caps are too large, cut them into pieces; if they are small, just cut them in half – you will find that the caps are hollow and unless they are cut in half the dirt cannot be removed. Brush off any dirt.

Heat the butter in a frying pan until it starts to sizzle, season the pieces of chicken wih salt and freshly ground pepper and seal them in the hot butter. Remove them from the pan and tip off the fat. Add the dry sherry and reduce until there is almost nothing left. Add 300 ml/½ pint of the reserved clam cooking liquor and reduce by three-quarters, then add the cream, bring back to the boil again and reduce until it starts to thicken. Add the pieces of chicken and allow to simmer over a very low heat until cooked, about 5 minutes.

To Serve

When ready to serve, add the morels and the clams to the sauce and allow to soak and gently warm through for about 1 minute. Divide the chicken and clams out equally between the plates or bowls, pour over the sauce and garnish with sprigs of fresh dill. NOTE When serving up, try to ensure that all the ingredients can be seen, especially the morels – after all, they are the expensive part, so why hide them?

Roast Quail with a Salad of Quails' Eggs and Crayfish Tails

SERVES 4

Method

Preheat the oven to 230°C/450°F/Gas Mark 8.

Poach the quails' eggs for 3 minutes and refresh in cold water when cooked.

Roast the quails in the oil and about 15g/½ oz of the butter for 10 minutes in the hot oven – 3 minutes on each leg and 4 minutes on their backs. When cooked, remove them from the pan and allow them to rest and cool.

Remove the intestinal tract from the crayfish by pinching the middle section of the tail between your thumb and forefinger, then twist and pull. Discard the fat from the pan, add the fish stock and dry sherry and bring to the boil. When boiling, plunge in the crayfish and cover with a lid. Cook the crayfish for 3 minutes in the liquid and then remove them and drain. Add the carrot and shallot to the liquid and continue boiling until it is syrupy. Meanwhile, remove the tail meat from the crayfish (save the shells as they are very good in a sauce or soup). Remove the legs and breasts from the quails.

To Serve

Reheat the quail meat in the oven. When the sauce is ready, add the cream and bring back to the boil, then add the crayfish tails. Remove from the heat and gradually add the remaining butter, stirring all the time until the butter has melted.

Arrange the lettuce leaves on the plates, place 2 eggs on each plate and spoon the vinaigrette over these and then top with the chopped chives. Divide the quail meat among the plates, allowing 1 leg and 1 breast each, and add the crayfish and sauce. Garnish with sprigs of fresh dill.

Ingredients
2 × 150g/5 oz oven-ready quails
I small carrot, finely sliced
I shallot, finely sliced
8 quails' eggs
I dessertsp oil
50 g/2 oz unsalted butter
85 ml/3 fl oz fish stock
50 ml/2 fl oz dry sherry
20 crayfish
I dessertsp double cream
Lettuce leaves (e.g. frizzy, corn salad, radicchio, red oak leaf)
2 tbsp vinaigrette
I dessertsp chopped chives

Garnish

Sprigs of fresh dill

Picture: page 99

SERVES 8

2 pairs best ends of lamb

8 scallops with nice roes

8 spinach leaves

½ recipe for scallop mousse (see page 200)

1 tbsp oil

15 g/½ oz butter

Salt and freshly ground white pepper

175 ml/6 fl oz dry white wine

300 ml/½ pint veal stock

2 sprigs fresh tarragon

450 ml/¾ pint double cream

Picture: page 100

Sautéed Fillet of Lamb with Scallops and Scallop Mousse

Fish with meat is not at all an unusual combination, and this is one of my favourites as it combines probably my two favourite foods, lamb and scallops. It is not the easiest of dishes to prepare or serve, but believe me the ingredients complement each other superbly and it is well worth the effort.

Method

The day before, remove the 2 eyes of meat from each pair of best ends; this should give you 4 strips of meat, 15 cm/6 inches long by 4 cm/1½–1¾ inches wide at the fat end and 2.5 cm/1–1¼ inches at the other. Remove the thin layer of sinew from the eyes of meat. Leave covered until needed.

On the day, preheat the oven to 180°C/350°F/Gas Mark 4. Shell, trim and wash the scallops, and dry well. Wash the spinach leaves well and blanch in boiling water for a few seconds, then refresh in iced water and drain and dry in a cloth. Line eight 40–50 ml/1½–2 fl oz buttered moulds with the spinach, leaving an overhang sufficient to fold over to enclose the mousse when full. Fill each mould with the scallop mousse and finish off by folding over the overhanging spinach. Cover each mould with a piece of buttered foil. Cook the scallop mousse moulds in a bain-marie in the oven for 8–10 minutes. Remove the moulds, and turn up the oven to 190°C/375°F/Gas Mark 5.

Remove the roes from each of the scallops and set aside. Slice each nut of white meat into 5 across the scallop. Cut each eye of lamb across in half, giving 2 pieces about 7.5 cm/3 inches long.

Heat the oil and butter in a frying pan until it sizzles. Season the fillets of lamb and gently sauté, turning once or twice until cooked – this will take 6–8 minutes. Once the lamb is cooked, remove it from the pan, cover and keep warm. Using the fat that is still in the pan, gently fry the slices of scallop meat for 3 seconds each side, and fry the reserved roes for about 5 seconds each side. Remove when cooked, cover and keep warm. Tip off the fat, add the white wine and reduce until there is almost nothing left. Add the veal stock and the tarragon and reduce by half, then pour in the cream and reduce until thickened. Check the seasoning and strain through a strainer.

To Serve

Place the lamb and the scallops in the hot oven for about 2 minutes to reheat, then slice each piece of lamb into 6. Divide the sauce out between the plates and lay the sliced lamb in a straight line just off-centre. Lay 5 slices of scallop next to the lamb and a roe next to that. Tip the mousses out of their moulds, cut a slice from each and lay the mousse and the cut slice next to the roes. If you have any good leaves of tarragon left, then sprinkle a few over the top of the lamb. By serving the dish like this, you should achieve a triangular effect which will emphasize both the lamb and the scallop mousse.

SERVES 2

1 best end of lamb with 6 bones
Salt and freshly ground white pepper
25 ml/1 fl oz dry white wine
115 ml/4 fl oz chicken stock
12 live crayfish
25 ml/1 fl oz veal stock (see page 30)
85 ml/3 fl oz double cream
12-14 fresh girolles

Garnish

A few flat parsley leaves

Roast Best End of Lamb with Crayfish and Girolles

This is slightly different from the normal Sunday roast; whatever you do, don't serve mint sauce!

Method

Preheat the oven to 230°C/450°F/Gas Mark 8.

Skin the lamb and remove the bones. Trim back the fat so that there is only about 1 cm/½ inch of fat around the eye of meat and remove the sinew that runs its length. Score the fat to give a criss-cross pattern using the point of a sharp knife. Heat a roasting pan and lightly season the meat. Place the lamb in the hot pan, fat side down, and roast in the oven for 18 minutes, turning the lamb over after 12 minutes. When cooked, remove the lamb from the pan and allow to rest in a warm place.

To make the sauce, tip the fat out of the roasting pan, add the white wine and swill around. Pour the wine and juices into a saucepan, bring to the boil and reduce until almost gone. Add the chicken stock and return to the boil. Remove the intestinal tract from the crayfish by pinching the centre of the tail between your thumb and finger, then twist and pull. When the stock is boiling, plunge in the crayfish and boil for 3 minutes. Remove the crayfish and allow to cool. When cold, remove the heads and shell the tails and put to one side. Crush the heads and shells and add to the stock. Return the stock to the boil and reduce by three-quarters. Strain the stock into a clean pan, add the lamb or veal stock and bring back to the boil. When boiling, add the cream and reduce slightly until it starts to thicken. Meanwhile, wipe the girolles to remove any dirt.

To Serve

Return the lamb to the oven for 1 minute just to heat through, then carve it into 5 mm/¼ inch thick slices. Add the girolles to the sauce and simmer for 2 minutes. Arrange the slices of lamb on the plates. At the last minute, add the crayfish tails to the sauce and spoon the sauce over and around the lamb, arranging the tails and girolles attractively. Garnish with a few leaves of flat parsley.

Roast Fillet of Veal with Dublin Bay Prawns

SERVES 4

1 × 900 g/2 lb fillet of veal
50 g/2 oz caul fat
32 Dublin Bay prawns (weighing about 1 kg/2-2¼ lb)
25 ml/1 fl oz oil
15 g/½ oz butter
1 clove garlic, crushed
1 shallot, roughly chopped
85 ml/3 fl oz dry vermouth
300 ml/½ pint fish stock
120 ml/4 fl oz veal stock (see page 30)
300 ml/½ pint double cream

Garnish

A few flat parsley leaves

Method

Preheat the oven to 220°C/425°F/Gas Mark 7.

Trim the fillet of veal, removing any sinews and fat, then wrap the fillet in the caul fat, which will help to keep it moist as it cooks. Remove the heads from the Dublin Bay prawns and roughly chop them up – these will be used to make the sauce.

Heat the oil in a roasting pan, add the butter and slightly brown the fillet, turning it from time to time. Transfer the pan to the oven and roast the veal for about 10 minutes, turning it occasionally. When cooked, the veal should still be slightly pink inside; if it is allowed to cook right through, it will be very dry. Remove the veal from the pan and keep warm.

Add the garlic, shallot, vermouth and fish stock to the pan and bring to the boil. Plunge in the tails of the prawns, cover with foil and boil for 4 minutes. When cooked, remove the tails from the stock and allow them to cool. Add the chopped heads and veal stock to the pan, bring back to the boil and reduce by three-quarters. Meanwhile, shell the tails, cut each piece of tail meat in half lengthwise and remove the black line that runs down their length. Cover. When the stock has reduced, strain it through muslin or a fine strainer into a clean saucepan and bring back to the boil. Add the cream and reduce until it starts to thicken.

To Serve

Return the fillet of veal and the prawns to the oven for 1 minute to reheat. When hot, remove the prawns and arrange equally between the plates in a circle around the edge. Pour the sauce over the prawns and around the plate. Carve the fillet of veal straight through into slices about 3 mm/⅛ inch thick and arrange these in a line in the middle of each plate. Finish off with a few leaves of flat parsley scattered over the prawns.

Glossary of Terms

Bain-marie A bath of warm water rather like a double saucepan into which a saucepan containing sauce is placed to keep warm and to prevent the sauce from boiling and spoiling.

Blanch This is to briefly immerse vegetables in boiling water to lightly cook them ready for future cooking and to heighten their colour. Also in order to remove the skins of certain vegetables they are first blanched and then peeled.

Cannelize To cut grooves into vegetables for decorative purposes, using a cannelizing cutter.

Court bouillon A strong stock for poaching all types of fish and shellfish (see page 31).

Julienne The term used for vegetables cut into fine strips, no more than 4 cm/1½ inches long, which are normally used for garnishing dishes.

Mirepoix Roughly-chopped vegetables for use in stocks and sauces when they will be strained out and discarded before serving. Normally consisting of onions, carrots and celery.

Papillote An envelope made from either paper or foil which is filled with fish or meat and then tightly sealed and baked. The cooked dish is normally served still in its envelope.

Pick To remove the leaves of herbs from their stalks for garnishing or chopping, and also to remove any yellowing or spoilt leaves.

Quenelle Fish mousse shaped between two spoons to form an egg shape and then poached.

Reduce To rapidly boil a liquid over a high heat to concentrate the flavour of a stock by means of evaporation. Also to reduce a sauce until it reaches its desired consistency.

Refresh Plunging into iced water to instantly halt the cooking process and to preserve and heighten colours, normally used for vegetables.

Sweat To soften vegetables normally for soups and sauces. It must be done in a pan with a tightly-fitting lid over a low to medium heat.

Turn The term used for shaping vegetables into small barrel or olive shapes for garnishing purposes, using a small knife.

Index

Index